Look&Learn™
FrontPage®

version
2002

By Shelley O'Hara & Kate Shoup Welsh

GW00708185

Hungry Minds™

Best-Selling Books • Digital Downloads • e-Books • Answer Networks • e-Newsletters • Branded Web Sites • e-Learning

New York, NY • Cleveland, OH • Indianapolis, IN

Look & Learn™ FrontPage®

Published by:
Hungry Minds, Inc.
909 Third Avenue
New York, NY 10022
www.hungryminds.com
www.dummies.com

Library of Congress Control Number: 20022101812

ISBN: 0-7645-3504-8

Printed in the United States of America

10 9 8 7 6 5 4 3 2 1

1B/QX/QT/QS/IN

Distributed in the United States by Hungry Minds, Inc.

Distributed by CDG Books Canada Inc. for Canada; by Transworld Publishers Limited in the United Kingdom; by IDG Norge Books for Norway; by IDG Sweden Books for Sweden; by IDG Books Australia Publishing Corporation Pty. Ltd. for Australia and New Zealand; by TransQuest Publishers Pte Ltd. for Singapore, Malaysia, Thailand, Indonesia, and Hong Kong; by Gotop Information Inc. for Taiwan; by ICG Muse, Inc. for Japan; by Intersoft for South Africa; by Eyrolles for France; by International Thomson Publishing for Germany, Austria and Switzerland; by Distribuidora Cuspide for Argentina; by LR International for Brazil; by Galileo Libros for Chile; by Ediciones ZETA S.C.R. Ltda. for Peru; by WS Computer Publishing Corporation, Inc., for the Philippines; by Contemporanea de Ediciones for Venezuela; by Express Computer Distributors for the Caribbean and West Indies; by Micronesia Media Distributor, Inc. for Micronesia; by Chips Computadoras S.A. de C.V. for Mexico; by Editorial Norma de Panama S.A. for Panama; by American Bookshops for Finland.

For general information on Hungry Minds' products and services please contact our Customer Care department; within the U.S. at 800-762-2974, outside the U.S. at 317-572-3993 or fax 317-572-4002.

For sales inquiries and resellers information, including discounts, premium and bulk quantity sales and foreign language translations please contact our Customer Care department at 800-434-3422, fax 317-572-4002 or write to Hungry Minds, Inc., Attn: Customer Care department, 10475 Crosspoint Boulevard, Indianapolis, IN 46256.

For information on licensing foreign or domestic rights, please contact our Sub-Rights Customer Care department at 212-884-5000.

For information on using Hungry Minds' products and services in the classroom or for ordering examination copies, please contact our Educational Sales department at 800-434-2086 or fax 317-572-4005.

Please contact our Public Relations department at 212-884-5163 for press review copies or 212-884-5000 for author interviews and other publicity information or fax 212-884-5400.

For authorization to photocopy items for corporate, personal, or educational use, please contact Copyright Clearance Center, 222 Rosewood Drive, Danvers, MA 01923, or fax 978-750-4470.

 is a trademark of
Hungry Minds, Inc.

About The Authors

Shelley O'Hara is the author of more than 100 books, including *Master VISUALLY Office XP* and many other bestselling computer titles.

Kate Shoup Welsh is a FrontPage expert and a freelance writer who has written on everything from sports to networking to computer graphics. She has co-written several books on computers, including *Easy Windows XP.*

Production Credits

Project editor: Mary Goodwin

Acquisitions editors: Michael Roney, Tom Heine

Technical editor: Lee Musick

Editorial manager: Rev Mengle

Project coordinator: Nancee Reeves

Layout and graphics: Beth Brooks, Kelly Hardesty, Shelley Lea, Laurie Petrone, Rashell Smith

Proofreaders: Andy Hollandbeck, Linda Quigley, Dwight Ramsey, Marianne Santy, Charles Spencer, Christine Tingleton

Indexer: Sharon Hilgenberg

Index art & layout: Barbara Obermeier

Acknowledgments

Shelley O'Hara: Special thanks to Michael Roney for inviting me to write this book; to Kate Welsh for co-authoring; to Mary Goodwin for excellent editing, courier service, and project management; and to all the other unheralded Hungry Minds staffers who worked on this project.

Kate Shoup Welsh: Many thanks to Shelley O'Hara for giving me so many professional opportunities during my career, and to Michael Roney for trusting us both with this title. Thanks, too, to Mary Goodwin for her expert editorial guidance, and to all the folks at Hungry Minds who had a hand at putting this book together. Finally, thanks to my daughter Heidi for napping at all the right times, and to my husband Ian, for taking such good care of us both.

Instant Information
That Sticks In Your Head

There are lots of ways to teach **computing** and **electronic design**. Books, videos, online courses, live seminars—you're familiar with them all. But while each method appeals to a specific learning style, none works so well as the inevitable training device of the future: a syringe to the brain. One day, you'll plunk down $19.99 at your local InfoMart and receive a cylinder of pure knowledge. Poke it in, push the plunger, and zap! You've upgraded your head.

We aren't quite at that level of technology yet, so we set to thinking: How can we accomplish the next best thing?

The answer is a book. A highly **visual tool** that conveys information «FAST» by showing it. A relatively short book «CONCISE» that you can absorb in a few sittings. A book that remains affordable by **maximizing** «EFFICIENT» page space. A book that page after page «COMPLETE» teaches the **most reliable techniques** in the business, and does so as **instantaneously** as humanly possible. A «LOOK & LEARN» book where you look at a page and, without delay, **learn** precisely what you need to know.

Fast   concise   efficient   complete.

These are the watchwords for **Look & Learn**, a new series of computer training guides designed for the visual mind.

How does it work? For starters, every word on every page relates to a graphic. This means that **features and steps appear in context**, so you can see how they work. It also permits you to hone in on the stuff you're most keen to learn. See an option, read the explanation, and you're ready to get back to work.

To speed your learning, dictionary-like **thumbtabs** show you where chapters start and stop. Each chapter gets a **unique icon**, so you know where you are in a flash. Contents @ A Glance (page vii) uses the thumbtabs to show you where to go.

Tips and insights **tip** are **clearly labeled** and highlighted. Commands, options, and other literal software text appear in bold type. **Color-coded callouts** reference related information within a discussion. And when the text refers you to another section, it tells you the **exact page number** to go to. (Shouldn't every book?)

Finally, when you're in a hurry to find information about a specific topic, turn to Look It Up & Learn (page 289), the only index that uses both words and pictures to point you toward the answers you need most.

Throw in **step-by-step tutorials**; succinct, no-nonsense writing; and unflinching discussions of even the most complex topics, and you have perhaps the best training value on the market. We hope you'll agree that no reference provides so much, so quickly and so clearly as **Look & Learn**.

The Editors

Contents

@ A Glance

Detailed Contents with steps

Detailed Contents with steps

6 Add & Edit Pictures   101

Add and manage graphics with FrontPage to lend life and visual interest to your Web pages.

7 Create Hyperlinks   131

Add hyperlinks to your Web, including links to bookmarks, other pages, e-mail addresses, and more.

8 Insert Tables   145

Learn how to use tables to display information within a page and to lay out the page.

Detailed Contents *with* steps

Detailed Contents with steps

(14) Publish A Web   257

After you create your Web site, share your content with the world by publishing your Web pages.

(15) Manage A Web   265

Use FrontPage to keep your site up-to-date and fresh with regular maintenance.

(16) Customize Your Workspace   283

Tweak the FrontPage workspace to better fit the way you like to work and to make you more efficient.

Index: Look It Up & Learn   289

This visual index uses words and pictures to point you toward the information you need most.

Get To Know FrontPage

Welcome to **FrontPage 2002,** the Web editing program that comes bundled with Microsoft Office XP. FrontPage provides the tools you need to create your own Web site and also edit, maintain, and publish your site.

If you are new to FrontPage, read this chapter to find out about the on-screen tools. You use these tools and the skills in this chapter throughout the process of creating and editing a Web site.

If you are an experienced FrontPage user, check out this chapter anyway. The 2002 version features a different interface with more tools to make it even easier to create and manage Web sites.

After you get to know FrontPage, you can begin creating and editing your own Web, with text, pictures, video, and all the other cool items you expect from a successful Web site.

The FrontPage Screen

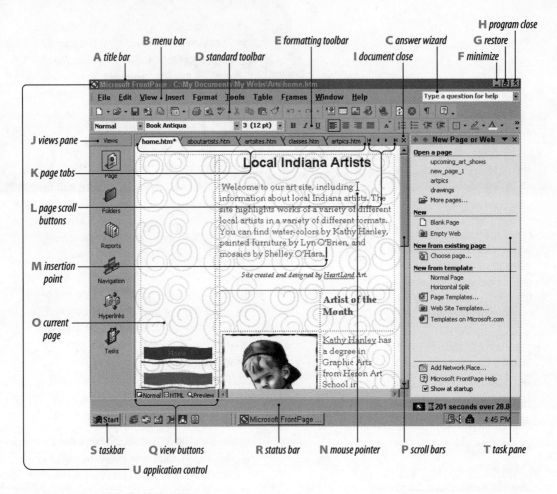

A title bar   **B** menu bar   **D** standard toolbar   **E** formatting toolbar   **C** answer wizard   **I** document close   **H** program close   **G** restore   **F** minimize

J views pane   **K** page tabs   **L** page scroll buttons   **M** insertion point   **O** current page

S taskbar   **Q** view buttons   **R** status bar   **N** mouse pointer   **P** scroll bars   **T** task pane

U application control

A title bar

The *title bar* lists the name of the program and the current open Web. The title bar also displays the name of the current page (O). If you haven't saved or named the Web, you see a generic title, such as **myweb7**. (By default, FrontPage names each Web **mywebx,** where "x" is an incremental number.)

B menu bar

The *menu bar* lists the names of the FrontPage menus. Click the menu name to display a list of *commands.* You can then choose the command you want to

execute. A command followed by an arrow displays a *submenu* (see Menus & Commands on page 12), and a command followed by an ellipsis (...) displays a *dialog box.* See Dialog Boxes on page 14 later in this chapter for more information on using dialog boxes.

> *tip* Most menu commands provide two different types of shortcuts: *toolbar buttons,* which you simply click, and *shortcut keys.* Both types of shortcuts are listed on the menu. See Keyboard Shortcuts on page 18 for more information.

C answer wizard

The *answer wizard* provides a quick way to get help without navigating through the Help menu and its commands. See Get Help With Answer Wizard on page 16 for more information.

D standard toolbar

The *standard toolbar* displays buttons for commonly used commands. Rather than choose the menu command for a particular action, you can click the toolbar button. For example, with the buttons in the standard toolbar, you can open, create, print, and preview a Web or Web pages. You can also perform common editing tasks such as cutting, copying, and pasting.

E formatting toolbar

The *formatting toolbar* provides fast access to frequently used formatting features. Some of these, like **Bold, Italic**, and **Underline**, are buttons; click the button to select that option. Some, like **Font** and **Font Size**, are drop-down lists; click the arrow next to the button and then choose from the drop-down list that appears.

If you aren't sure what a button does, you can put the mouse pointer over the button to display the ScreenTip or button name.

> *tip* You can set up FrontPage to display the standard and formatting toolbars together in one row or separately in two rows. To make this change, choose **Tools ⟶ Customize.** Click the Options tab and then check or uncheck **Show Standard and Formatting toolbars on two rows,** depending on your preference. If you display the toolbars as one row, you access all the buttons by scrolling through the standard toolbar (D).

F minimize

When you want to close the program window, but keep the program running, you can **minimize** the program window. You might do this, for instance, so that you can view or work in another program or access desktop icons such as folders. When the program window is minimized, you can click the taskbar button that represents the program to restore the program window to its full size.

G restore

When the program window is maximized (fills the entire screen), you see a *restore* button in the title bar (A). In most cases, you want to keep the window maximized so that you can see as much of the screen as possible. If you want to see a smaller version of the program window, click the restore button.

The window doesn't fill the entire desktop and has borders. Also, after you click the restore button, it changes to a **maximize** button. Click the maximize button to maximize the window again.

maximize button

> *tip* When a window isn't maximized, it has borders, and you can resize the window by dragging the window border. You can also move the window around on the desktop by dragging the title bar (A). You can't move a maximized window or resize it by dragging.

H program close

You can click the program's *close* button to exit the program. If you haven't saved your work, the program prompts you to do so before closing.

I document close

In addition to a program close button, each document has its own *close* button. You can click this button to close the document. Again, if you haven't saved the work on the document (in FrontPage, the pages that make up a Web), the program reminds you to do so.

J views pane

The *views pane* displays icons for each of the different views you can work in in FrontPage. Each view is appropriate for a certain task or action in the entire process of building a Web. For example, *page view*, shown here, is used when you build pages. You can change to another view by clicking the appropriate view button. See The Views Pane on page 10 for more information.

K page tabs

A Web usually consists of a set of pages, each one represented by a *page tab*. You can open and work on the various Web pages by clicking the page's tab.

> *tip* When you add a new page, FrontPage assigns it a generic name, but you can rename the page with a more descriptive name. Chapter 4, Edit Web Pages, covers adding, deleting, and renaming pages.

L page scroll buttons

If all of the page tabs can't be displayed at once, you see *page scroll buttons*. You can click these buttons to move to the first tab, previous tab, next tab, or last tab.

M insertion point

When you need to edit, select, or add text, you start by placing the *insertion point*, a blinking vertical line, next to the text you want to work on or on the spot where you want to insert text. To place the insertion point, move the mouse pointer to the location and then click the mouse button.

N mouse pointer

The *mouse pointer* appears on-screen and moves when you move the mouse on your desktop. You use the mouse pointer to choose menu commands, click

buttons, select page tabs, and more. The pointer changes shape depending on what action you perform. See Mouse & Pointer on page 6 for more information.

O current page

The *current page* is displayed in the main part of the program window. Chapter 3, Create Web Pages, tells you how to create Web pages and add them to your FrontPage Web.

P scroll bars

When a page has more contents than can be displayed in the window at one time, *scroll bars* appear. You use these bars to scroll horizontally and vertically through the document.

Click the up arrow to scroll up, and click the down arrow to scroll down. You can also drag the scroll box to scroll at a faster pace through the page.

To scroll horizontally, click the left arrow to scroll left, and click the right arrow to scroll right. You can also drag the scroll box.

Q view buttons

You can display a Web page in several different views, including **Normal, HTML,** and **Preview.** To change to a different view, click the appropriate view button.

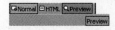

R status bar

The *status bar* displays messages about current actions. The right-most section tells you how long the page will take to display on the modem speed listed. For example, here, the page will take 201 seconds on a 28.8 modem.

S taskbar

The *taskbar* displays buttons for all the document windows, programs, and content windows (such as a folder window) that are open. You can use the taskbar to switch to a different document or program. To do so, click the button for the window you want.

> **tip** If you want more screen space, you can hide the taskbar. When the taskbar is hidden, you can point to the taskbar area to make the taskbar pop up. To make this change, right-click a blank area of the taskbar and choose **Properties.** Check the **Auto Hide** checkbox and then click **OK.**

T task pane

The *task pane*, a new Office XP feature, lets you display common tasks. In some cases, the task pane appears automatically when you select a certain command. For example, if you click the File menu and choose Open, the New Page or Web task pane may appear. Check out the sections, The New Page Or Web Task Pane, on pages 20 and 38 for more information on using this helpful task pane.

You can hide or display the task pane by opening the view menu and checking or unchecking the task pane command.

Other task panes include the Clipboard task pane (used to copy multiple items at a time) and the Search task pane, which helps you locate text and files. See The Task Pane on page 11 for more information on the task pane.

U application control

The window controls (which include the **Minimize, Maximize, Restore,** and **Close** options) provide fast access for controlling your window. You can also select these same options from the *application control button*, which you find located in the top left corner of the FrontPage window.

Click the button to display the **Control** menu. Then choose the command you want.

If a command is dimmed, it is unavailable. For example, you can't move a maximized window, so this command appears dimmed when the window is maximized.

Customize The FrontPage Screen

You can customize the FrontPage screen in several ways to fit your personal working style. For example, you can choose to always display toolbars that you use frequently so that you can get to them quickly while you work. You might, for instance, display the drawing toolbar if you add lots of graphical elements, like WordArt text and Clipart images, to your pages. You can also build your own custom toolbars with features for buttons you use often; doing so allows you to access just the features you need.

FrontPage also lets you customize the contents of menus. *Short menus* display only the commands you use most frequently. You can still display all the commands, but initially you see just a set of the most commonly used commands—*your* most commonly used commands. Or you might prefer to always see all the commands. FrontPage lets you make that choice.

In short, you can make the FrontPage screen appear as you want. Customizing FrontPage is the topic of Chapter 16, Customize Your Workspace. Turn to that chapter to find out how to make FrontPage more efficient for you.

As you read this book, keep in mind that we always show the complete standard and formatting toolbars on two rows. Also, the Windows taskbar is hidden to show as much of the FrontPage screen as possible. Finally, we always show full menus.

Mouse & Pointer

The mouse is one of the main input devices, along with the keyboard. You use the mouse to choose commands; select text; draw, resize, and move objects; and more.

The pointer, which follows the movements of the mouse, appears on-screen. You can tell what action you are performing by how the pointer looks. FrontPage uses several different mouse pointers, and we explain the most often-used pointers here.

↖	A arrow	⊘	J unavailable
+	B marquee	↖?	K help
⧖	C busy	✎	L pencil
I	D I-beam	◿	M eraser
↕	E vertical resize	▲I	N format painter
↔	F horizontal resize	↖	O move text
⤢	G diagonal resize	☞	P select dynamic effect
✛	H move object	↓	Q select table, column, or row
☜	I link select	I	R insertion point

A arrow
Of all the cursors, you see the arrow and the insertion point (R) the most. The arrow appears when you choose a command, move the insertion point, click a toolbar button, and use the scroll bars.

B marquee
This icon appears when you use the drawing tools to draw on-screen. For example, you see the marquee pointer when you draw a text box, a rectangle, or a frame.

C busy
When FrontPage is busy performing some task, you see this pointer. If you try to perform some other action while this pointer is on-screen, you hear a beep telling you that you can't perform that action until FrontPage completes the current task.

> **tip** Sometimes the busy pointer is different, depending on the theme and version of Windows that you have installed. You may see an hourglass or a round clock, for instance.

D I-beam
To select text, you drag this pointer across the text. It is called an I-beam because it kind of looks like a capital I.

E vertical resize
When you select an object (a table, picture, text box, and so on), *selection handles* appear around the object. You can change the size by dragging the appropriate selection handle. When you resize vertically, the pointer looks like this.

F horizontal resize
Like vertical resize (E), you can resize objects horizontally. If the pointer looks like this, you are resizing only the horizontal size of the object.

G diagonal resize
If you want to resize both horizontally and vertically, you can click a selection handle in any of the corners of the selected object. The pointer looks like this when you resize horizontally and vertically at the same time.

H move object
To move an object to a different position, you click it to select it and then drag. This pointer appears when you move an object.

> **tip** If you want to copy an object, hold down the **ctrl** key and drag the object. This copies and moves the new object at the same time.

I link select

When the pointer hovers over a hyperlink, it appears as a hand with a pointing finger. Clicking the link takes you to that page or Web site. You learn more about hyperlinks in Chapter 7.

J unavailable

If you try to do something that is not allowed, this pointer appears. For instance, if you drag an object to move it and that placement is not allowed, you see this pointer.

K help

You can get help about on-screen commands or elements using the help pointer.

L pencil

This pointer appears when you draw a table on a Web page. You can select the thickness, color, and style of the line from the tables toolbar. Tables are covered in detail in Chapter 8.

M eraser

When you draw a table, you can use the eraser tool to erase a line or table border. When you erase, this pointer appears.

N format painter

You can copy formatting from one selection of text or paragraph to another. When you do so, the pointer looks like this. Copying formatting is covered in Chapter 5.

O move text

You can move text using commands or toolbar buttons or by dragging. When you drag text to move it, this pointer appears.

> **tip** You can also copy text by dragging. To do so, hold down the **ctrl** key as you drag across the text that you want to copy. A pointer should appear that looks nearly the same as this one, only you also see a plus sign, indicating that you are copying the text rather than just moving it. After you copy the text, you are free to place the cursor in the text's new location and paste away.

P select dynamic effect

This pointer appears when you select a dynamic effect added to a page such as a page banner, hit counter, or link bar. See Chapter 10, Apply Dynamic Effects, for information on adding these elements.

Q select table, column, or row

You can select a row or column in a table to make changes. This pointer appears when you select table items.

R insertion point

Next to the arrow (A), this pointer appears most often. It is the blinking vertical line in the text that shows where new text will appear if you start typing.

Common Mouse Operations

You can use the mouse to perform a variety of actions. The main mouse skills include the following.

Click
Press the left mouse button. Click is most commonly used to place the insertion point and select menu commands.

Right-click
Press the right mouse button. Use right-click to display a shortcut menu.

Double-click
Press the left mouse button twice in rapid succession. Double-clicking is used to open an icon or file.

Key-click
Press and hold down a key on the keyboard and then click. This is indicated as **shift+click** or **ctrl+click** in this book. These actions are used for special purposes. Shift+clicking is

often used to select multiple items. Ctrl+clicking is used to test a hyperlink on a page.

Drag
Press and hold down the mouse button and drag the mouse. Dragging is used to move and resize objects. You also drag across text with the I-beam pointer to select text.

The Standard Toolbar

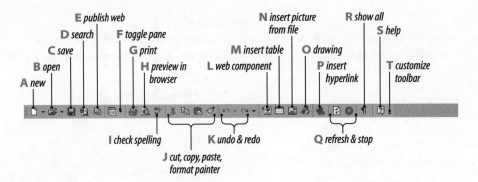

Labels for the toolbar:

- **A** new
- **B** open
- **C** save
- **D** search
- **E** publish web
- **F** toggle pane
- **G** print
- **H** preview in browser
- **I** check spelling
- **J** cut, copy, paste, format painter
- **K** undo & redo
- **L** web component
- **M** insert table
- **N** insert picture from file
- **O** drawing
- **P** insert hyperlink
- **Q** refresh & stop
- **R** show all
- **S** help
- **T** customize toolbar

For fast access to frequently used commands, you can use the buttons on the **standard toolbar.** These buttons provide features for working with the overall Web page and include a variety of options. If you prefer buttons over menu commands, familiarize yourself with what each button does.

The standard and formatting toolbars are on by default, but they may share a row. We show them on two separate rows throughout this book.

> *tip* To change how the toolbars are displayed, choose **Tools➥Customize.** On the Options tab, check or uncheck **Show Standard and Formatting toolbars on two rows.**

A new
Click this button to create a new page. Click the down arrow next to this button to create a new page, Web, folder, document library, list, survey, or task.

B open
Click this button to display the **Open File** dialog box, which lets you open a page. Click the down arrow and choose **Open Web** to open a Web.

C save
Click this button to save the current page.

D search
Click this button to display the **Basic Search** task pane to search for text.

E publish web
Click this button to publish your Web. Chapter 14 covers this process.

F toggle pane
To display a folder list, click this button. Click it again to hide the folder list. You can also click the down arrow to display the **Folder List** or **Navigation Pane.**

G print
Click this button to print the current page to your default printer.

H preview in browser
Click this button to preview the current page in your default browser.

I check spelling
To start a spell check, click this button.

J cut, copy, paste, format painter
Use this set of buttons to cut, copy, and paste text or objects. Use Format Painter to copy formatting.

K undo and redo
To undo the last action, click **Undo.** To "undo" the undo, click **Redo.**

> *tip* You can click the down arrow next to these buttons to select other actions (not simply the last action) to undo or redo.

L web component

Use this button to insert *Web components* such as hit counters, table of contents, link bars, and other elements.

M insert table

Click this button to insert a table onto the page. Tables are the topic of Chapter 8.

N insert picture from file

Click this button to display the **Insert Picture** dialog box. From this dialog box, you can select a picture to add to a Web page.

O drawing

Click this button to display the drawing toolbar. You can use this toolbar to draw and add graphic elements to your Web pages. Chapter 6 covers the drawing toolbar in detail. Click the button again to hide the toolbar.

P insert hyperlink

Click this button to display the **Insert Hyperlink** dialog box. Using the options in this dialog box, you can create links to other pages in your Web, to other Web sites, or to an e-mail address.

Q refresh & stop

Use these buttons to refresh a page or to stop the display of a page.

R show all

To show non-printing characters, such as hard returns, tabs, and spaces, click this button. Click it again to hide these elements.

S help

Click this button to get help on FrontPage features.

T customize toolbar

You can use this drop-down arrow to add other buttons to the toolbar or to customize the toolbar. Click the down arrow and then choose **Add or Remove Buttons➡Customize.** Any buttons that are checked appear on the toolbar. You can check buttons to add them or uncheck buttons to hide them. At the bottom of the menu is a down arrow; click this arrow to display additional buttons to choose from.

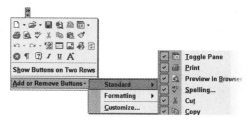

Navigate Combined Toolbars

A resize handle

B down arrow

If you combine the standard and formatting toolbars on one row, the toolbar looks like this. To resize the toolbar to display more or fewer of the buttons, drag the resize handle (A). To display additional buttons, click the down arrow and then select the button you want (B). FrontPage keeps track of the buttons you use and adjusts the default buttons that appear, replacing ones you haven't used with ones you have.

The Views Pane

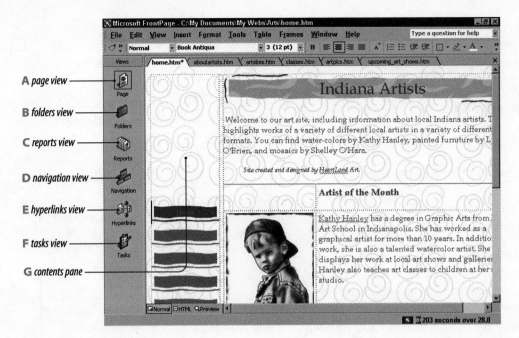

A *page view*

B *folders view*

C *reports view*

D *navigation view*

E *hyperlinks view*

F *tasks view*

G *contents pane*

FrontPage provides several views, each suitable to a particular task. You can switch to a different view by clicking its button in the views pane. The **contents pane** (G) displays the selected view. (Here you see page view.) We tell you about using these various views throughout the book.

> *tip* You can also select the view from the View menu. Open the View menu and then select the view you want.

A page view

Use this view to create Web pages. You work in page view most often when creating a Web.

B folders view

This view shows the hierarchical structure of the various Web folders and files. This view is covered in detail in Chapter 15.

C reports view

You can select from various reports that give you information about links, updated files, and a wealth of other valuable information for managing your Web. Reports are covered in Chapter 15.

D navigation view

This view helps you see how the pages are related within your Web. You can check the navigation flow and make adjustments, as covered in Chapter 12.

E hyperlinks view

This view displays the links from pages within the Web and to other Web sites.

F tasks view

You can set up a list of tasks to accomplish and monitor them from this view. See Chapter 15 for more information.

G contents pane

In page view, you see the content of the current page in the main pane or *contents pane*. In this area, you can type text, add graphics, and basically build the content of your page.

The Task Pane

The task pane is a new feature in all Office XP programs, including FrontPage. When you select some commands, the task pane appears automatically. For example, if you click the Search button, you see the Basic Search task pane. You can also manually display the task pane by choosing **View➥Task Pane.**

The task pane provides links for common tasks and options for performing a task (like searching). For example, in the New Page or Web Task pane, you can select to open a page, create a new page or Web (blank or empty), create a new page or template from a template, or access related links such as Microsoft FrontPage Help.

The title bar of the task pane includes features for working with the task pane.

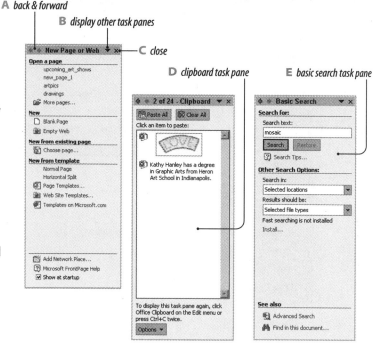

A *back & forward*

B *display other task panes*

C *close*

D *clipboard task pane*

E *basic search task pane*

A back & forward
Click these buttons to navigate back to the previous page or forward to the next page (if you have gone back).

B display other task panes
To display other task panes, click this down arrow and then choose from the list of task panes that appears.

C close
Click this button to close the task pane.

> You can resize the task pane by dragging the left border, making the task pane smaller or larger.

D clipboard task pane
This task pane comes in handy when you copy multiple items to the clipboard, or if you want to use special paste options. Use the **Paste All** button to paste all items on the clipboard. To clear items, press **Clear All**. The **Options** button lets you choose whether to display the clipboard task pane automatically, whether to represent it on the taskbar with an icon, and other options.

E basic search task pane
The **Search** task pane helps you find text and files. In this task pane, you can tell FrontPage the text to search for, the folders and drives to search, and the file type.

Menus & Commands

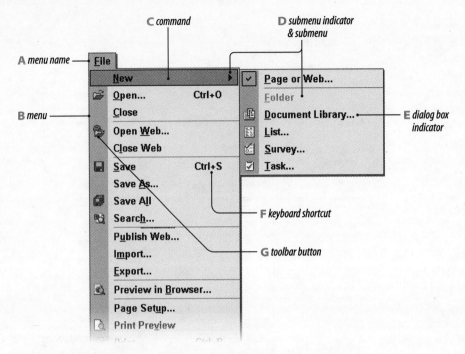

C command

D submenu indicator & submenu

A menu name — File

B menu

- New
- Open...   Ctrl+O
- Close
- Open Web...
- Close Web
- Save   Ctrl+S
- Save As...
- Save All
- Search...
- Publish Web...
- Import...
- Export...
- Preview in Browser...
- Page Setup...
- Print Preview

Submenu:
- ✓ Page or Web...
- Folder
- Document Library... — **E** dialog box indicator
- List...
- Survey...
- ✓ Task...

F keyboard shortcut

G toolbar button

When you want to perform an action in FrontPage, you choose the appropriate *menu command*. Front-Page includes a set of menus which you access through the menu bar. To use a menu, click its name; the menu list appears. From the menu, click the command you want. In some cases, the command is executed immediately. In others, a *submenu* appears (indicated by an arrow); you can then choose the desired command from the submenu. In other cases, a *dialog box* appears (indicated with an ellipsis). A dialog box enables you to provide additional information about how the command is carried out—for instance, how many copies of a page to print.

The menu itself provides other information, such as the appropriate keyboard shortcut and toolbar button for the command.

A menu name
Each menu name tells you something about the contents of that menu. For example, the **Insert** menu contains commands for inserting different elements such as pictures, comments, or files.

B menu
Lists the commands for that particular menu.

C command
You find the commands for performing various actions listed in the menu. The currently-selected command appears highlighted; click the command to execute it.

D submenu indicator & submenu
Commands followed by an arrow display a submenu when you select them.

E dialog box indicator
Commands followed by an ellipsis display a dialog box when you select them.

F keyboard shortcut
If a command has a keyboard shortcut, you see the shortcut listed next to the command name.

G toolbar button
If the command has a toolbar button equivalent, the icon precedes the menu name.

> *tip* To close a menu without making a selection, click the **esc** key or click outside the menu.

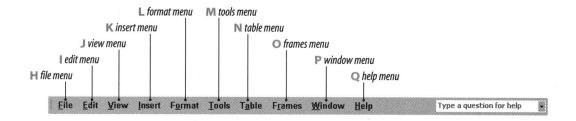

H *file menu*   I *edit menu*   J *view menu*   K *insert menu*   L *format menu*   M *tools menu*   N *table menu*   O *frames menu*   P *window menu*   Q *help menu*

H file menu

Use the **File** menu commands to open, close, and save Webs and Web pages. You can also publish the Web; import and export data; preview, set up, and print pages; send a page as an e-mail attachment; exit the program, and perform other file-related tasks.

I edit menu

Use the **Edit** menu commands to move, copy, and paste text and objects. You can also undo and redo actions, find and replace text, and set up tasks.

> **tip** If a command is dimmed, the command is unavailable. For example, if the Undo command is dimmed, you can't undo the last action.

J view menu

Use the **View** menu to choose from several views. You can also select which on-screen elements, such as the task pane and toolbars, are displayed. Items that are checked are displayed. To turn off an item, select that command and remove the checkmark. For more information on different views, see Views on pages 32 and 33.

K insert menu

The **Insert** menu enables you to insert breaks, lines, the date and time, symbols, comments, navigation elements, banners, web components, pictures, files, hyperlinks, and other key elements that you use to build a Web page.

L format menu

Use the **Format** menu to make formatting changes to text and other objects. Most of the formatting

commands are covered in Chapter 5, Enhance Page Design.

M tools menu

The **Tools** menu is kind of a miscellaneous grab bag of features, from spell-checking to customizing FrontPage.

N table menu

The **Table** menu contains commands for creating, editing, and formatting tables. See Chapter 8, Insert Tables, for help on using these commands.

O frames menu

You can divide a page into frames and arrange them using the commands in the **Frames** menu. Chapter 11, Divide A Page Into Frames, provides information on these commands.

P window menu

Use the **Window** menu to move among the different pages that are open. The current page is indicated with a checkmark. To select another page, click its name.

Q help menu

Access help features from the **Help** menu. See Get Help With Answer Wizard and Get Help With Table Of Contents on pages 16 and 17 in this chapter.

> **tip** You can also access commands using the keyboard. See Keyboard Shortcuts on page 18 for more information.

❶ Get To Know FrontPage: Menus & Commands   **13**

Dialog Boxes

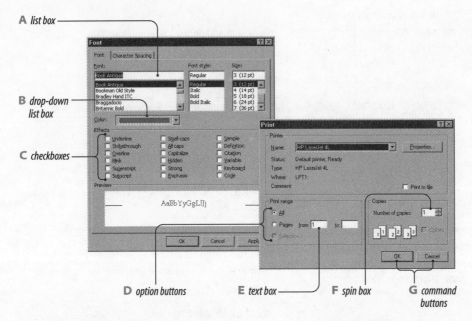

A *list box*

B *drop-down list box*

C *checkboxes*

D *option buttons* **E** *text box* **F** *spin box* **G** *command buttons*

When you need to make choices about how a command is performed, a *dialog box* appears to let you make those choices. You then select options in the dialog box and click OK (or some other command button appropriate to the dialog box) to carry out the command. All Windows programs, including FrontPage, share the same types of dialog box options.

A list box

Select an option from the list. You can scroll through the list to see all of the available options. The items are usually listed alphabetically.

B drop-down list box

In this type of list box, only the first option is displayed. Click the down arrow to display other options; then click the option you want.

C check boxes

Click a checkbox to select that option (indicated with a checkmark). Click it again to remove the checkmark and turn off that option. You can select as many checkbox options as you want.

D option buttons

Click an option button to select it; the button appears darkened. You can select only one option button in a set of option buttons.

Some dialog boxes have more than one set of option buttons. In this case, you can select one option for each set.

> **tip** Instead of using your mouse to move among the various elements in a dialog box, press the tab key to jump from option to option.

E text box

You can type desired options into a text box, such as the pages to print or the file name when saving a file.

F spin box

For some text boxes that contain values, you can type the value or use the spin arrows to increment the value.

G command buttons

The main command buttons are **OK**, which carries out the command, or **Cancel**, which cancels and closes the dialog box. Some dialog boxes have additional buttons; clicking these buttons displays other dialog boxes.

Shortcut Menus

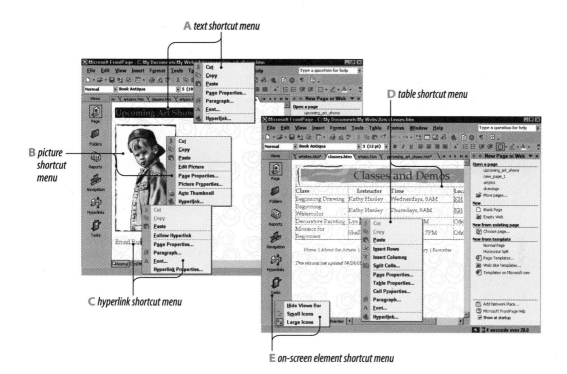

A *text shortcut menu*

D *table shortcut menu*

B *picture shortcut menu*

C *hyperlink shortcut menu*

E *on-screen element shortcut menu*

In addition to the menus that you find in the menu bar, FrontPage offers a number of *context-sensitive* command menus. When you right-click text or an object, a list of appropriate commands appears in a shortcut menu. Some of the most common shortcut menus are described here.

> *tip* If you display a shortcut menu by mistake, press **esc** to close the shortcut menu without making a selection.

A text shortcut menu

When you right-click a selection of text or within text, you see commands that relate to working with text. You can cut, copy, and paste selected text as well as choose formatting options or make the text a hyperlink.

B picture shortcut menu

Right-click a picture and you see a set of commands for cutting, copying, and pasting the picture, as well as commands for setting picture and page properties.

> *tip* When you click a picture, the pictures toolbar appears by default. You can read more about working with pictures in Chapter 6.

C hyperlink shortcut menu

The shortcut commands for a hyperlink enable you to follow (display) the link, change the appearance of the link, and change link properties.

D table shortcut menu

As you might expect, right-click within a table, and you see commands for working with the table. You can insert rows or columns, split cells, set cell properties, and more.

E on-screen element shortcut menu

You can also right-click most on-screen items, such as the views pane or the toolbars, to customize them using the shortcut menu that appears.

It's difficult to remember how to perform the myriad of tasks and use the many commands and features of any program, let alone one as powerful and complex as FrontPage.

To assist you, FrontPage provides online help, and the fastest way to access that help is by using the **answer wizard** textbox in the menu bar.

1 type question

The faint type "Type a question for help" is just a reminder for what answer wizard does. Just click in the textbox and type your question. Press **enter** to submit your question.

> 🗨️ You don't have to type an entire question; you can type just a few keywords. Try to use the feature name, if you know it, or describe the task you want to perform in as much detail as you can to get the most relevant matches.

2 select help topic

You can click any of the listed topic links to display help on that topic. If you don't see quite the topic you think you need, click the **See more...** link.

3 review help info

The **help window** appears displaying the related help information.

4 print help info (optional)

Click the **Print** button to print the help information.

5 get additional help (optional)

You can click any of the highlighted text to display additional information. If you click a term, you see a definition. If you click a How? link, the steps expand to show exactly how to perform the step in more detail.

6 click close

When you finish reviewing the information, click the **close** button to close the help window.

1 *type question*

2 *select help topic*

3 *review help info*

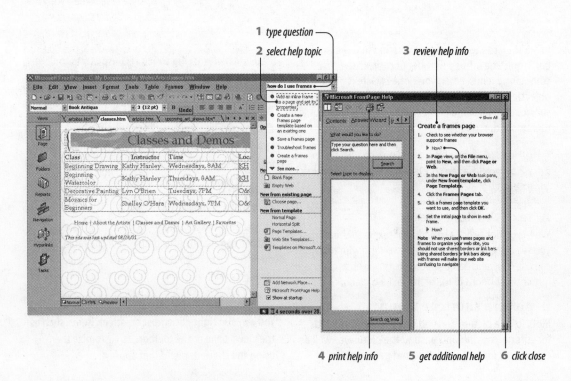

4 *print help info*   **5** *get additional help*   **6** *click close*

FrontPage provides other methods for getting help, including browsing through the help feature's table of contents and using the index. Browsing is good when you want to get an overall sense of the type of topics; it's similar to browsing the table of contents of a book to find information. Using the index is helpful when you want to look up a particular feature, and you know the exact name of the feature.

1 open help window
Choose **Help➔Microsoft FrontPage Help.** As a shortcut, you can also press **F1.**

2 click contents tab
You see a list of topics; think of these topics as chapters in a book. To get to the page level, you have to open the chapter until you find the right "page."

> *tip* If the Office Assistant appears, you will probably want to turn it off—this feature annoys most users. It lets you type a question and then select from the matching topics, just like the answer wizard.
>
> To hide the Office Assistant, right-click it. (Usually the Assistant looks like an animated paper clip, but you can change the animation figure if you choose to keep the Assistant around.) Then choose **Options.** On the Options tab, uncheck **Use the Office Assistant** and then click **OK.**

3 display help page
Click the plus sign next to the topic of interest. The list expands to show related topics.

4 select help page
Click the topic that most closely matches what you want to look up. When you do so, the right pane shows the help information.

In some cases when you click a help page, you see several options in the right pane that relate to the help topic. Click the help link that seems most related to the help you need.

5 click close
When you finish reviewing the help information, click the **close** button to close the help window.

> *tip* To use the help feature's index, you follow the same basic steps: Open the **help** window and then click the **Index** tab. You then type the keywords you want to match and click **Search.** You can then select from the list of found topics in the **Choose a topic** list.

1 *open help window*

2 *click contents tab*

3 *display help page*

4 *select help page*

5 *click close*

Keyboard Shortcuts

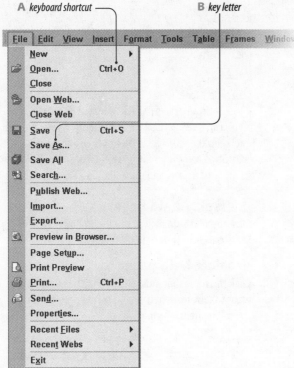

A *keyboard shortcut*

B *key letter*

File Edit View Insert Format Tools Table Frames Window

New ▶
Open...   Ctrl+O
Close
Open Web...
Close Web
Save   Ctrl+S
Save As...
Save All
Search...
Publish Web...
Import...
Export...
Preview in Browser...
Page Setup...
Print Preview
Print...   Ctrl+P
Send...
Properties...
Recent Files ▶
Recent Webs ▶
Exit

Some users, especially those who are fast typists and don't relish moving their hands away from the keyboard to the mouse, like to use *keyboard shortcuts* to perform commands.

For many commands, you can use either a keyboard shortcut or a key letter to perform the command from the keyboard.

A keyboard shortcut

A *keyboard shortcut* is usually a combination of keys that when pressed in order perform a command. The keyboard shortcut for a command appears next to the name of the command in the menu. For example, the keyboard shortcut for the Save command is **ctrl+S.** To use the shortcut, hold down the **ctrl** key and press the **S** key.

Some keyboard shortcuts aren't key combinations, but are function keys instead. As an example, you can press **F1** to get help.

B key letter

The *key letter* of a command or menu is underlined. To open a menu, press **alt** and then press the key letter of the menu name. For instance, to open the File menu, press **alt+F.**

To choose a command, press the underlined key letter of that command. For example, to choose the Save command, press **S.**

> 💡 Dialog boxes also have key letters which you can use to select options.

Use Keyboard Shortcuts

Take command of the keyboard by using these common keyboard shortcuts.

Command	Shortcut				
Save	ctrl+S	Copy	ctrl+C	Italic	ctrl+I
Open	ctrl+O	Paste	ctrl+V	Underline	ctrl+U
Print	ctrl+P	Undo	ctrl+Z	Align Left	ctrl+L
Cut	ctrl+X	Select All	ctrl+A	Center	ctrl+E
		Find	ctrl+F	Align Right	ctrl+R
		Replace	ctrl+H	Spelling	F7
		Insert Hyperlink	ctrl+K	Help	F1
		Bold	ctrl+B		

Create A New Web Site

In FrontPage, the term *Web* refers to the container that holds all of the relevant pages within a particular site. The starting point of any Web site is creating a new Web.

FrontPage provides some helpful tools for creating a Web. If you are new to FrontPage, you may want to use a *template* or *wizard* to create your Web. The templates and wizards, which are modeled on common site types, give you a structure that you can then modify to fit the needs of your particular site. Of, if you prefer, you can start from scratch by creating an empty Web.

After you create a Web, you can add pages, the contents of your Web site. (Creating pages is the focus of Chapter 3.) You can work on your Web in several different views, each appropriate for common Web-publishing tasks; this chapter also introduces these views. Finally, we also tell you how to open and close a Web.

The New Page Or Web Task Pane

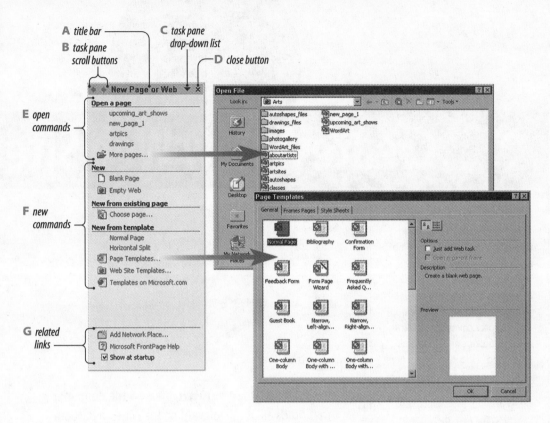

A *title bar*

B *task pane scroll buttons*

C *task pane drop-down list*

D *close button*

E *open commands*

F *new commands*

G *related links*

The *New Page or Web task pane,* which you display by choosing **File➥New Page or Web,** is your launching pad when you create a Web.

From this task pane, you can make all sorts of choices about your Web, including whether you want to use a wizard or template as the Web's foundation, or whether you want to start out with a completely empty Web. Read on for more information to help you get the most out of the New Page or Web task pane.

A title bar

FrontPage offers a variety of task panes. The title bar lists the name of the task pane. It also contains features that help you use the task pane.

B task pane scroll buttons

To display other task panes, click the **Forward** or **Back** buttons in the task pane title bar (A).

C task pane drop-down list

Click this arrow to choose from a list of available task panes. Do this when you want to perform tasks such as inserting a clip art image, viewing clipboard contents, or searching for a file.

> 🔖 For some tasks, FrontPage automatically displays a task pane. For instance, when you insert a clipart image, the **Insert Clip Art task pane** appears. You can also specify which task panes to display using the task pane drop-down list (C).

D close button

To close the task pane, click its **Close** button. You can also hide the task pane by choosing **View➥Task Pane** and unchecking the name of the pane.

E open commands

The names of the last four pages you worked on are displayed in the **Open a page** area. You can click the name of a page in this list to open it.

If the page you want to open isn't listed, click **More pages.** When you click More Pages, you see the Open File dialog box. From this dialog box, you can navigate to the folder and drive that contains the file you want to open. See Open A Web on page 35 for more information on opening Webs and pages.

F new commands

If you haven't created any pages or Webs, you can do so using the commands in the **New task pane** area.

You can create empty or blank Webs and pages, pages based on existing pages, or pages or Webs from templates. For example, if you click **Page Templates** under New from template, you see the Page Templates dialog box. From this dialog box, you can then select a template on which to base your new page.

> *tip* For information on creating new Web pages within a Web, see Chapter 3, Create Web Pages.

G related links

The bottom of the task pane displays related links, folders, or sites that you might open. If you are connected to a network, you can go to selected network folders by using the **Add Network Place** link. If you want to display help, click **Microsoft FrontPage Help**. Doing so opens the help window. See Get Help With Table Of Contents on page 17 for more information on using FrontPage's help features.

> *tip* If you always want the New Page or Web task pane to be displayed when you start FrontPage, check the **Show at startup** checkbox in the related links area (G).

Wizards & Templates

If you want some help creating a Web, or if you want to create your Web quickly, consider using a template or a wizard.

A *wizard* is a series of dialog boxes that asks you questions about your new Web. Based on your choices, FrontPage creates a Web to your specifications.

FrontPage features several different wizards, including a corporate presence wizard, a database interface wizard, and a discussion web wizard that help you create different types of Webs. See Create A Web From A Wizard on page 22 for more information on these wizards.

After you use the wizard to create a Web, you then edit each page

created by the wizard, replacing the filler text with your own content.

A *template* is a Web with pages and formatting already completed. You simply replace the content supplied by the template with your own. (Unlike a wizard, a template doesn't prompt you to select options for each page.)

You can choose a customer support template, a personal web template, or a project web template. See Create A Web From A Template on page 26 for more information.

After you use a template to create a Web, you can edit the pages in the template, adding your own content and formatting. You aren't limited to the pages in the template; you can

add new pages as well. Likewise, you can delete any pages in the template that you don't want to use.

Of course, you don't have to use a wizard or a template to create your Web. If you know the structure and format of the site, you can start with an empty Web and then add the pages and contents, building the site from the ground up. This is obviously a more advanced way to create a Web, but this may be the way to go if none of the templates or wizards comes close to matching your needs.

Turn to Create An Empty Web on page 28 for more information about this option.

Create A Web From A Wizard

To help you get started, FrontPage includes several wizards, each geared toward creating a specific kind of Web. You can find wizards for creating a corporate presence Web, a discussion Web, a database interface Web, and other types of Webs.

The steps vary depending on the particular wizard you select, but the process is the same. You start the wizard, make selections in the wizard's dialog boxes, and click **Next** to move from step to step.

1 open new page or web task pane
Open the **New Page or Web** task pane by choosing **File➡New**.

2 click web site templates
To select the wizard you want to use, click **Web Site Templates** under New from template.

3 select wizard
Click the wizard you want to use. You can tell the difference between wizards and templates by the icon. Wizards include a wand; templates don't.

The *Corporate Presence* wizard builds a Web with pages for what's new, products and services, table of contents, a feedback form, and a search form.

The *Database Interface* wizard connects an Access database to your Web site. For more information on using FrontPage with databases, see Chapter 13, Build Forms.

The *Discussion Web* wizard creates a discussion group where visitors can review posted messages as well as post new messages. This Web, by default, includes a table of contents and a search page for full-text searching.

You can use the *Import Web* wizard to create a Web from other documents and folders on your system.

4 select web location
Enter the path for storing the Web and its various pages. You can type the path, select it from the drop-down list of recently-used servers, or click **Browse** and select a folder from the **New Web Location** dialog box.

You have several choices for storing a Web. You can store the individual pages, just like regular documents. This method works for simple Webs without a lot of pages.

1 *open new page or Web task pane*   **2** *click web site templates*

3 *select wizard*   **4** *select web location*

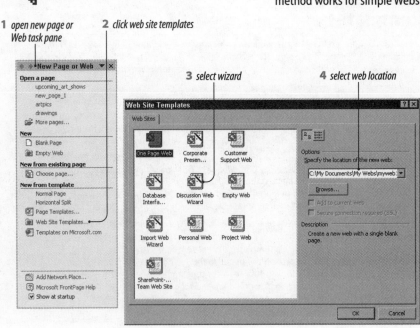

You can also store the Web as a folder; this is called a *disk-based Web*. Within the folder, you can then store the pages as documents. You can also include subfolders for storing images and other files. You might use this option when creating a Web for a company intranet.

As another option, you can store the pages and files on a Web server, one you access via a dial-up, LAN, or home network connection. See Chapter 14, Publish A Web, for information on storing or publishing pages to a network.

After you make your selection, click **OK**.

5 review intro

The first page in the wizard describes how the wizard works and the goal of the particular wizard you selected. Click **Next** to move to the next screen.

6 select pages to include

Next, the wizard has you select the pages to include in the Web. The list of pages varies depending on the wizard you use. By default, the wizard includes all the pages in the list; uncheck any pages you don't want in the completed Web. Click **Next** to move to the next step.

tip The home page is required, but all other pages are optional. Keep in mind that you can always add other pages or remove pages you don't need. See Chapter 3, Create Web Pages, for help on adding and creating new pages and Delete A Page on page 69 for help on deleting pages.

7 select home page topics

The *home page* is the first page a visitor sees on your site; the home page also navigates a visitor to other pages at the site. Check any of the topics you want to include, and then click **Next** to move to the next page.

8 select other page topics

The wizard asks you to select topics for any other pages you chose in step 6. The topics vary depending on the page type. Check the desired topics and then click **Next** until you have selected topics for each page in the Web.

9 select top & bottom page options

Here you choose what appears at the top and bottom of each page. Options for the top include your company's logo, the page title, and links to your main Web pages. Options for the bottom include links to your

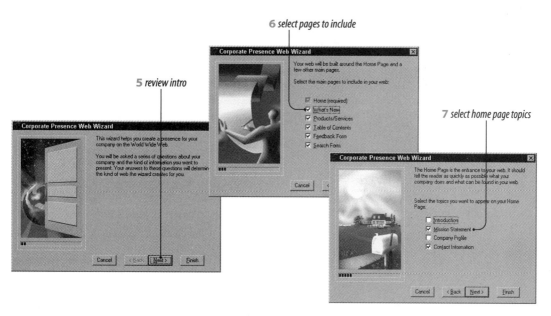

6 *select pages to include*

5 *review intro*

7 *select home page topics*

main Web pages, the e-mail address of the Webmaster, a copyright notice, and the date the page was last modified. Click **Next** to move to the next step.

> *tip* If you include links at the top, don't include them also at the bottom. Consider using the default options; they work best in most situations or at least until you get a feel for the site and its structure. For example, it's good to include the date the page was last modified so that you can keep track of changes to the site.

10 select under construction icon
(optional)

When you use a wizard, FrontPage inserts filler text for the content, which you eventually replace with your own content. To keep track of which pages are finished and which aren't, you can use an **Under Construction** icon. Select **Yes** or **No** and then click **Next**.

11 enter your info

You are next prompted to enter information about yourself and/or your company. This information is then plugged into the content of the pages at the appropriate spots, such as in the Contact Information on the home page. Type the information and click **Next**.

For example, in the Corporate Presence wizard, you are prompted to type your full company name, a one-word title for the company, and your company's street address. The wizard then asks you for the phone number, the fax number, the e-mail address for the Webmaster, and the e-mail address for general information.

12 finish wizard

You've answered all the questions! Now, click **Finish** to create the Web. In addition to creating the Web and the pages in the Web, FrontPage generates a list of common tasks needed to complete the Web.

8 *select other page topics*

9 *select top & bottom page options*

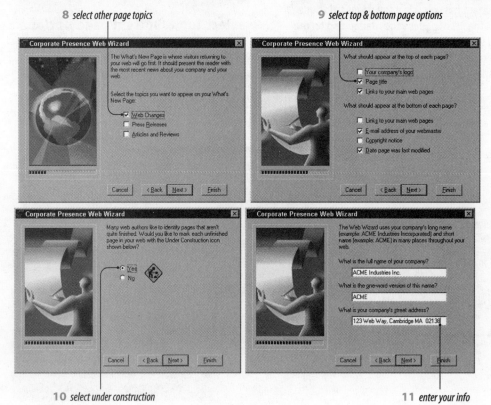

10 *select under construction*

11 *enter your info*

24 ② **Create A New Web Site:** Create A Web From A Wizard

> *tip* You can choose a *theme,* a set of coordinated fonts, colors, and graphics used to format the pages in the Web. Click the **Choose Web Theme** button, select the theme you want to use, and click **OK**.
>
> Click **Next** to move to the final step.
>
> For more information on Web themes, see Apply A Theme on page 173.

13 view web

The default view for viewing the new Web is **Tasks** view. (See Views on page 32 for more information on the various views you can use to work with your Web.) Here you see a list of all the stuff you have to do to complete your Web.

14 add content

To complete the Web, open each page and replace the placeholder content supplied by the wizard with your own original information. For example, on the home page, you need to replace the filler text for the introductory paragraph, mission statement, and other information. The various sections of the page match up to the topics you selected to include for each page in step 8.

> *tip* To see detailed information about each task, double-click it. You see the Task Details dialog box listing the task name, person to whom the task is assigned, modification dates, description, and priority. You can use this dialog box to track the progress for each task. For more information on working in Tasks view, see Chapter 15, Manage A Web.

We tell you how to make all kinds of changes and additions to your site throughout this book; refer to the table of contents or the index for a detailed list of all these possibilities.

13 *view web* **14** *add content*

12 *finish wizard*

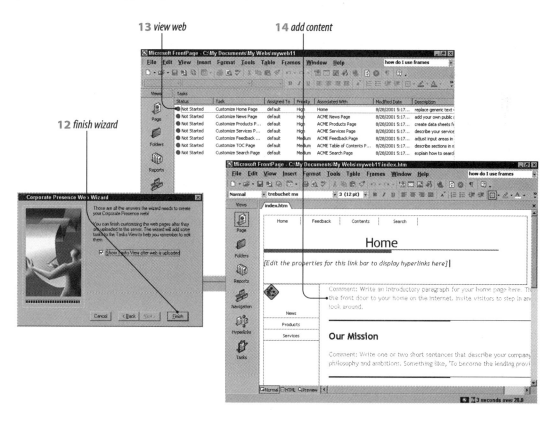

Create A Web From A Template

If you want a site that isn't suited to one of the wizards, you can try one of FrontPage's templates. *Templates* are basically pre-constructed Webs—the structure and style of the Web is complete, and all you have to do is open each page and amend the filler text (and make any other changes that you want).

Like the Web wizards, the templates also focus on sepcific types of Webs, including a customer support Web, a personal Web, a project Web, and a team Web.

tip You can get additional FrontPage templates on the Microsoft Web site. Just connect to the Internet and then click **Templates on Microsoft. com** under New from template in the New Page or Web task pane. You see the Microsoft Office Tools on the Web page. Click your location and then use any of the links on the Template Gallery page to display and download templates on a wide variety of categories, including letters, marketing, legal, business forms, finance and accounting, career, and others. This page also features templates for several Office document types, not just Webs.

1 open new page or web task pane
Make this pane appear by choosing **File➡New**.

2 click web site templates
You find this option under **New from template**.

3 select template
Click the template you want to use. (The icons with the boxed arrow in the top left corner are for templates; the icons with the magic wands are for wizards.)

tip If you aren't sure what a template does, select it and then review the description.

4 select web location
Enter the path for storing the Web and its various pages. You can type the path, select it from the drop-down list of recently-used servers, or click **Browse** and select a folder from the New Web Location dialog box. See Create A Web From A Wizard on page 22 for more information on your storage options.

After you select the template and location, click **OK**. FrontPage creates your Web based on the template.

5 check pages in template
The new Web includes the default pages for the site template. You can get a good overview of the structure of the site and the pages it contains in Navigation view. Click the **Navigation** button. This view shows the home page as well as all the other linked pages in the template.

The pages vary depending on the template. Here you see the pages

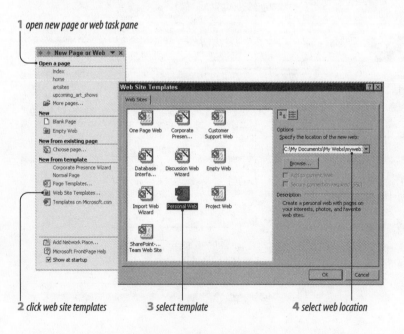

1 *open new page or web task pane*

2 *click web site templates* 3 *select template* 4 *select web location*

for the personal web template, including a home page, About Me, Interests, Favorites, Photo Gallery, and Feedback.

welcome, favorite links, weather, and others. You also get a title box, table of contents (called a *shared border*), a hit counter, and formatting.

tip You can combine Webs, adding the content of a template to an existing Web. To do so, open the Web to which you want to add the content, select the template, and then check the **Add to current Web** checkbox.

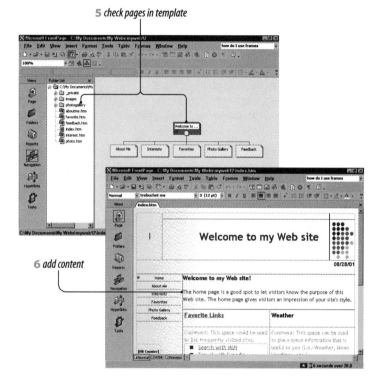

5 *check pages in template*

6 *add content*

6 add content

To complete the Web, you open each page and modify the content of the page so that it includes your information. You can open a page from Navigation view by double-clicking the page.

Each page features the theme for the template and includes placeholders for common elements. For example, on the home page of the personal Web template, you have places for a

FrontPage Templates

FrontPage 2002 includes the following templates:

One Page Web	Creates a new web with a single blank page.
Customer Support Web	Creates a web used for customer support, designed particularly for use by software companies.
Empty Web	Creates a blank web. See "Create an Empty Web" on page 28.
Personal Web	Creates a web used for personal home pages and

includes pages for listing your interests, photos, and links to your favorite Web sites.

Project Web	Creates a web used for managing a project and contains pages with a list of members, a schedule, a status, and a discussion and archive page.
SharePoint-based Team Web Site	Creates a web for managing a team and includes an events calendar, a library for shared documents, a task list, and a contact list.

steps Create An Empty Web

Sometimes using a template or wizard is not the best method to create a Web. If you have to undo a lot of changes made in the wizard or template—if you have to add or delete several pages, for instance—you might be better off starting with an empty Web and then adding the pages you want.

An *empty Web* is simply a container, usually a folder, to which you add pages, text, pictures, and the other elements that make up your Web site.

1 open new page or web task pane
Open the New Page or Web task pane by choosing **File→New**.

2 click empty web
Click **Empty Web** under New in the task pane. You see the Web Site Templates dialog box, with Empty Web selected. This dialog box appears so that you can type a name for the Web.

The default name assigned to new Webs is **mywebx,** where *x* is a sequential number. These Webs are stored within the *My Documents\My Webs folder.*

You don't have to use the default naming scheme. In fact, if you plan to create many sites, it's a good idea to use a more descriptive name, a name that reminds you of the site's purpose so you can find it easily in the future.

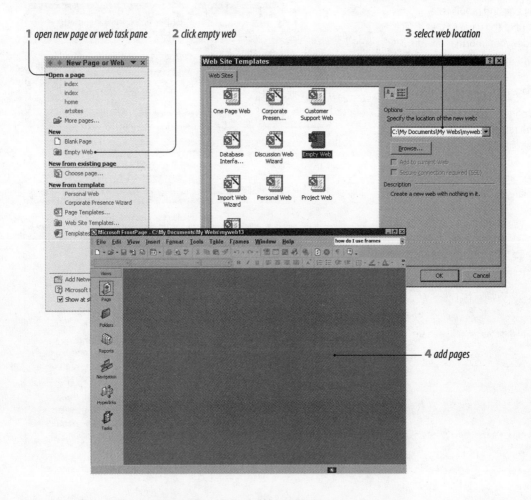

1 *open new page or web task pane*   2 *click empty web*   3 *select web location*

4 *add pages*

You can also select another folder in which to place the Web; we recommend keeping all the Web folders within the My Webs folder.

3 select web location

Enter the path for storing the Web and its various pages. You can type the path, select it from the drop-down list of recently-used servers, or click **Browse** and select a folder from the New Web Location dialog box. See step 4 in Create A Web From A

Wizard, page 22, for more information on your storage options.

After you select the template and location, click OK. FrontPage creates the Web.

4 add pages

After you click OK, you see a blank screen—your empty Web waiting for you to fill it with pages. See Chapter 3, Create Web Pages, for information on adding pages to your new, empty site.

Plan Your Web

Having a plan for your site before you start building it helps make your site more cohesive overall and cuts down on time and work in the long run. It's easier to decide on a strategy and follow it than it is to change structure midstream while creating the pages.

Form a clear-cut purpose or goal for the Web

What do you want to accomplish? Sell a product? Provide information? Promote a company?

Clearly understanding your goal helps you design a site to accomplish that goal.

Understand your audience

What visitors do you want to attract? What is the goal of the visitor when visiting your site? How can you best reach this user?

List the contents of the site

Do you need to provide company background information? A feedback form? A product list? Links to other sites?

Brainstorm about what the site should contain and then list all of the elements you think are important.

List the pages

Once you have a list of the types of information you need to include, use that list to determine how many pages you need to include and the contents of each page. Each page should have a clear focus.

Map the pages

To organize the pages, map out how a visitor will navigate from one page to another. How should the pages be linked? Sketch a flow chart or an organization chart of the Web structure.

Collect text for the site

You need text for the pages, which you can create on the fly as you build the site. Or you can use documents you already have. Chapter 3, Create Web Pages, tells you how to add text as well as move or copy text.

Collect pictures for the site

In addition to text, consider what illustrations, pictures, diagrams, or clip art you might include at the site.

For example, you might want to scan or create a company logo for the site. If you are selling a product, you might use a digital camera to add photos of each product. Chapter 6,

Add & Edit Pictures, covers all you need to know about adding pictures.

Consider the look of the site

You have many choices for formatting and enhancing page design, the topic of Chapter 5. Have some idea of the effect you want—silly, professional, or artsy, for example.

Think about the page structure

You can use different FrontPage elements to lay out a page, including tables or frames.

Sketch out the pages, finding the best placement for text, pictures, tables, and frames. This sketch can help you determine the appropriate page structure.

Assign tasks and get feedback

Many sites are the work of a group rather than an individual. If this is the case, you can assign tasks using Tasks view (which we tell you about in Chapter 15).

You also may need to get approval for the site contents and structure. Think about your team's resources before you create the site.

Create Web Pages In Other Programs

Depending on the purpose of your site and your working style, you might create some pages in other programs and then incorporate them into your FrontPage Web. For example, you might use Microsoft Word, a word processing program, to type and format documents, or you might want to use Excel to create spreadsheets for your site. Many programs, especially Microsoft programs, let you save a document as a Web page, and you can easily add these pages to your FrontPage Web.

1 create document

Use any of the program's features to create the document. Here, we use Microsoft Word.

2 save document

Instead of saving the document as the default file type, use the **Save as Web page** command. (The name of this command may vary slightly from program to program.) In Microsoft programs, you choose **File➡Save as Web page**.

When you choose the command, you see the Save As dialog box, and the Save as type is set to Web page.

3 select web folder

Locate the folder in which you want to save the document. To keep your pages organized, you should save the document to the Web folder.

> *tip* Display the **Save in** drop-down list to select another folder or drive. Click the **Up One Level** button to move up through the folder structure. You can also click any of the buttons in the Places bar to open one of the listed folders, including History, My Documents, Desktop, Favorites, or Web Folders.

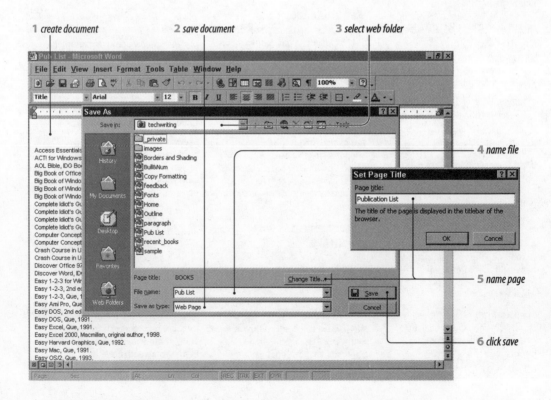

1 *create document*   2 *save document*   3 *select web folder*

4 *name file*

5 *name page*

6 *click save*

4 name file

Type a descriptive file name for the file. This is the name that will identify this particular file on your system.

7 *open page*

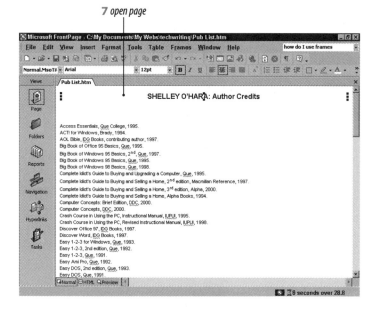

5 name page

If you don't like the current page title, click the **Change Title** button, type a new title, and click **OK**. The *page title* appears in the title bar of the browser window when this page is displayed. Use a descriptive name that helps visitors understand the contents of the page.

6 click save

Click the **Save** button to save the file.

7 open page

You can then open the page in FrontPage and modify it. You can add it to a current Web either by opening it and saving it with the Web or by inserting the file. See Insert A Text File on page 50.

Office Programs & Web Publishing

All Microsoft Office programs from version 2000 on include features for Web publishing. This list gives you an idea of some of the things you can do with each program, including Word, Excel, Access, and Power-Point. (For more specific information, consult the program's documentation or online help.)

In **Word,** you can create a document and then format the text, align paragraphs, add tables, insert hyperlinks, and so on. When you save a document as a Web page, these formatting changes are translated to *HTML* (hypertext markup language), a language used to format Web pages.

Most of your document formatting should translate to the resulting

Web page, but the formatting may not be exactly as you planned. For example, shading translates to a background color. Some formatting options, such as columns, headers and footers, page numbers, page borders, tabs, and others, don't carry over into the resulting Web document at all.

Excel lets you publish entire workbooks on the Web. The data appears just like in a workbook, and you can click any of the worksheet tabs to view the information. You can choose to publish a "snapshot" of data, which a user can't change, or you can create a Web page from a worksheet which lets users enter, format, calculate, analyze, sort, and

filter data. You can also create interactive charts or data pivot tables.

In **PowerPoint,** you can publish a presentation to the Web. As an example, you might publish a presentation on a company intranet so that others could view the presentation at their convenience. You could also publish a presentation on a Web so that your visitors could view the presentation.

With **Access,** you can publish different types of Web pages, the most common being a data access page. You can use the Database Interface wizard to publish data from a database. You can also create HTML versions of your database records. See Chapter 13 for more information on data access pages.

Views

FrontPage lets you display the contents of your Web, and specific pages, in several different views. The Views bar lists buttons for each of the Web views. To switch to another view, click the appropriate button.

You can also use the View buttons to view a page in Normal, HTML, or Preview modes. From Page view, click the view you want to use.

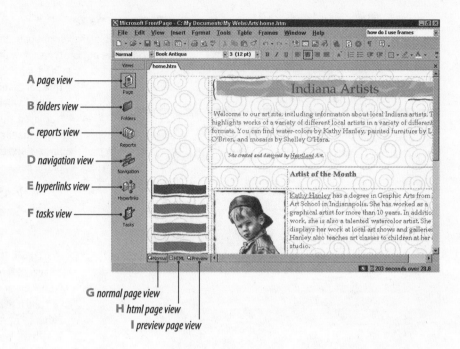

A *page view*
B *folders view*
C *reports view*
D *navigation view*
E *hyperlinks view*
F *tasks view*

G *normal page view*
H *html page view*
I *preview page view*

A page view

This view, which is the default view, displays the contents of the current page. You see formatting, graphics, and text as they will appear online.

B folders view

When you want to work with the folders and files within a Web, switch to *Folders* view. This view displays a Folder List as well as a contents pane. You can see file information, such as the name, title, size, and modification date for each page, and the folders for your Web. Chapter 4, Edit Web Pages, covers handling the many files that make up a Web.

> *tip* When you switch to Folders view, the Folders List appears. The *Folders List* is a hierarchical list of folders and files. You can choose to display this list in other views so that you can view the folder and file organization. To do so, choose **View➧Folder List.** Click the **close** button for the list to close it.

C reports view

You can use *Reports* view to view a list of common reports such as uncompleted tasks, broken hyperlinks, slow pages, and other useful reports that help you manage your Web. Chapter 15, Manage A Web, covers the various FrontPage reports.

> *tip* In addition to clicking the buttons in the View bar, you can also choose different views from the View menu. Some views, such as Reports, contain submenus. For example, you can select the specific report you want to view from the Reports submenu.

D navigation view

This view gives you an overall sense of the structure of a Web. Chapter 12, Add Navigation Elements, covers working in this view.

E hyperlinks view

Use this view to see the links to pages and other sites within your Web. See Chapter 7, Create Hyperlinks, for information on this view.

H *html page view*

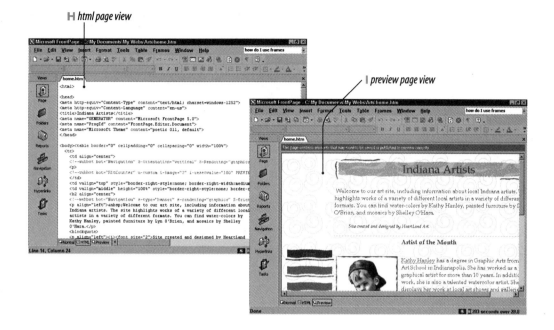

I *preview page view*

> 📝 **tip** You can display a navigation pane within the page view. You might do this if you want to display the overall structure as you work on a page. Choose **View→Navigation Pane** to display the pane. Choose the command again to hide the pane.

F tasks view

Using a *task list* is especially helpful if more than one person is creating, editing, or managing a Web. You can assign tasks to keep track of what needs to be done and who's assigned to do it. Chapter 15, Manage A Web, covers using this view.

G normal page view

Within page view, you can select several other views for displaying the current page. The default is normal view, which shows the page and its content.

H html page view

If you want to view the underlying HTML (*hypertext markup language*) codes within a document, click **HTML**. You can edit the document using this view if you are familiar with HTML.

> 📝 **tip** Viewing the page in HTML view gives you an idea of how the coding works. For example, you can see codes such as <align="center"> and pretty much guess what they do. Other codes might not be as self-explanatory, but you can match the results of the page with the code used to create that effect. To become a more proficient Web publisher, you may need to learn HTML in greater detail, and you can familiarize yourself with the codes using this view.

I preview page view

To preview a page as it should appear in a browser, click the **Preview** button. You get a sense of how the page will look online. (To see the actual results of your work, you should first publish and then preview the site.)

> 📝 **tip** To preview a page within the browser, choose **File→Preview in Browser**. For more information on previewing pages, see Preview A Page on page 72.

The Open Web Dialog Box

A *look in drop-down list*

B *places bar*

C *back button*

D *up one level button*

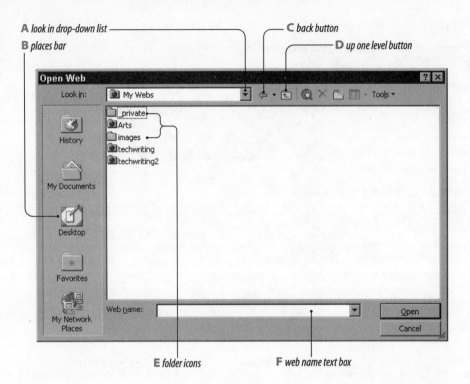

E *folder icons*

F *web name text box*

Before you can work on a Web—before you can add pages, open and edit existing pages, and make formatting changes—you've got to open the Web. Enter the Open Web dialog box for this very purpose.

To make this dialog box appear, choose **File➡Open Web.** The Open Web dialog box lists the folders and files on your system, and you can navigate to the appropriate folder to open the Web you want.

A look in drop-down list

When the Open Web dialog box appears, you see the last folder that was opened. Root through this drop-down list to select another drive or folder on your system.

B places bar

The Places bar includes icons for commonly used folders. Click the icon for the folder or location you want to open.

C back button

If you have moved to another folder and need to backtrack a step, click the Back button.

D up one level button

If you need to back up one level in the folder structure, click the Up One Level button. You see the containing folder or drive for the current folder.

E folder icons

You can open any of the folders listed in the contents pane. To do so, double-click the folder icon.

F web name text box

The easiest method to open a Web is to navigate to the Web and select it. If you know the exact name and path to the Web, though, you can type it here rather than navigate to it.

🔵 Open A Web

Using the Open Web dialog box, you can open a Web you want to work on. Remember that opening a Web isn't the same thing as opening a Web page. (Opening the pages within a Web is covered in Chapter 4.)

When you open a Web, you are really opening the Web folder, which contains all of the pages you have added and saved to the Web. By default, you see the Web in page view, with no pages open. You can open any pages you want to work on.

1 choose open web

Choose **File➡Open Web** to display the Open Web dialog box.

> 💡 If you recently worked on a Web, you can open it from the File menu by choosing **File➡Recent Webs.** From the list of recently opened Webs, choose the one you want to open.
>
> As another shortcut, you can click the down arrow next to the Open button and then click **Open Web** to display the Open Web dialog box.

2 locate web folder

Open the folder that contains the Web you want to open. You can use the tools for navigating the Open Web dialog box as covered in The Open Web Dialog Box on page 34.

3 select web

Select the Web you want to open. Keep in mind if you have created disk-based Webs, the Web icon is a folder icon.

4 click open

You may think nothing is open because you don't see any pages. You can confirm the Web is open by checking the title bar. You can now open any of the pages within this Web. See Open & Edit A Page on page 57.

> 💡 You can open more than one Web at a time, with each Web in a separate FrontPage window. You can switch among open Webs using the taskbar buttons for each of the windows.

1 *choose open web*

2 *locate web folder*

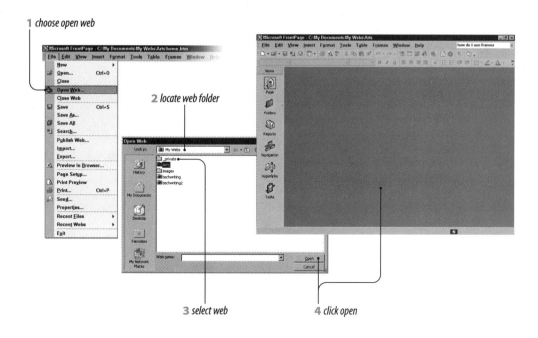

3 *select web*   **4** *click open*

Close A Web

When you finish working, you need to save your work and close the Web. FrontPage doesn't have a command for saving a Web. Instead, you save each of the Web pages you have created or modified. (Chapter 3 covers creating and saving Web pages.)

To close the Web, you use the Close Web command, which puts away the Web and all of its pages. However, when you close a Web, FrontPage remains open. If you want to close the Web and exit the program, you can do that also.

1 save pages

Save each of the open pages by choosing **File→ Save.** See Save A Page on page 43 for help with this step.

If you forget to save and close the Web, the program prompts you to save each of the modified or new pages. Click **Yes** to save the page.

> *tip* To save all open pages, choose **File→Save All.**

2 close web

Choose **File→Close Web.** The open Web is closed, but FrontPage remains open. You can now open another Web or exit the program.

> *tip* To exit the program, choose **File→Exit** or click the **close** button for the FrontPage window. If you want to both close a Web and exit FrontPage, you can simply choose **File→Exit** rather than closing the Web and then exiting.
>
> In addition to the menu commands, you can use the following keyboard shortcuts for opening, saving, and closing a Web or Web page.

Press	To
Open a Web page	Ctrl+O
Save a Web page	Ctrl+S
Close a Web page	Ctrl+F4
Close a Web and exit FrontPage	Alt+F4

1 *save pages*   **2** *choose close web*

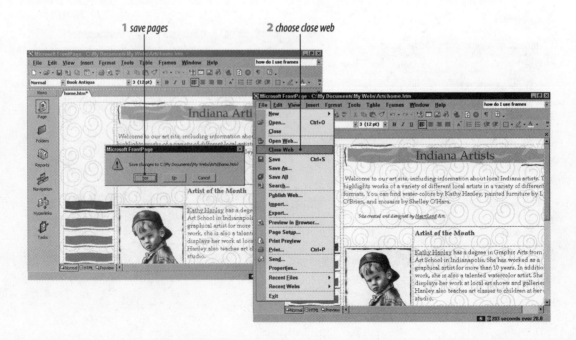

Create Web Pages

chapter

3

If you use a wizard or a template to create your Web, then you start out with a set of pages generated by FrontPage. These pages contain filler text, and it's your job to go in to every page and replace this placeholder text with your own award-winning words and images. Should you desire more space, you can also add new pages to a template- or wizard-based Web.

If you start with a blank, empty Web, then you don't have any pages to play with until you create them, and their content, yourself. You can make a page from scratch, or you can use a *template*, which includes pre-designed formatting as well as sections for pertinent topics.

Web pages can contain text, graphics, links, tables, sound, and videos. This chapter tells you how to add text, including special symbols and the date and time. Later chapters in this book cover adding other Web page elements.

The New Page Or Web Task Pane

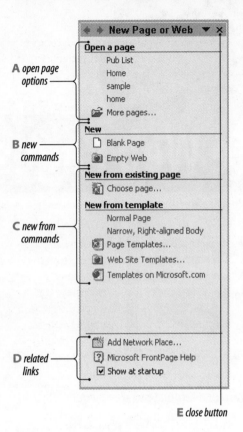

A *open page options*

B *new commands*

C *new from commands*

D *related links*

E *close button*

If you have experienced the thrill of creating a new Web (which we tell you about in Chapter 2), then you are already familiar with the all-helpful New Page or Web task pane. (Choose **File➥New➥Page or Web** to make this pane appear.)

After you make your Web, you are poised and ready to add new pages to the Web; you can create a blank page, a page based on a template, or a page based on an existing page. Options in the New Page or Web task pane let you tell FrontPage your choices for creating a new page. The related links area in this task pane also helps you navigate to folders or sites that you may want to access while building your Web site.

A open page options

FrontPage lists the last several pages you have opened. You can click any of the page names listed here to open that page. See Open & Edit A Page on page 57 for information about opening pages.

> *tip* You can use the scroll buttons and the drop-down list at the top of the task pane to display other task panes. See The New Page Or Web Task Pane on page 20 for a description of other task pane elements.

B new commands

When you want to create a plain old vanilla-flavored blank page, then you choose the **Blank Page** option under the New area. See Create A Blank Page on the next page for more information on creating blank pages.

C new from commands

In addition to blank pages, you can create pages based on existing pages or pages from templates. Use the options in the New from existing page and New from template area. See Use A Template on page 40 and Create A Page From Another Page on page 45 for more information on these options.

D related links

The bottom of the task pane displays related links, folders, or sites that you might open. Check the **Show at Startup** checkbox to display the New Page or Web task pane every time you open FrontPage.

> *tip* To quickly access FrontPage help, click the **Microsoft FrontPage Help** link in the Related Links area. See Get Help With Table Of Contents on page 17 for more information.

E close button

To close the task pane, click its close button.

Create A Blank Page

When you already know what you want a page to contain and you can't find a template that is close to what you want, it's probably most expedient to create a blank page to which you can add your content, rather than trying to amend a page created by a template. To your blank page you can add sections, headings, text, and other Web page elements to your heart's desire.

1 choose page or web
Summon the New Page or Web task pane by choosing **File➡New➡Page or Web**.

2 choose blank page
In the task pane, click **Blank Page** under the New heading. FrontPage fills your order and adds a new page. Note that the page has a tab which includes the default name. The insertion point is at the top of the page, and you can start typing text at any time.

> *tip* You can also click the **New** button to create a blank page.

3 create page contents
Use the following list to find the information you need to create the page:

To add text to the page, see Add Text on page 46.

To change the look of the text, see Chapter 5, Enhance Page Design. You can change the font, font style, and color. You can indent text, add bullets, use paragraph borders, and more.

To add a picture or other illustration to the page, see Chapter 6, Add & Edit Pictures. You can add clipart images (Insert Clipart on page 107), insert pictures from a file (Insert A Picture From A File on page 114), or draw a picture using the Drawing toolbar (The Drawing Toolbar on page 124).

To insert a hyperlink, see Chapter 7, Create Hyperlinks. You can insert hyperlinks to other documents (Link To A File Or Page on page 134), to another Web site (Link To A Web Site on page 136), to a bookmarked section within a document (Link To A Bookmark on page 139), or to an e-mail address (Create An E-mail Link on page 140).

To add a table, see Chapter 8, Insert Tables.

To add other elements, such as a hit counter, sound, or Java application, see Chapter 10, Apply Dynamic Effects.

> *tip* By default, FrontPage names the pages **new_page_x.htm** where x is an incremental number. To better keep track of your pages, rename them to something more descriptive. You can change the name when you save the page (see Save A Page on page 43 of this chapter), or you can rename the page after it has been created and saved. See Rename & Retitle A Page on page 70 for information on renaming a page.

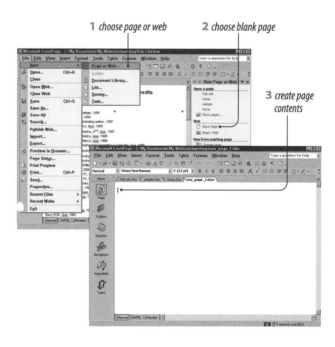

1 *choose page or web* **2** *choose blank page*

3 *create page contents*

Use A Template

To help you get started creating pages, FrontPage includes several *templates*. The templates feature pre-made formatting and layouts based on common page types or page layouts. For example, you can use a template to create a feedback form, photo gallery, or table of contents, or you can create a page with a one-column-with-two-sidebars or two-column-with-staggered-body layout. The name of each template describes what the template does, but the best way to decide which template works for your new page is to check out the preview of the template in the Page Templates dialog box.

1 choose page or web

Choose **File➧New➧Page or Web** to display the New Page or Web task pane.

2 click page templates

In the task pane, click **Page Templates** under the New from template heading. You see the Page Templates dialog box. If necessary, click the General tab.

tip You can also click the down arrow next to the New button and then select **Page** to display the Page Templates dialog box.

3 select template

The dialog box includes a scroll bar so that you can scroll through the long list of templates—FrontPage includes close to 30 different general templates for you to choose from. Click the template you want to use.

tip The templates are displayed as icons. You can display more templates at a time by changing to List view. Just click the **List** button to change to this view.

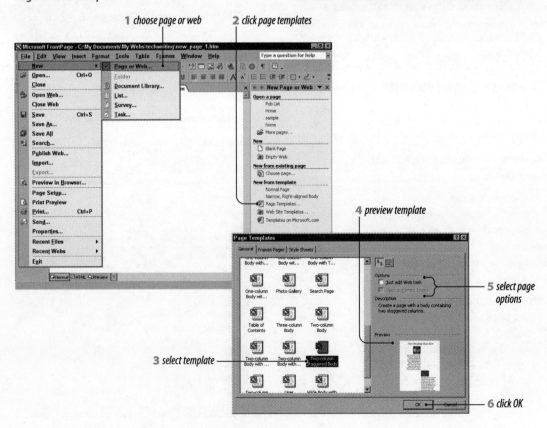

1 *choose page or web* 2 *click page templates*

4 *preview template*

5 *select page options*

3 *select template*

6 *click OK*

4 preview template

You can get a good idea of how the page is structured by checking out the preview. You can also read the description of the selected template.

> **tip** You may have noticed that the dialog box includes tabs for other templates. You can create a frames page using the Frames Pages tab. For information on using the frames page templates, see The Frames-Page Templates on page 204. You can also change the look of the page using a style sheet. For information on the style sheet templates, see The Cascading Style-Sheet Templates on page 169.

5 select page options

If you don't want to add the page, but you do want to add a Web task for creating the page, select **Just add Web task**, which adds a task to the task list. See Chapter 15, Manage A Web, for help on working with the task lists. Note that this option is not available unless you have a Web open.

If you have a page open and that page is set up as a frames page, you can create and open the new page in the current frame of that page. For information on creating frames pages, see Create A Frames Page on page 206.

6 click OK

Click OK to create the page based on the template.

7 replace filler contents

Unless you chose to only add the task back in step 5, FrontPage creates the page and includes filler text for the text parts of the page. You can then replace this filler text with your own content. Depending on which template was selected, FrontPage may also insert sample pictures as *picture placeholders*. Just like the filler text, you can replace these picture placeholders with the images you want to use. Chapter 6, Add & Edit Pictures, explains how to add images to your page.

> **tip** If you have already created and saved a page and want to create a similar page, you can create a new page based on the saved page. See Create A Page From Another Page on page 45.

7 *replace filler contents*

The Save As Dialog Box

A *save in drop-down list*   **B** *folder list*

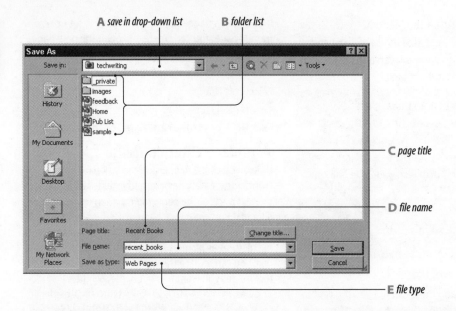

C *page title*

D *file name*

E *file type*

Each page is its own document, saved in the special Web folder (the Web itself). As you add new pages or edit existing pages, you need to save your changes. When you save a page for the first time, by choosing **File**➡**Save,** you enter a name for the file, a title for the page, and a location for the file in the Save As dialog box. If you have already saved a page, but want to change the name, location, or title, choose **File**➡**Save As** to make these changes in the Save As dialog box.

A save in drop-down list

The Save in drop-down list displays the name of the current folder, which should be the same name you used when you created your Web. Use this list to select another folder or drive on your computer, if you wish.

B folder list

Any folders within the Web folder appear here. You can double-click any of these folders to open them and save the document within that folder.

C page title

The current page title is displayed here. (The *page title* is what you see in the browser title bar when a page is

displayed. The page title also appears on the page tabs.) To change the title, click the **Change title** button.

> **tip** FrontPage uses the main Web as the *containing folder.* Within this folder, you also have a private folder and a folder for storing images. You can place pages you don't want your visitors to see in the private folder. For complex Webs, you may decide to organize the pages into folders. Use the **Create New Folder** button to create new folders. For simple Webs, you can just store the pages in the main Web folder.

D file name

The current file name is listed here. You can type a different name for the file as needed.

E file type

When you save a Web page, the file type is *Web Pages.* You can change this if you want to save a page as a template or a style sheet, for example. Just click the down arrow and choose the appropriate file type. See Save As A Template on page 44 for more information.

steps Save A Page

When you save a page for the first time, you assign the page a file name, page title, and location. As you work on your Web page, you should save it periodically—not every time you make a change, but after every couple of changes. Doing so minimizes the risk of a tragic loss of work should you have a sudden power failure.

> *tip* If you create a page and don't need it, you can close it without saving by choosing **File→Close**.

1 choose save
Choose **File→Save**. If you have already saved and named the page, the page is saved with the default name in the current location. You can skip the remaining steps. If this is the first time you have saved the page, you see the Save As dialog box.

> *tip* As a shortcut, click the **Save** button to save a page. To save all open pages, choose **File→Save All**.

2 select location
You can change to another drive or folder by using the Save in drop-down list or the Up One Level button or by double-clicking any of the listed folders.

3 name file
Type a file name. You can use up to 255 characters. This is the name that is assigned to the actual file on your computer. When you browse through file and folder lists, you see this name.

Note that when you save the first page in your Web, FrontPage uses the default name *index.htm;* this name appears in the File name text box.

4 name page
FrontPage assigns a default page title based on the first heading in the page. You should use a descriptive name for the page title; this name appears in the title bar of the browser window when the page is displayed. Click the **Change title** button, type a new title, and click **OK**.

5 click save
Click the **Save** button to save the page. FrontPage saves the file, updates the page title if you changed it, and redisplays the page.

> *tip* Don't wait until the page is complete to save, and don't just save one time. Save often so that the saved version (the one stored on your computer) reflects the changes you have made to the displayed version (the one on your screen).

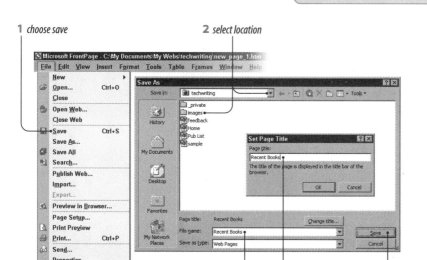

1 *choose save*   2 *select location*

3 *name file*   4 *name page*   5 *click save*

steps Save As A Template

You may spend a lot of time getting a page perfect, with just the right layout, background, formatting, and other options. You may like your perfect page so much that you want to use it as the basis for other pages. Rather than re-create this page each time, you can save the page as a *template*. Then your page becomes just like a FrontPage page template, allowing you easy access to your perfected layout, background, and other formatting.

Note that you can also create a new page based on existing pages, pages that aren't saved as a template. Use this method for creating new pages when you just need to copy a page or two. (See Create A Page From Another Page on page 45 for more information.) Go ahead and save a page as a template if you want to use a page's structure to create many new pages, or if you want to use the template in other Webs. Saving as a template helps you quickly find the template you want to use because it is listed in the Page Templates dialog box.

1 choose save as
Choose **File➡Save As** to make the Save As dialog box appear.

> **tip** Everything within the page will be saved with the template—all text, images, formatting, and so on. If you have included some elements in the page that you don't need in the template, delete them. For example, you may want to delete the text or images, leaving just the placeholders.

2 select file type
Display the Save as type drop-down list and select **FrontPage Template**. When you select this file type, FrontPage changes to the Pages folder (windows\ application data\microsoft\frontpage\pages). Saving the template in this folder ensures that it appears in the Page Templates dialog box.

3 name file
Type a descriptive file name for the template. You can use up to 255 characters.

4 click save
Click the **Save** button to save the page as a template. Now, when you click the New from Template option in the New Page or Web task pane, you see your new page template listed with the file name you entered for step 3.

1 choose save as

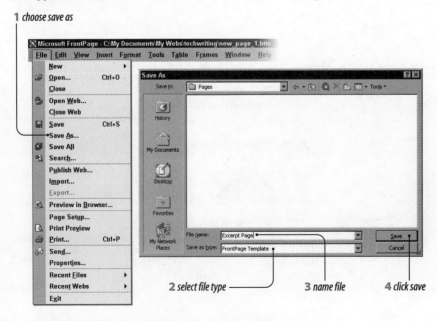

2 select file type　　　*3 name file*　　　*4 click save*

Create A Page From Another Page

You spend hours creating a good-looking page, adding graphic elements such as lines or pictures, formatting the headings, and making other changes. You like the look of this page so much that you want to add another page to your Web with exactly the same look, but slightly different content. Don't spend hours re-creating the look! Instead, create a brand new page based on the original page.

Note that if you want to use the same layout and formatting often and in other Webs, consider saving it as a template. Doing so places it in a special folder and makes it available in the Page Templates dialog box. See Save As A Template on page 44 for more information. The page that you want to use as the basis for your new page must be saved.

1 choose page or web
Choose **File➔New➔Page or Web** to display the task pane.

2 click choose page
Under the New from existing page area, click **Choose page.** You see the New from Existing Page dialog box. The name of the current Web folder is listed in the Look in box.

3 select base page
If the desired page isn't within the existing Web, open the Web folder that contains the page. You can use the Up One Level button to change to another folder.

4 click create new
Select the page on which to base the new page and then click the **Create New** button. FrontPage creates a brand new page with the same formatting and text as the page you selected. You can then edit this new page, saving it with a different name.

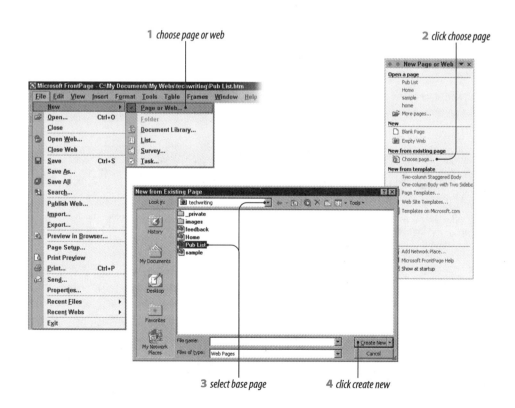

1 choose page or web

2 click choose page

3 select base page　　*4 click create new*

Add Text

Just about all Web pages contain some text. In fact, some pages may contain nothing but text! You can add text to a blank page, or you can add text to existing content. Note that if you used a template or wizard to create your Web or page, the page may include filler text that you will want to replace with your own words. See Select & Edit Text on page 47 for help on doing that.

1 move insertion point
The flashing vertical line indicates where new text will be inserted when you type. Start by pointing to where you want to add text and clicking. The insertion point moves to that location.

2 type text
Type as much text as you want. When FrontPage reaches the end of a line, it automatically wraps the text to the next line. By default, FrontPage uses the font Times New Roman, 12-point, as the typeface. You can change this and other formatting options; check out Chapter 5, Enhance Page Design, for more information.

To end a paragraph and start a new one, or to insert a blank line, press **enter**.

To insert a line break within the paragraph, keeping the text as one paragraph for formatting purposes, choose **Insert➞Line Break** and click **OK**. You can insert special line breaks if you have pictures in the margin and want to move them down. Use the **Clear left margin**, **Clear right margin**, or **Clear both margins** options, depending on the placement of the figure.

> *tip* The shortcut key for inserting a line break is **shift+enter**.

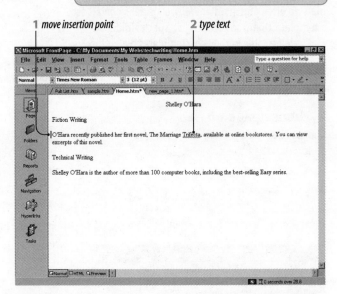

1 move insertion point   *2 type text*

Typing & Page Layout

Format text
One way to control where text is placed on the page is to format the text. You can change line-spacing, divide a document into columns, and make other changes. Chapter 5, Enhance Page Design, covers formatting options. As another way to format text, you can use style sheets, the topic of Chapter 9.

Use text boxes
Another way to place text on the page is to draw text boxes where

you want to include text and then type text within these graphic elements. See Chapter 6, Add & Edit Pictures, for information on drawing text boxes and using special text effects called *WordArt*.

Use tables
Another way to structure the page is to create a table. Tables work not only for tabbed lists, but also for the underlying structure of a page. You can include pictures, paragraphs of text, headings, and other page ele-

ments within the structure of a table cell. Many of the templates, for instance, use a table to organize a page's contents. See Chapter 8, Insert Tables, for help on creating tables on a page or for page layout.

Divide a page into frames
Finally, you can divide a page into frames and structure the text and other elements of the page using frames. Chapter 11, Divide A Page Into Frames, explains how to use this method to lay out a page.

steps Select & Edit Text

Pages that were created by a template or wizard may include filler text that you will want to change. To add your own content, you select and replace this text. You may also select text when you want to make other editing changes. For instance, the first step in formatting text is to select the text you want to change. To move or copy text, you start by selecting the text.

Selecting text is the cornerstone of nearly all text editing and formatting. You will select and edit text a zillion times over the course of your Web-editing career; now's the time to get good at it.

1 highlight text

You have two ways to select (*highlight*) text: with the mouse or the keyboard. To use the mouse, click at the start of the text to place the insertion point. Then hold down the mouse and drag across the text you want to select.

To select text with the keyboard, use the movement keys to move to the start of the text. Then hold down the shift key and highlight the text by pressing the left, right, up, or down arrow.

tip You can also use several shortcuts for selecting text. For example, double-click a word to select it. Triple-click the mouse to select the paragraph. To select all the text on a page, choose **Edit➡ Select All** or press **ctrl+A**.

For selecting text in tables, see Chapter 8, Insert Tables.

2 edit text

Once the text is selected, you can do any of the following:

To replace the text with new text, start typing the new text. Use this editing method to replace the filler text in a template or to replace outdated text with new content.

To delete the text, press the **delete** key. You can delete filler text or old content, for example. Or you might want to clean up text you have added by getting rid of repetitious or unneeded text.

To format the text, make any formatting changes using the **Formatting toolbar** or **Format** commands. See Chapter 5, Enhance Page Design, for complete information on formatting.

1 *highlight text*

2 *edit text*

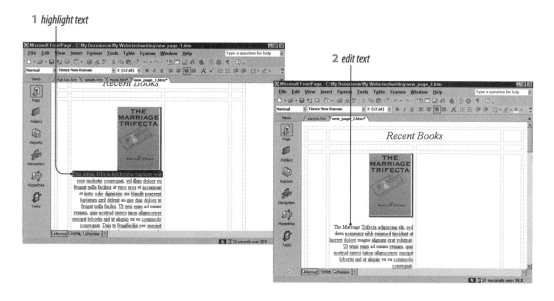

steps Move & Copy Text

When working with the text on a page, you may want to rearrange the text. You might change the order of the sections on a page, or you might want to rearrange the sentences in a paragraph, for example.

To move text, you cut it from the current location and then paste it into the new location. Likewise, you may want to copy text that you want to use again. To copy text, you copy and then paste. Moving and copying are similar tasks, and so we describe them together for you here.

1 select text

To start, select the text you want to move or copy. See Select & Edit Text on page 47 for information on this step.

2 choose copy or cut

To move text, choose **Edit➥Cut** or click the **Cut** button. To copy text, choose **Edit➥Copy** or click the **Copy** button.

3 place insertion point

Move the insertion point to where you want to place the selected text. You can click the mouse to place the insertion point or use the cursor movement keys.

> **tip** You can also copy or cut text from one page to another. To display another page, click its tab and then select the location on that page. You can also use the **Window** menu to display other open pages.
>
> To copy or move text to another Web, open both Webs and then select the text to move or copy. Click the taskbar button for the other Web and then select the page and location.

4 choose paste

When the cursor is where you want to paste the cut or copied text, choose **Edit➥Paste** or click the **Paste** button. The text appears in the desired new location.

> **tip** To undo the copy or move, choose **Edit➥Undo** or click the **Undo** button.

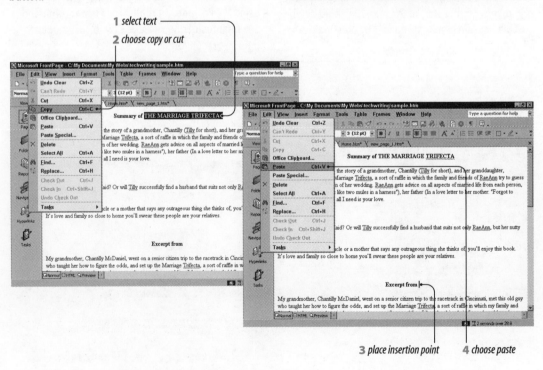

1 *select text*
2 *choose copy or cut*
3 *place insertion point* **4** *choose paste*

Use Text From Another Program

If you have created text or data in other programs and want to use some information from those documents in your Web page, you can copy text or data from these documents and paste it into your page. Use this method if you want to use just some of the data from a document. If you want to insert an entire document, check out Insert A Text File on page 50. If you want to insert the document and keep the two separate, but linked, insert a hyperlink to that document. Chapter 7, Create Hyperlinks, covers inserting a link to a document.

source formatting from the original file or paste just the text only.

> 💡 You can use the **Clipboard** task pane to view items you have cut or copied. You can then select from the list of items which you want to paste. You can even paste them all. To view this task pane, choose **Edit→Office Clipboard**. To paste from the task pane, click the item that you want to paste.

1 select text
Select the text you want to move or copy. See Select & Edit Text on page 47 for information on this step.

2 choose copy or cut
To move text, choose **Edit→Cut** or click the **Cut** button. To copy text, choose **Edit→Copy** or click the **Copy** button.

3 select text location
Move back to FrontPage, using the taskbar buttons. Then click the insertion point at the spot on the page where you want to place the selected text.

4 choose paste
When the cursor is where you want to paste the cut or copied text, choose **Edit→Paste** or click the **Paste** button.

5 select paste options
The text is pasted, and the **Clipboard Smart Tag** appears. If you want to change how the copied or cut data is pasted, click the down arrow next to this button and then select the option. For example, you can choose to keep the

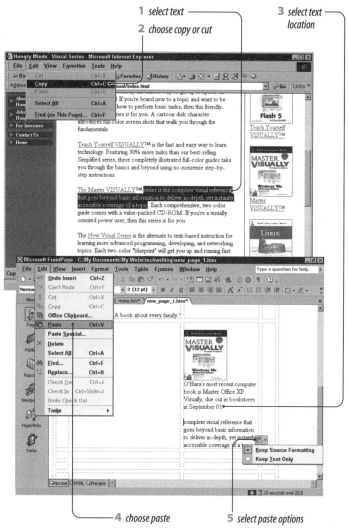

1 select text

2 choose copy or cut

3 select text location

4 choose paste

5 select paste options

steps Insert A Text File

If you have created content in another program, you can insert that file into a page in FrontPage. You can insert several file types, including HTML documents, Word documents, and others. Note that you can also copy text from one program and then paste it into FrontPage. See Use Text From Another Program on page 49. You can also save some documents as Web pages. For instance, in Word, Excel, and PowerPoint, you can save a document as HTML (Web) pages. See Create Web Pages In Other Programs on page 30 for help with this task. Finally, you can create a link to a document, keeping the files separate, but linked. See Link To A File Or Page on page 134 for help on inserting this type of link.

1 select page
Select the page where you want to insert the file.

2 choose import
Choose **File→Import** to display the Select File dialog box. The name of the current folder is displayed.

3 locate file to insert
Change to the drive or folder that contains the file you want to insert. You can change to another drive or folder by using the Look in drop-down list or the Up One Level button or by double-clicking any of the listed folders.

If you don't see the file listed, it's probably because the list is showing a different file type. Look in the Files of type drop-down list and select the appropriate file type.

4 select & open insert file
Select the file you want to insert and click **Open**. The file opens and is inserted on the current page (the page you selected in step 1).

> **tip** If the converter for the file type you selected wasn't installed when you first installed FrontPage, you see a message prompting you to install the necessary filter. Insert your FrontPage CD and then click **OK** to install the filter.

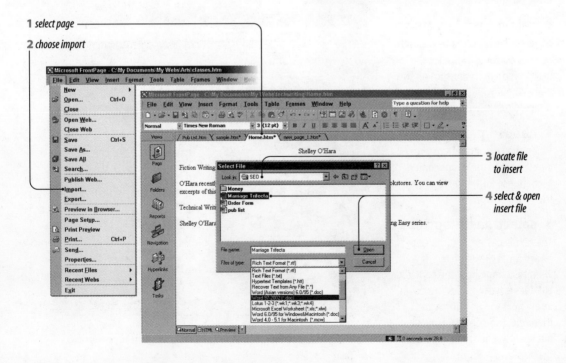

1 select page

2 choose import

3 locate file to insert

4 select & open insert file

Make Simple Formatting Changes

Once you have entered the text for your page, you can use some simple formatting changes to make certain text stand out. For example, you may want to make the document headings bold or to italicize key words. You also have the option of underlining, but do so sparingly. By default, hyperlinks appear underlined. You don't want to confuse the audience by including underlined text that isn't a link.

> *tip* You can also make simple editing changes. To delete a character, move the insertion point next to it. Then press **delete** to delete characters to the right of the insertion point. Press **backspace** to delete characters to the left of the insertion point. To add text, click where you want new text and start typing. To delete a large section of text, don't delete it one character at a time. Select it and then press **delete**.

1 select text

To start, select the text you want to change. See Select & Edit Text on page 47 for information on this step.

2 format text

Do any of the following:

Click **Bold** (A) or press **ctrl+B** to make the text bold.

Click **Italic** (B) or press **ctrl+I** to make the text italic.

Click **Underline** (C) or press **ctrl+U** to underline the text.

FrontPage obeys your every command and formats the text as you asked.

> *tip* To help your audience navigate from one page to another and to find the key sections of a page, use heading styles to format the headings. See Chapter 9, Work With Styles, for more information. You also can find more information on the many formatting features of FrontPage in Chapter 5, Enhance Page Design.

a *or press **ctrl+B***

b *or press **ctrl+I***

c *or press **ctrl+U***

2 *format text*

1 *select text*

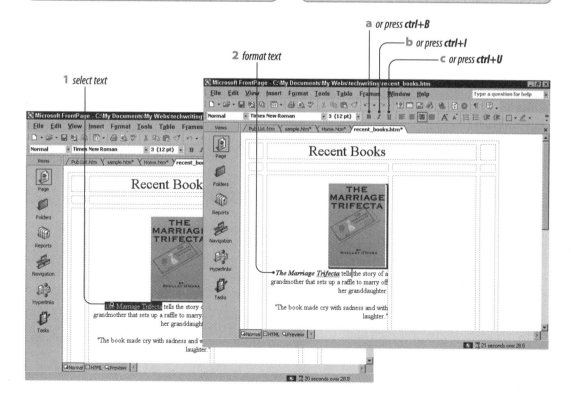

Insert A Horizontal Line

Horizontal lines break up the content and add visual interest to your page. You can insert a horizontal line in any part of the page. You can also tell Front-Page how you want the line to appear.

> **tip** Other ways to add lines are to add page or paragraph borders, covered in Add A Box Border on page 94 and Add A Custom Border on page 95. As another alternative, you can divide a page into frames (Chapter 11) or create a table (Chapter 8).

1 place insertion point

Click the spot on the page where you want to insert the line. The line will be inserted above where you place the insertion point.

2 choose horizontal line

Choose **Insert→Horizontal Line**. FrontPage places the line on the page for you. If you like the look of the line, you're finished. If you want to change the appearance of the line, follow the remaining steps.

3 choose horizontal line properties

Right-click the inserted line and select **Horizontal Line Properties**. You see the Horizontal Line Properties dialog box.

4 select options & click OK

You can select a width measured by *percent of window* or height measured in *pixels*. The larger the number, the bigger the line. Select an alignment (left, center, or right). Display the color drop-down list and select a color. Finally, you can choose to create a solid line, rather than the default shaded line. Click **OK**. The line is modified.

> **tip** If you don't want the line to stretch from margin to margin, select **Center** as the alignment and then make the line shorter. You can measure the width in percent of window (100% is margin to margin) or in pixels.

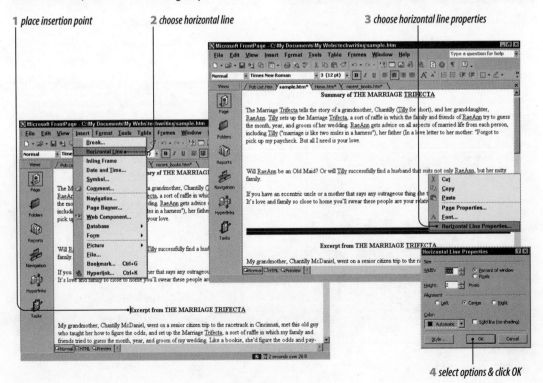

1 *place insertion point*   2 *choose horizontal line*   3 *choose horizontal line properties*

4 *select options & click OK*

Insert A Symbol

Another item you may want to include within a page is a special symbol such as a trademark (™) symbol, a copyright (©) symbol, a mathematical symbol (≈), or a Greek symbol (Ω). To display and print symbols, FrontPage uses special fonts that are nothing but symbols. You can choose from any of the symbol fonts installed on your computer. Common symbol fonts include **Symbol**, **Webdings**, and **Wingdings**.

1 place insertion point

Click where you want to insert the symbol on the page.

2 choose symbol

Choose **Insert➡Symbol.** You see the Symbol dialog box displaying the available symbols in the default symbol font.

3 select font

In the Font drop-down list, select the font that contains the symbol you want to insert. The list of fonts installed on your computer will vary, but expect to find common symbol fonts including Symbol, Webdings, and Wingdings.

4 select & insert symbol

Scroll through the list of symbols to find the one you want to insert. You can also choose from the palette of recently used symbols. Click the symbol you want to insert and then click **Insert.** The symbol is inserted, and the dialog box remains open. Click **Close** to close the dialog box.

> **tip** Unlike most Microsoft programs, you can't type AutoCorrect entries to insert a symbol. (If you type (c) in Word, for instance, it's replaced with ©). You also can't assign shortcut keys to commonly used symbols.

1 *place insertion point*
2 *choose symbol*

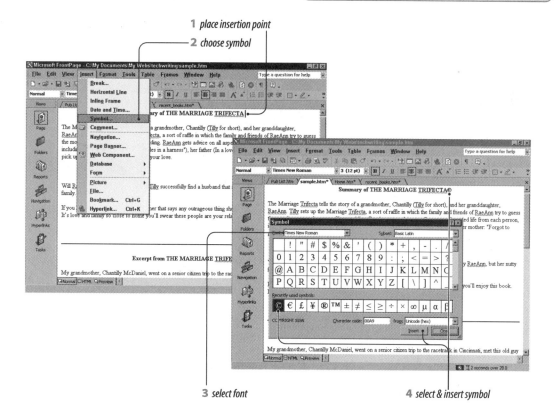

3 *select font*   4 *select & insert symbol*

Insert The Date & Time

To keep track of the date for your content, you can insert the date and time directly onto the page. This information helps you and your audience keep track of when the content was created or modified. You may want to insert this information within the body of a page. You can choose to insert the date the page was last edited or the date the page was automatically updated. Finally, you have several formats for the date and time.

1 place insertion point
Click where you want to insert the date or time.

2 choose date and time
Choose **Insert→Date and Time.** You see the Date and Time dialog box.

3 select date option
You can insert the date the page was last edited or the date the page was last automatically updated. Use the first option if you want to track when you or someone on the Web team actually made a change. Use the second option if you have certain content that

is automatically updated (such as a hit counter or other automatic features) and if you want to update the date each time the page has been changed, not necessarily by you or your staff.

4 select format
In the Date format drop-down list, select a format. Sample formats include 07-03-01, Jul-01, and Tuesday, 03 July 2001. Then display the Time format drop-down list and choose a format for the time. Formats include 07:57:19 TZ, 07:57 AM TZ, and others where TZ is your time zone. If you don't want to include the time, set it to None. Likewise for the date.

5 click OK
FrontPage inserts the date and time just as you have requested.

> *tip* Note that the date is actually a code that will be updated when the page is updated either manually or automatically. You can delete the code by clicking to the left of it and pressing **backspace**. To update the code, select it and press **F9**.

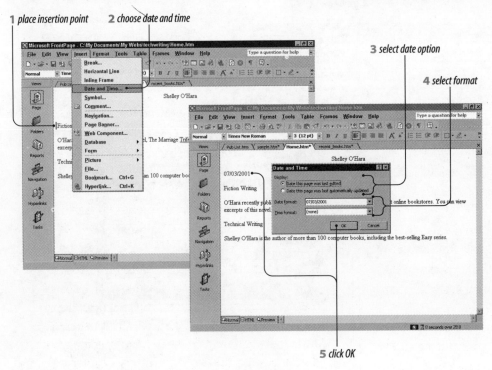

1 *place insertion point* **2** *choose date and time*

3 *select date option*

4 *select format*

5 *click OK*

chapter 4
Edit Web Pages

Creating and maintaining a Web page is an ongoing process, and editing plays a part in every phase of the process. In the beginning, when you first put your site together, you need to fine-tune and check the accuracy of your content. After your Web is up and running, you need to continually update the content, adding new attractions, replacing outdated material, changing the look, and so on. People who visit your Web regularly start to consider your site stale and boring if the content is frozen and staid. To keep your Web fresh, exciting, accurate, and effective, you need to edit the pages.

This chapter first shows you how to open pages for editing. Then you see how to make all kinds of changes—everything from finding and replacing text and using the thesaurus to deleting pages. We also show you how to do the nitty-gritty editing, like checking your spelling. Finally, this chapter also shows you how to preview your page before posting it for the world to see.

The Open File Dialog Box

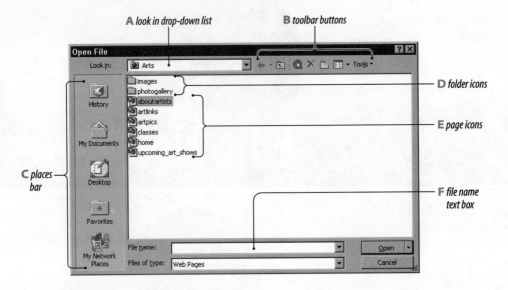

A *look in drop-down list*

B *toolbar buttons*

D *folder icons*

E *page icons*

C *places bar*

F *file name text box*

To work on a particular page in your Web, you first need to *open* the page. Opening a page is similar to opening a Web (see Open A Web on page 35). You use the **Open File** dialog box, rather than the Open Web dialog box, to do so, but the features of these dialog boxes are similar. To display the Open File dialog box, choose **File➡Open.** You can also click the **More Pages** link in the Open area of the New Page or Web task pane.

> *tip* You can open a page without opening the Web it belongs to, but opening the Web first makes it possible to view all the pages in other views such as Navigation view, Folders view, and so on.

A look in drop-down list
When you choose **File➡Open,** you see the contents of the last folder you opened. If you want to work on another page in another drive or folder, use the Look in drop-down list.

B toolbar buttons
The dialog box includes a toolbar which lets you navigate from folder to folder. Click the **Up One Level** button to move up a level.

To change how the contents of the dialog box are displayed, click the down arrow next to the View button and choose another view.

C places bar
The Places bar includes icons for commonly-used folders. Click the icon for the folder or location you want to open. For instance, click **My Documents** to open that folder.

D folder icons
You can open any of the folders listed in the contents pane. To do so, double-click the folder icon.

E page icons
After you change folders and drives to locate the page icon for the particular page you want to work on, you can double-click the icon to open that page.

F file name text box
If you know the name of the file you want to open, you can type the name in this text box and click the **Open** button.

Open & Edit A Page

To make any type of change to a page, you must first open the Web (see Open A Web on page 35) and then open the page. You can open a page from the **New Page or Web** task pane very easily; first choose **File→New→Page or Web** to make the task pane appear. FrontPage keeps track of the last pages you worked on and lists them in the Open a page section of the task pane. (If you don't see the name of the page in this list, click **More pages.**) When you locate the name of the page, you can click it to open that page. Skip the remaining steps and go straight to editing. If the page isn't listed, or if you prefer not to use the task pane, you can choose the page to open from the **Open File** dialog box.

> *tip* If you want to open all the pages in the Web, or at least more than one, you can't do so in the Open File dialog box, but you can do so in Folders view. Click the **Folders** view button and then ctrl+click each file you want to open. Right-click the selected files and then click **Open.**

To delete text, drag across the text to select it, and then press **Delete**.

To change the appearance of the page (the text, the paragraphs, or the page itself), select the text you want to change and then use any of the buttons in the Formatting toolbar or any of the commands in the Format menu. See Chapter 5, Enhance Page Design, for help on formatting pages.

To insert a text hyperlink, type the text for the hyperlink or insert the hyperlink by choosing **Insert→Hyperlink.** Chapter 7, Create Hyperlinks, covers all the details of inserting a hyperlink.

> *tip* Remember to save changes to a page as you edit. Click the **Save** button, press **ctrl+S**, or choose **File→Save** to save the page.

You can insert several types of pictures, including clipart, digital photographs, WordArt, and others. See Chapter 6, Add & Edit Pictures, for more information on working with these visual elements.

1 display open file dialog box

Choose **File→Open** or click the **Open** button.

2 locate page to open

You can change to another drive or folder by using the **Look in** drop-down list or the **Up One Level** button or by double-clicking any of the listed folders.

3 open page

When the page you want to open is listed, double-click it to open the page. You can also click the page and then click the **Open** button. The page appears on-screen.

4 edit page

To add new text, click where you want to insert the text and start typing.

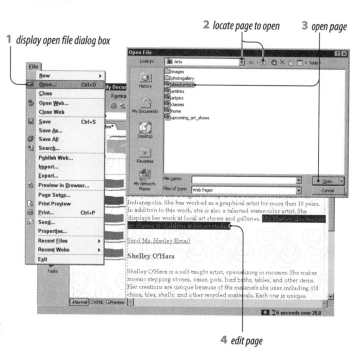

1 *display open file dialog box*

2 *locate page to open*

3 *open page*

4 *edit page*

Set Page Margins

1 *display page properties* **2** *set margins*

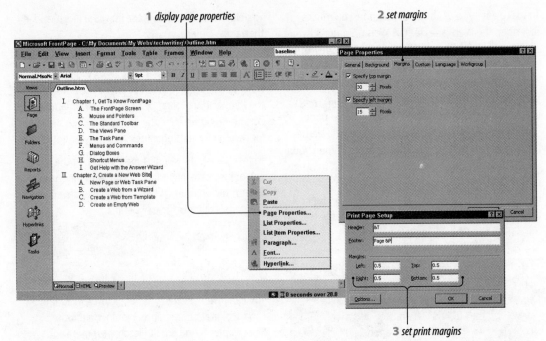

3 *set print margins*

If you want to change the margins for the page, you can do so. You might make the margins smaller, for instance, if you want to print more on a page.

Because documents viewed on-screen aren't limited to a paper size, you need to set only the top and left margins. For printed page options, you set the margins for all sides. The default printed page margins are .5 on all sides.

1 display page properties
Right-click a blank section of the page and select **Page Properties**.

2 set margins
Click the **Margins** tab. Check the **Specify top margin** checkbox and then type the margin for

the top of the page, in pixels. To set the left margin, check **Specify left margin** and enter the margin in pixels. Click **OK**. This step sets the margins for the Web page.

3 set print margins (optional)
To set the margins for the *printed* page, choose **File➥Page Setup**. Type the margins, in inches, for the left, top, right, and bottom margins. Click OK.

> *tip* You can click the **Options** button to display the **Print** dialog box. Then click **OK** to print. For information on printing Web pages, see Print A Page on page 60.

Header & Footers

You can't include headers or footers on a Web page, although you can add shared page borders (see Chapter 12, Add Navigation Elements). When printing a page, though, you can include headers and footers.

To add a header or footer, display the **Print Page Setup** dialog box (choose **File➥Page Setup**) and then type the header and/or footer text to include.

Preview A Printed Page

In addition to previewing a page in a browser, you can preview the page as it will appear when printed. You might do this if you think your visitors will print the page or if you plan to print the page and include it in other publications.

Previewing shows how the text and other page elements flow on the page. You can also add headers and footers to the printed page. (See Set Page Margins on page 58 for information on adding these elements.) For information on previewing a page in the browser, see Preview A Page on page 72.

1 open page
Open the page that you want to preview.

2 choose print preview
You see a preview of the page as it will appear when printed. Note that by default the page includes the

page name as the header and the page number as the footer.

3 zoom in (optional)
In the default view, you can't read the text. You can zoom in (and then back out) to view more details of the page by clicking the **Zoom In** button. You can click this button twice to zoom in to a closer view. You can also simply click the pointer (which looks like a magnifying glass) on the page to zoom in. To zoom out, click the **Zoom Out** button.

> *tip* If the Web page is more than one printed page, click **Next Page** to view the next page; click **Prev Page** to view the previous page. Click the **Two Page** button to view two pages at once.

4 click close
To close the preview window, click the **Close** button.

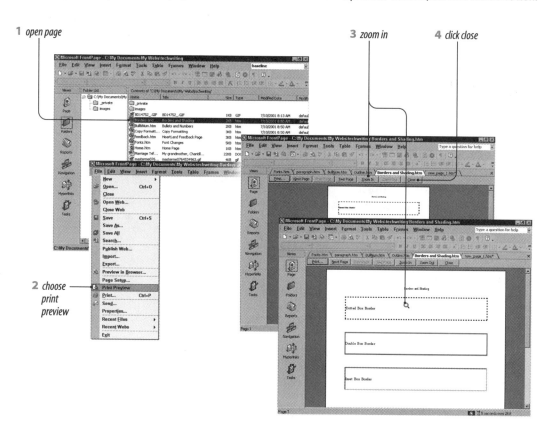

1 *open page*

2 *choose print preview*

3 *zoom in*

4 *click close*

steps Print A Page

At some point, you may want to print a page to use in a report, presentation, or other publication. You may also find it easier to proofread text on a printed copy rather than on the screen. Or you may need to print out pages for your staff to review and comment on. In any case, you can print a page from the **Print** dialog box.

1 choose print

To make the Print dialog box appear, choose **File→Print.**

> *tip* If you want to send a page directly to the printer without setting print options, click the **Print** button.

2 select printer (optional)

FrontPage displays the default printer in the **Name** drop-down list box. You can display the list of installed printers and select another printer.

3 select page range (optional)

If the page is more than one printed page, you can select the range of pages to print. The default is All, but you can select **Pages** and then enter the page(s) to print.

> *tip* To print just part of a page, select the text to print and then choose **File→Print.** Or, in the Print dialog box, click the **Selection** radio button.

4 select number of copies (optional)

If you want to print more than one copy, enter the number of copies to print in the **Number of copies** spin box. You can also click the spin arrows to increment the value.

5 click OK

Your print-outs should be hot off the presses.

> *tip* You can't print pages in Folders view or Hyperlinks view, but you can print a page from Navigation view. Select the page to print and then click the **Print** button.

1 *choose print*

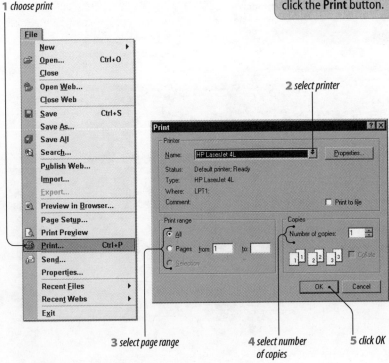

2 *select printer*

3 *select page range*

4 *select number of copies*

5 *click OK*

steps Check Spelling On The Fly

To present the most professional site, you should check the spelling of your site's text and correct any misspelled words. To help with this task, FrontPage lets you check your spelling as you type. Each time you type a word that FrontPage doesn't recognize, you see a red squiggly line under the word. This mark indicates that FrontPage couldn't find this word in its dictionary. Note that the word may not be misspelled; some terms and names may be flagged as misspelled just because FrontPage didn't recognize them. If the word is misspelled, you can display the **Spelling** shortcut menu and make changes as you type.

As an alternative, you can ignore the flagged words and check your spelling all at once. See The Spelling Dialog Box and Check Spelling on pages 62 and 63.

1 open spelling menu

When you see a flagged word, right-click the word to display the shortcut menu. If FrontPage has any suggested replacement spellings, they are listed at the top of the menu. The rest of the menu displays spelling commands.

tip If you don't want FrontPage to check for spelling errors, choose **Tools→Page Options.** On the **General** tab, uncheck the **Check spelling as you type** checkbox. You can also hide all errors in all documents (all flagged words) by checking **Hide spelling errors in all documents.** When you do want to check spelling, be sure to turn off this option.

2 choose correction

To replace the word with one of the listed spellings, choose the appropriate replacement in the shortcut menu.

To ignore the word and all of its occurrences in the document, choose **Ignore All.** Use this option for uncommon words that are spelled correctly and shouldn't be flagged.

To add the word to the dictionary so that it's not flagged, choose **Add to Dictionary.** Use this option for words that are flagged and that you often use. Rather than continually flagging them, FrontPage adds the word to the dictionary so that it recognizes the word in future documents.

1 *open spelling menu*   **2** *choose correction*

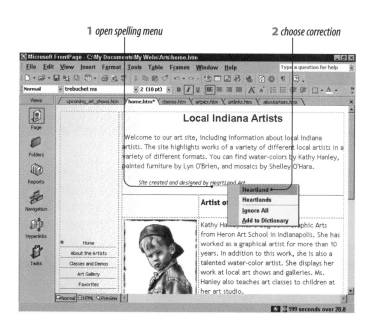

The Spelling Dialog Box

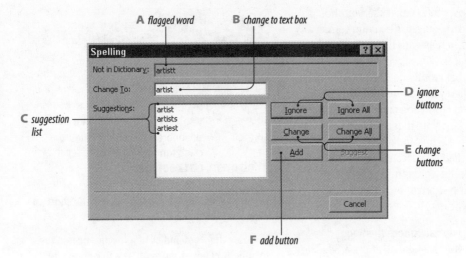

A *flagged word*   **B** *change to text box*

D *ignore buttons*

C *suggestion list*

E *change buttons*

F *add button*

As mentioned, you can check spelling as you go. Or you may prefer to concentrate on writing the content and go back later to check spelling. In this case, you can start a spell-check by choosing **Tools**➡ **Spelling** and working in the **Spelling** dialog box. During a spell-check, FrontPage goes through the entire page and checks the words against the words in its dictionary. Any words that FrontPage doesn't find in its dictionary are flagged. When the Spelling dialog box opens, you see the first flagged word and lots of options for fixing the error.

A flagged word

The first word in the page that isn't listed in the Front-Page dictionary appears in the **Not in Dictionary** text box. You can't edit this word in the text box; you have to choose options in the dialog box to edit the word.

B change to text box

The same word is listed in the **Change To** text box. In some cases, FrontPage flags a word but is unable to list a replacement spelling. Or the replacements may not be what you intended. For example, a common mistake is to forget a space between two words. In the Change To text box, you can edit the word as needed.

C suggestion list

If possible, FrontPage lists suggested correct spellings for the flagged word. If one of the listed words is correct, you can select it and use it as the replacement.

> **tip** If no suggestions are listed, click the **Suggest** button.

D ignore buttons

If the word is spelled correctly, you can ignore the misspelling. When you ignore the spelling, the wavy red line disappears. You can ignore this instance by clicking **Ignore** or all instances by clicking **Ignore All**. Use Ignore if you want to verify other places that use this word. Use Ignore All if you are sure that all instances are acceptable as is. If you choose Ignore All, Front-Page won't flag any other instances of the word.

E change buttons

If you edit a word or select a replacement, click one of the Change buttons to make the change. Click **Change** to change this instance or **Change All** to change all instances.

F add button

If the word is commonly used, you can add it to the dictionary so that it isn't flagged in the future. Click the **Add** button to do so.

🌀steps Check Spelling

During a spell-check, the **Spelling** dialog box appears for each unfound word. You can then change or ignore each of the flagged words.

> *tip* Just because a word is flagged doesn't mean it is misspelled. Uncommon terms and proper names, for instance, may be spelled correctly even though they are flagged. Likewise, just because the document doesn't contain any flagged words doesn't mean it is error-free. You still need to proofread your document. FrontPage can't discern whether you used the correct word; it only recognizes the spelling. For example, FrontPage won't flag *to, too,* or *two* if you have used them incorrectly, as long as you have spelled them right. Be sure to proofread to avoid embarrassing errors.

1 choose spelling

Choosing **Tools➥Spelling** or clicking the **Spelling** button starts the spell-check and makes the **Spelling** dialog box appear.

2 edit flagged word

You can tell FrontPage to change or ignore the word, or add it to the dictionary. See The Spelling Dialog Box on page 62 for more information on each of these options. Do this for each word that FrontPage has flagged.

> *tip* FrontPage also flags double words, a common typing mistake. When a double word is flagged, you can ignore it (if the double word is correct) by clicking **Ignore** or delete the second occurrence by clicking **Delete**.

3 click OK

When the spell-check is complete, you see a message stating so. Click **OK** to close the message box and return to the page.

> *tip* If you want to check the spelling of more than one page, switch to Folders view, Navigation view, or Hyperlinks view and then click the **Spelling** button. In the dialog box that appears, check the selected page(s) or the entire Web and then click **Start**. You can then check several pages at once.

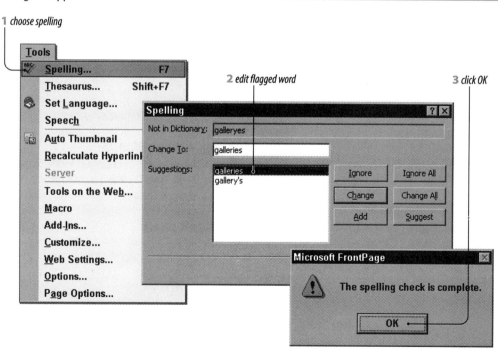

1 *choose spelling*

2 *edit flagged word*

3 *click OK*

The Find And Replace Dialog Box

A *find what text box*

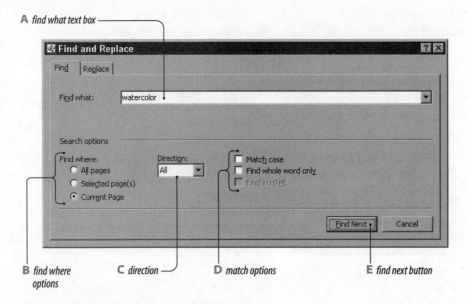

B *find where options*   **C** *direction*   **D** *match options*   **E** *find next button*

If you are looking for a particular word or phrase on a page, you can scan the page to find it, but it's much faster to *search* for it. The **Find** dialog box helps you search for and locate a word or phrase in the blink of an eye. However, often when you search, you can end up with too many matches or matches that you didn't intend. To limit the search, you can use any one of several options available in the **Find and Replace** dialog box, which you summon by choosing **Edit➡Find.**

The **Replace** tab in the Find and Replace dialog box lets you search for a particular word or phrase and then replace it with another word or phrase. Like finding text, you can select where to search, the direction, and how to make the matches. Choosing **Edit➡Replace** makes this dialog box appear if the Find and Replace dialog box isn't already on your screen.

The first set of options on the Replace tab are the same ones you find on the Find tab, and you use these options the same way. That is, you type the

text to find and replace in the find what text box, select the find where options, select a direction, and set match options.

A find what text box
To search for a word or phrase, type it in this text box.

> 📝 If you have previously performed a search, you can click the down arrow next to this textbox and choose from previous search strings.

B find where options
You can search all pages, the selected pages, or the current page (the default). If you want to search the entire Web, select **All pages.** If you want to search selected pages, select them first and then choose **Selected page(s)** here.

> 📝 You can select multiple pages within a folder, but only in Folders view. Click the Folders view button. You can ctrl+click to select each page, or to select pages next to each other, click the first page, hold down the shift key, and click the last page. All pages, including the first and last, are selected.

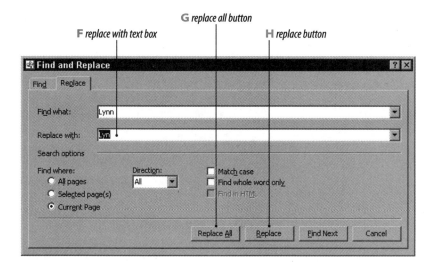

F *replace with text box*

G *replace all button*

H *replace button*

C direction

You can search all directions (from the location of the insertion point down to the end of the document and then back through from the top to the current location). Or you can search up or down.

D match options

If you want to match the entry exactly as you typed it, check **Match case.** As an example, if you type *Art,* FrontPage flags *Art,* but not *art* or *ART.* To limit the search to whole words, check **Find whole words only.** Again, if you type *art* and check this checkbox, Front-Page finds *art,* but not *heart, artistic,* or other words that contain *art.*

> *tip* If you choose **Edit→Find** from views other than Page view, you can search for a HTML code. Select **Find in HTML.** This option isn't available when searching a single page from Page view.

E find next button

Use the **Find Next** button on either tab to start the search. Note that if you are searching multiple pages, this button is called **Find in Web.**

F replace with text box

The **Replace** tab contains the preceding items, but adds a Replace with textbox. Here you can type the entry to use as the replacement text.

> *tip* If you have previously performed a replace, you can click the down arrow next to this text box and choose from previous replace strings.

G replace all button

When FrontPage finds a match after clicking the Find Next button (E), it is highlighted, and you can then choose whether to make replacements one at a time or all at once.

> *tip* It's a good idea to at least go through a few replacements and confirm that the entries are being handled as you expected. Otherwise, you may end up with replacements that you didn't intend to make.

H replace button

To make a replacement and move to the next match, click this button.

> *tip* If FrontPage finds a match and you don't want to make the replacement, you can click the Find Next button to skip this match and move to the next one.

steps Find Text

To search for a word or phrase, perhaps to verify or make changes to the text, start by displaying the page you want to search in Page view or selecting the page to search in Navigation or Hyperlinks view. For instance, you may want to confirm someone's name or a site you've listed on a page. Rather than manually read through the page, you can find the word or phrase much more quickly by searching for it.

1 choose find

Choosing **Edit➥Find** makes the **Find and Replace** dialog box appear.

2 type text to match

Type the text that you want to find in the **Find what** textbox. You can type a partial word, a whole word, or a phrase. The more specific the word, the better the results. For example, if you search for *art* on a site for artists, you are likely to end up with too many matches.

If you search for *etchings,* though, you greatly improve your odds of finding the section you want.

3 select search options

Select any search options you want to use to limit the search. See The Find And Replace Dialog Box on page 64 for more information on the various options.

4 click find next

Click **Find Next** to start the search. FrontPage moves to the first match, and the Find and Replace dialog box remains open. Click Find Next to find the next match.

If you are searching the entire Web, the Find and Replace dialog box expands to include the search results. Also, you click **Find in Web** to start the search. The results display the page(s) where the match was found as well as the number of matches on each page.

Click **Cancel** to close the dialog box when you're done.

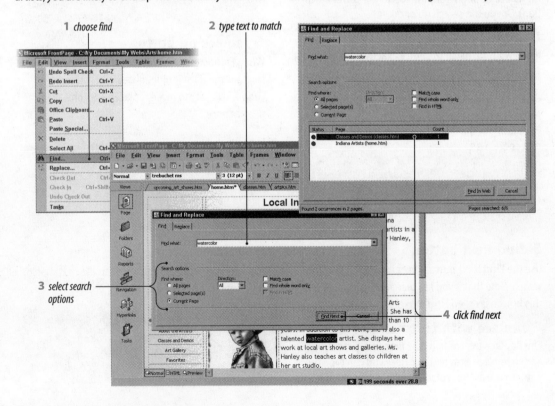

 **Replace Text**

After you type the text for a page, you may find that you need to make some *global replacements*. For example, you may need to change the name of a company throughout a page, or you might have misspelled a name and need to correct the spelling everywhere it appears. Rather than make these changes manually, you can have FrontPage find all of the incorrect entries and replace them with the appropriate text.

1 choose replace

Your good friend, the **Find and Replace** dialog box, appears. This is where you tell FrontPage what errant text you want to find, and what you want to replace that text with.

2 type text to find

Type the text that you want to find and replace.

3 type replacement text

Type the entry to use as the replacement text.

4 select search options

Select any search options you want to use to limit the search. See The Find And Replace Dialog Box on page 64 for more information on the various options.

tip These options are more critical when you replace text. If you don't limit a replace, you may end up with replacements you didn't intend. As an example, suppose that you replace *art* with *craft*. If you don't limit the search to entire words, you can end up with replacements such as changing *artist* to *craftist*.

5 click find next

Click **Find Next** to start the search. FrontPage moves to the first match, and the Find and Replace dialog box remains open.

6 make replacement

Click **Replace** to replace this occurrence, **Find Next** to skip making this replacement and move to the next match, or **Replace All** to replace each occurrence. Do this for each match found.

If you are searching the entire Web, FrontPage searches through each page, prompting you to confirm you are finished with one page and want to go to the next page. Go through each page until you search and replace in all pages and then return to the list.

When you're done, click **Cancel** to close the dialog box.

1 *choose replace*   **2** *type text to find*   **3** *type replacement text*

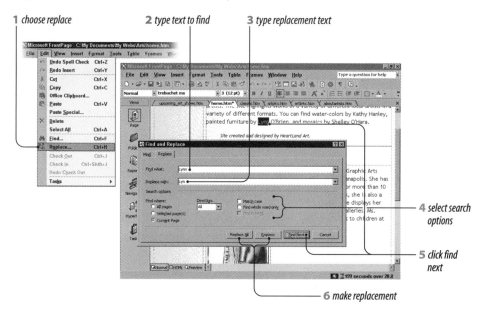

4 *select search options*

5 *click find next*

6 *make replacement*

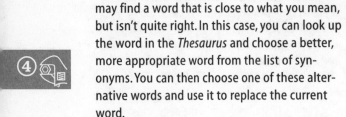

Use The Thesaurus

As you type or review the content for a page, you may find a word that is close to what you mean, but isn't quite right. In this case, you can look up the word in the *Thesaurus* and choose a better, more appropriate word from the list of synonyms. You can then choose one of these alternative words and use it to replace the current word.

1 click word

Click within the word that you want to look up.

2 choose thesaurus

You see the **Thesaurus** dialog box listing the synonyms for the selected word.

> *tip* You can also select the word and press **shift+F7** to look up synonyms.

3 select meaning (optional)

Some words may have more than one meaning. In this case, the meanings are listed in the dialog box, and you can pick the meaning closest to yours to display related synonyms.

4 look up more synonyms (optional)

In some cases, the synonyms that are listed are closer to the meaning you want to convey, but still not exactly what you want. In this case, you can select that synonym and click **Look Up** to display synonyms for this new word. If you look up other found words, you can also click **Previous** to return to a previous list of synonyms.

5 make replacement (optional)

If you find a word that better conveys your meaning, you can select it and click **Replace** to replace the selected word with the new word. If you don't find a word, you can close the dialog box by clicking **Cancel**.

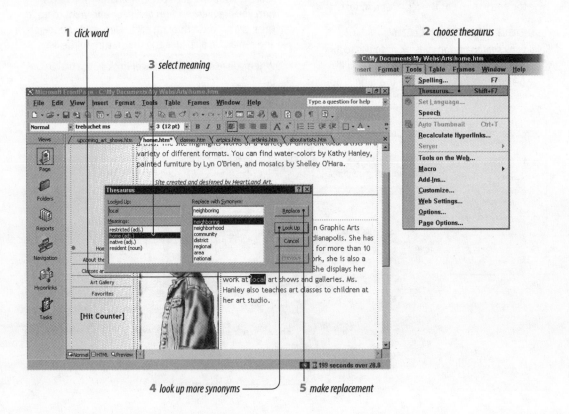

1 *click word*

3 *select meaning*

2 *choose thesaurus*

4 *look up more synonyms*

5 *make replacement*

steps Delete A Page

If your Web contains a page that you no longer need, you can delete it from the Web. Doing so ensures that the Web isn't cluttered with unnecessary files.

Deleting a page is also handy if you used a template to create the Web and the template included pages you don't want to use. (See Use A Template on page 40 for more information on using a template to create a Web.)

1 display folder list
You can't delete a page in Page view unless the Folders list is displayed. Choose **View➤Folder List** to display this list.

Note this list is displayed by default in Folders view. You can also change to this view to delete a page.

2 select page
In the folder list, click the name of the page you want to delete.

tip You can delete a page in Navigation view; in this view you are given the option of removing the page from the navigational structure or deleting the page from the Web. Select the option you want and then click **OK**.

3 delete page
Choose **Edit➤Delete**, right-click the page and choose the **Delete** command from the shortcut menu, or press the **delete** key. FrontPage displays the **Confirm Delete** dialog box. Click the **Yes** button in the **Confirm Delete** dialog box to permanently delete the page.

tip You can't undo a page deletion. You can't even retrieve the item from the Windows Recycle Bin. Be sure that you want to delete the page. If you change your mind, click **No** to cancel the deletion. If you do delete the page, you have to re-create it to get it back.

1 *display folder list*   **2** *select page*   **3** *delete page*

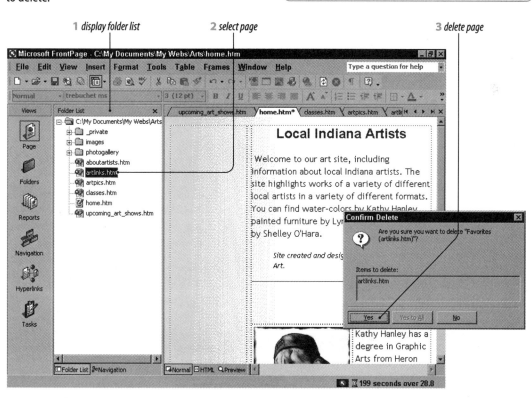

steps Rename & Retitle A Page

When you save a Web page, you assign a *file name* and *page title*. You can change either of these. You may want to use a more descriptive file name if the name you originally used doesn't accurately reflect the page contents. Also, when saving, you may not have changed the page title, but used the default title. You may choose, again, to use a more descriptive title to better identify the page to your visitors. When working with files or pages, you can select the page icon in Folders or Navigation view. Or you can select the file icon in the Folder list, which is available in any view. Using the Folder List is the method covered here.

1 display folder list

You may have to choose **View➥Folder List** to make the list appear on the screen. However, this list is displayed by default in Folders view.

2 rename page

Right-click the file you want to rename and choose **Rename.** Type a new name or edit the name and then press **enter.** Be sure not to change the extension, which can cause problems.

3 update links

If this page is linked to other pages, you are prompted to let FrontPage update the links. Click **Yes** to do so.

> *tip* If you choose **No,** you may have broken links in your Web. You can view a Broken Links report and make any necessary changes. See Hyperlink Reports on page 142.

4 retitle page

To change the page title, right-click the page and then choose **Properties.** Type the new title and click **OK.** Remember that the title appears on the page tabs and page icons in FrontPage and in the browser title when the page is displayed.

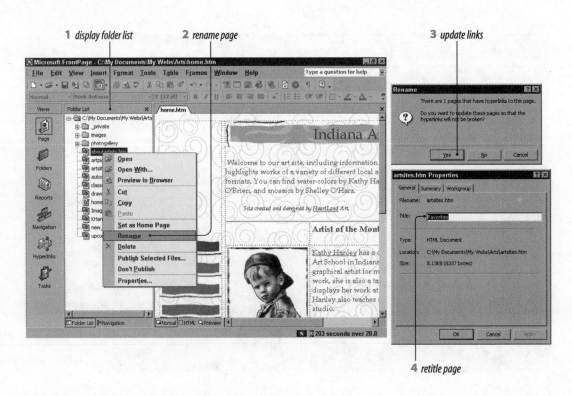

1 *display folder list*   2 *rename page*   3 *update links*

4 *retitle page*

steps Copy Formatting

Sometimes you apply several formatting options to a paragraph or section of text and want to use the same set of options again. If you plan to use the set of options often, you should create a *style* (covered in Create A New Style on page 166), but if you just need to use the formatting once or twice, you can copy it using the **Format Painter** button in the Formatting toolbar. For example, you might format a section heading using a certain font, font style, and border.

Rather than select these same commands again for a similar section heading, pick up the formatting from the first heading and copy it to the second.

> *tip* If you want to copy the formatting more than once, double-click the **Format Painter** button. You can then drag across as many text selections as you want. To quit copying, press the **esc** key.

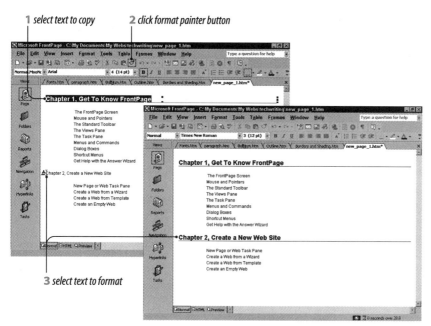

1 *select text to copy*   **2** *click format painter button*

3 *select text to format*

1 select text to copy

Select the text that is formatted with the options you want to copy.

2 click format painter button

When you click this button, the pointer changes to a paint-brush.

3 select text to format

Drag across the text you want to format with the selections. The formatting is copied.

Remove Formatting

Formatting can be a trial-and-error process. You may find that you have made so many changes that now the text is overdone. You can undo the changes, but sometimes you may need to start from scratch—that is, remove all the formatting from the text. You may find that you want to remove formatting if you

are updating a page from another source or if you have inserted a page using a template and the style is not what you need. You can remove the formatting, returning to the bare bones, and then start again.

To remove formatting, follow these steps:

1 Select the text that contains the formatting you want to remove.

2 Choose **Format▸Remove Formatting**. The formatting is removed. The keyboard shortcut for the Remove Formatting command is **ctrl+shift+Z**.

For more information on formatting, see chapter 5, Enhance Page Design.

Preview A Page

Testing, or *previewing,* your pages lets you see your pages as your viewers will see them, which helps you make sure that your pages appear on the screen as you intended. FrontPage lets you preview a page in any browser installed on your computer. Test your pages in as many browsers as possible— at the very least, test them in the two most popular browsers, *Microsoft Internet Explorer* and *Netscape Navigator.* To preview a page in the Internet Explorer window, click the **Preview in Browser** button. To preview a page using Internet Explorer or another browser installed on your computer, you need to use the **Preview in Browser** dialog box.

1 choose preview in browser

The **Preview in Browser** dialog box appears.

2 select browser

The **Preview in Browser** dialog box lists the browsers that FrontPage finds on your computer. To select a browser, click it.

tip If you want to add a new browser to the list, and that browser is installed on your computer, click the **Add** button. Then type the browser name and the path to the program file for the browser. You can also click the **Browse** button in the **Add Browser** dialog box to navigate to and select the program file.

3 select window size

Click a radio button to select the *resolution,* or the size, of the browser window and its contents. If you choose Default, the page will be displayed at the default resolution of the viewer's browser. If you choose 640 x 480, 800 x 600, or 1024 x 768, the browser's window size will be set

to that resolution. (The *resolution* is a measurement of pixels or picture elements. The higher the number, the finer, and smaller, the contents of the window.)

4 check automatically save page

Before you preview the page, you should save it. If your computer tends to crash when you start one more program than its memory can handle, automatically saving avoids losing hours of work that you have already done.

5 click preview

After you select all the options from the dialog box, click the **Preview** button. FrontPage opens the browser you selected in step 1 and displays the current page.

tip To preview the page within FrontPage, click the **Preview** button in the View area. This allows you to see how the text flows on the page, which really helps when working on the formatting. Use the Preview in Browser view when the page is complete.

1 choose preview in browser *2 select browser*

3 select window size

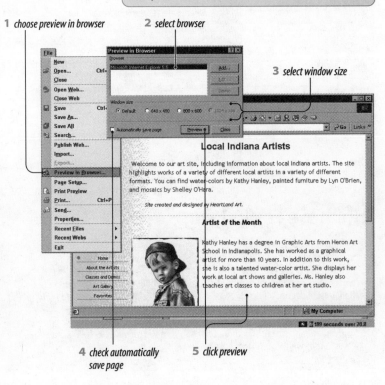

4 check automatically save page *5 click preview*

Enhance Page Design

To make your Web pages easy to read and understand, you should spend some time working with the look of the pages. You can change the formatting of text, paragraphs, and pages to help your site be interesting and easy to follow.

As an example, you may want to make your headings bold and big so that the sections on a page stand out. As another example, if you have long passages of text, you may want to indent the text to break it up into digestible chunks or change the line spacing to make the text easier on the eyes. In addition, you can add bullets and numbering, and other text effects, to help break up the text and other elements on your pages.

Formatting is the same in FrontPage as it is in most word processing programs. You can use either the **Formatting toolbar** or the commands in the **Format menu** to make your formatting changes. This chapter explains all of FrontPage's basic formatting features.

The Formatting Toolbar

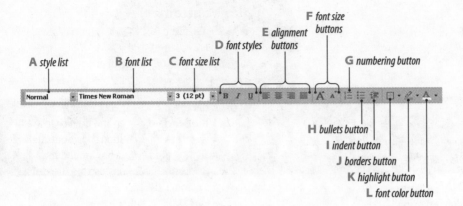

A style list   **B** font list   **C** font size list   **D** font styles   **E** alignment buttons   **F** font size buttons   **G** numbering button   **H** bullets button   **I** indent button   **J** borders button   **K** highlight button   **L** font color button

The fastest way to make a formatting change is by using the **Formatting toolbar.** You can use the buttons in this toolbar to change the font, text alignment, text size, or text color quickly. You can also add bullets or numbers and indent the text. Use the Formatting toolbar if you want to make a quick change. If you have several, more complicated changes, and you want to preview and apply the changes before making them, use the Format commands as covered in this chapter.

A style list
Display the **Style** drop-down list and apply a style. For more information on styles, see Chapter 9, Work With Styles.

B font list
To change the look of the text, display the **Font** drop-down list and choose the font you want. The most recently used fonts are listed first.

tip FrontPage only lists fonts that are installed on your computer. You can purchase additional fonts from computer retail stores or online and then install them in Windows. A popular font Web site is *www.myfonts.com;* you can view and purchase fonts directly from this online source.

C font size list
To change the size of the font, display the **Font Size** drop-down list and choose a size. Note that FrontPage displays both a *relative* size (such as 3) and an *absolute* size (12 pt). This font-sizing method comes into play when the browser doesn't have the font or font size; in that case, the browser can pick a relative size that matches.

D font styles

These three buttons—**Bold, Italic,** and **Underline**—let you change the style of the font, making it bold, italic, underline, or a combination of the three. Make Simple Formatting Changes on page 51 covers these simple formatting commands.

> **tip** Be careful when using underline—hyperlinks also appear underlined. You don't want your visitors confusing underlined text with hyperlinks.

E alignment buttons

You can change how text is aligned on the page by clicking the **Align Left, Center, Align Right,** and **Justified** buttons.

F font size buttons

Another way to change the size of text is to use the **Increase Font Size** and **Decrease Font Size** buttons. Click these buttons to bump the font size up or down to the next size for the selected font.

> **tip** By default, FrontPage displays both the Formatting and Standard toolbars. (See The Standard Toolbar on page 8 for information on the Standard toolbar.) This book shows each toolbar in its own row. If your screen shows the two sharing a row and you'd prefer separate rows, choose **Tools→ Customize.** Click the **Options** tab and then check **Show Standard and Formatting toolbars on two rows.** Click **OK.**

G numbering button

Use numbered lists to indicate items in a sequence, such as a series of steps. You can apply the default numbering style by selecting the paragraphs to number and clicking the **Numbering** button.

H bullets button

Use a bulleted list for items in a list of equal importance, such as items in an agenda. Select the paragraphs you want to add bullets to and click the **Bullets** button. For more information on adding bullets, see Add Bullets on page 87.

I indent button

You can indent the text by clicking the **Increase Indent** button; each click indents the text a little more. To unindent the text, click the **Decrease Indent** button.

J borders button

To apply a border to a paragraph, click the down arrow next to the **Borders** button and then choose a border placement. The default button shows outside borders; clicking this style places a box around the paragraph. For more border options, use the **Borders and Shading** command. See The Borders Tab on page 92 and The Shading Tab on page 93.

K highlight button

If you want to highlight a particular word or sentence, you can do so using the **Highlight** button. The default color is yellow, but the *color palette* (click the down arrow next to this button) lets you change the color. See Select Web-Safe Colors on page 100 for more information on using the color palette.

L font color button

To change the color of the font, select the text to change, click the down arrow next to the **Font Color** button, and then choose the color you want to use. Note that if you have applied a theme, the colors in the palette are those used in the theme. For more information on using themes, see Apply A Theme on page 173.

The Font Dialog Box

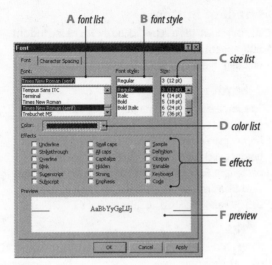

A *font list*   B *font style*

C *size list*

D *color list*

E *effects*

F *preview*

The Formatting toolbar is the fastest way to make font changes, but if you have several changes to make at once and you want to see a preview of all these changes together, you can use the **Font** dialog box. This dialog box also offers special effects, such as blinking text, hidden text, or special text styles (citation, computer code, and others). To display the Font dialog box, choose **Format➡Font.**

A font list

Type the name of a font in this textbox or choose a font from the list, which includes all the fonts installed on your computer.

B font style

Select the font style—bold, italic, regular, or bold italic—from this list. To remove boldface and/or italics, select **Regular.**

> *tip* You can use these shortcut keys to apply font styles to selected text quickly: **ctrl+B** for bold, **ctrl+I** for italic, and **ctrl+U** for underline.

C size list

Select the font size from this list. Make sure that the text is readable on-screen; 8-point type is okay for fine

print, but use a larger font for the body text on a page. Commonly, you also use a larger size than body text for headings.

D color list

Open the **Color** pop-up palette to select a color for selected text. The default color is **Automatic** (usually black). Click **More Colors** to open the **More Colors** dialog box. (To learn about the **More Colors** dialog box, see Select Web-Safe Colors on page 99.)

E effects

To turn on a special effect, check its checkbox. You can select more than one special effect at a time, but be judicious. See Apply Text Effects on page 80 for an explanation of each of these effects.

> *tip* Not all browsers support some of these effects. Test the page in your browser if you really want to use a specific special effect.

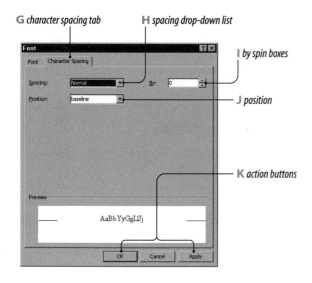

G *character spacing tab* **H** *spacing drop-down list*

I *by spin boxes*

J *position*

K *action buttons*

F preview

One benefit of using the Font dialog box is that you can preview all of your formatting choices here. If you don't like what you see, make a change.

G character spacing tab

Click this tab to change the spacing and position of text on the *baseline*. The baseline is the position of regular text (text that isn't raised or lowered). Use this option when you want to raise or lower text, but keep it the same size. Use *subscript* or *superscript* (see J) when you want to raise or lower text and make it smaller.

H spacing drop-down list

The **Spacing** drop-down list lets you create special spacing effects by expanding or condensing the text. Use **Expanded** to move selected characters farther apart. For example, you can increase the spacing between selected characters in a heading so that the heading is as wide as the width of a line of smaller body-text words on the next line. As the point size of the text in a heading increases, the letters and digits tend to move apart until the heading seems to be composed of separate characters; the heading no

longer looks like a single word. Choose **Condensed** to make the characters take up less space. (The default is normal.)

I by spin boxes

Once you have chosen **Expanded** or **Condensed**, fine-tune the spacing by increasing or decreasing the value in the **By** option box to the right of the **Spacing** list. For Expanded, the higher the value, the more the text is spread out. For Condensed, the higher the value, the more the text is pushed together.

J position

To change the position of the text relative to the *baseline,* display the **Position** drop-down list and choose **sub** (below), **super** (above), **top, middle, bottom,** or any of the other options.

K action buttons

The three action buttons let you complete or cancel an action. Click **OK** or press **enter** to apply your changes and close the dialog box. Click **cancel** to close the dialog box without any formatting taking place. Click **Apply** to apply the changes but keep the dialog box open for further formatting.

steps Change Font & Size

You can affect a certain mood for a page at your Web by changing the font. Some fonts make your text look fun or silly. Some fonts are professional and business-like. Some fonts are fancy, some plain.

You can also change the font size for various reasons. You might want to make the font smaller to fit more text on a page. Or you might want to make certain text larger so that it stands out. FrontPage uses two measurements to specify a font size: a *relative measurement*, such as 1, 2, or 3, and an *exact measurement*, such as 12 point.

> *tip* Fonts are measured in *points,* and there are 72 points to an inch. The bigger the number, the larger the text. This is true for specific font sizes as well as relative font sizes.

1 select text

Select the text that you want to change. To select all the text on a page, choose **Edit➡Select All** or press **ctrl+A.**

2 choose font

Click the down arrow next to the **Font** list and choose the font you want to use.

> *tip* To bump up the font size to the next larger size, click the **Increase Font** button. To decrease the size to the next smaller size, click the **Decrease Font** button.

3 choose font size

Click the down arrow next to the **Font Size** list and choose your new font size. Use your best judgment when selecting fonts and sizes. You don't want too much busy-ness to detract from your message. Also, make sure that the font is a readable size. Finally, consider sticking with common fonts. If you select an uncommon font, it may not display properly if a visitor doesn't have that font installed.

> *tip* To change the default font, choose **Tools➡ Page Options.** On the Default Font tab, select the default proportional and fixed-width fonts you want.

1 *select text*

2 *choose font*

3 *choose font size*

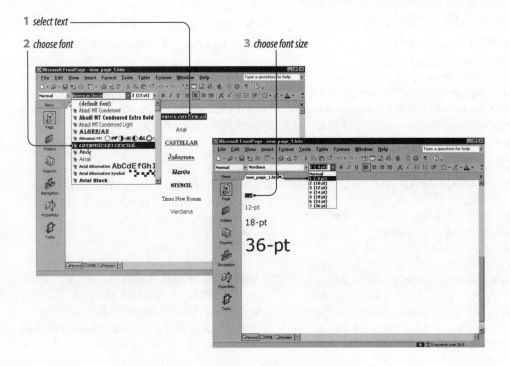

Change Font Color & Highlight

You can also make text stand out by changing its color. If you created your page with a theme, the colors you find in the **Font Color** button's palette are those colors used in the theme. If you haven't applied a theme, the standard colors are available in the color palette. (For more information on themes, see Chapter 9, Work With Styles.) As another option for adding color, you can highlight text to make it stand out. You might use highlighting as an editing tool, highlighting passages that need to be verified or reviewed. You can also use highlighting to call attention to key ideas in a page.

1 select text
Select the text whose color you want to work on.

2 choose font color
Click the down arrow next to the **Font Color** button and then click the color you want. FrontPage changes the font color from the default to your new chosen color.

Stick with a few basic colors on a page; otherwise, the text becomes too busy. Also, most hyperlinks are formatted in a different color. When choosing a color, be sure not to confuse the text color with the color used for hyperlinks. If you have applied a background picture or color (see Add Background Or Foreground Color on page 96 and Shade With A Picture on page 97), be sure the font color is readable. Finally, consider using one set of colors consistently throughout the Web, rather than a mishmash of colors, to provide additional continuity for your site.

> *tip* If you have applied a theme to the page, the colors from that theme are listed under Document Colors. See Apply A Theme on page 175.

3 apply highlight
Click the down arrow next to the **Highlight** button and choose a color for the highlighting. Front-Page highlights the text with the color you specified.

If the color palette doesn't contain the color that you want, click **More Colors** for either the Font Color or Highlight. In the **More Colors** dialog box, select the color you want to use by clicking on it in the color wheel. See Select Web-Safe Colors on page 99 for more information.

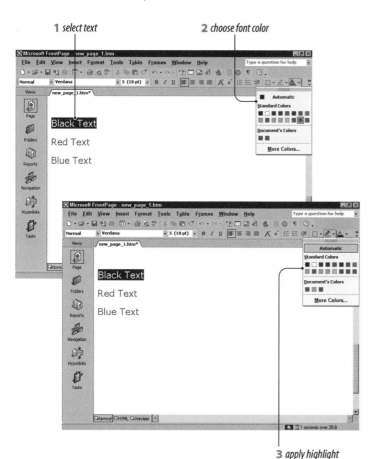

1 *select text*   2 *choose font color*

3 *apply highlight*

steps Apply Text Effects

The **Font** dialog box includes some special text effects not available on the Formatting toolbar. For example, the Font dialog box lets you make your text *small caps, all caps, hidden, blinking, superscript,* and *subscript.* You can also choose character styles for certain elements of the page. For example, if the page includes computer coding, use **Code.** For text you want the reader to enter, use **Keyboard.** When you select this effect, a particular font style is used for that text.

> *tip* If you don't know what an option does, you can select it and view the preview. As another option, right-click the option and then choose **What's This?** to display a ScreenTip explanation.

As with font changes, use special text effects sparingly. First, you don't want your message to get lost if the effects are too overwhelming. Second, some browsers may not display all effects properly. To check your page, publish and then preview it. See Preview A Page on page 72.

1 select text

Select the text that you want to add special effects to.

2 choose font

Choosing **Format➥Font** makes the **Font** dialog box pop up.

3 choose special effects

Check any of the special effects to turn them on. Take a peek at the preview to view sample text formatted with the effect(s). When the text appears the way you want it, click **OK.**

> *tip* You can select more than one text effect, but some overwrite others. For instance, you can't select Small caps and All caps or All caps and Capitalize. You can't select Superscript and Subscript at the same time. If you select one of these options and then select a conflicting option, the new option is checked, but the conflicting one is unchecked or turned off.

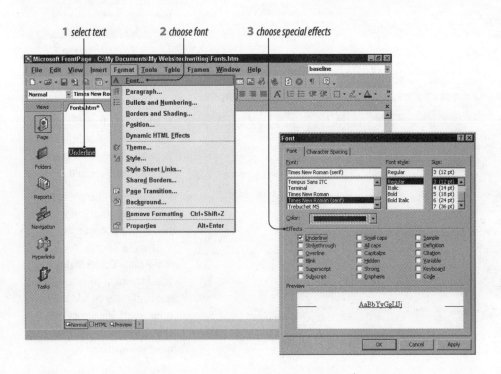

Font Effects

The following table lists each of the effects available in the **Font** dialog box, tells what the effect does, and gives the name of the *counterpart HTML element*. If you prefer to edit or format pages using HTML, you can use these codes to apply a specific effect. When editing in HTML, codes to turn on an effect come in pairs: one to turn the effect on and one to turn it off. For instance, to apply underline, you would use this set of codes:

| u | turns on |
| /u | turns off |

The text to be underlined would appear between these two codes. Do you need to bother with the codes? If you are curious , maybe. If you want to learn more about HTML, sure. And if you are an expert, you may use HTML or Reveal Tags to debug a page. For instance, you might find a missing code in the pair, and this error may be effecting the appearance of the page.

Some effects are actually *styles,* and applying these effects gives them not only a special appearance but codes them so that the browser recognizes the style. Common styles recognized by browsers include definition, sample, keyboard, and code.

Effect	What Effect Does	HTML Element	Example Use
Underline	Underlines text	**U** element	Underline
Strikethrough	Draws a line through text	**S** or **STRIKE** element	Strikethrough
Overline	Places a line over text	None	Overline
Blink	Makes text blink on and off	None	Blink
Superscript	Moves text up and makes it smaller	**SUPER** element	Superscript
Subscript	Moves text down and makes it smaller	**SUB** element	Subscript
Small caps	Makes text small uppercase	None	SMALL CAPS
All caps	Makes text regular uppercase	None	ALL CAPS
Capitalize	Makes text initial uppercase	None	Capitalize
Hidden	Hides text from view	None	Hidden
Strong	Applies boldface	**STRONG** element	Strong
Emphasis	Applies italics	**EM** element	Emphasis
Sample	Creates sample computer program output	**SAMP** element	Sample
Definition	Applies the Definition style	**DFN** element	Definition
Citation	Cites a book, paper, or excerpt	**CITE** element	Citation
Variable	Highlights a variable	**VAR** element	Variable
Keyboard	Indicates keyboard input	**KBD** element	Keyboard
Code	Applies computer-code font	**CODE** element	Code

The Paragraph Dialog Box

A alignment

B left & right indents

C first line indent

D paragraph spacing

E line spacing

F word spacing

G preview

Like formatting characters, you can select paragraph formatting options using the toolbar or the menu command. For example, you can change the indents by clicking **Increase Indent** or **Decrease Indent** or change alignment by clicking one of the align buttons (**Align Left, Center, Align Right,** or **Justified**). You can also use the **Paragraph** dialog box to make these kinds of changes. This dialog box enables you to make the same choices, but also includes other options for setting line spacing and paragraph spacing. To open this dialog box, choose **Format➡Paragraph.**

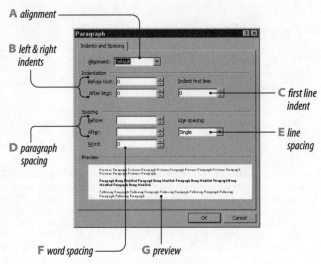

A alignment

To change the alignment of highlighted text, display this drop-down list and select the alignment you want (**Left, Right, Center,** or **Justify**).

B left & right indents

Use the **Before text** spin boxes to set a *left* indent and the **After text** indent boxes to set the *right* indent. Enter the measurement in *pixels*. You can type a value or use the spin arrows to increment the value.

> **tip** A *pixel* as defined by FrontPage's online help is "a single unit of measurement that your computer's display hardware uses to paint images on your screen." These units, which often appear as tiny dots, compose the pictures displayed by your screen; measurements for on-screen elements are often given in pixels.

C first line indent

To specify a first line indent, enter the value here. Enter a negative number to create a *hanging indent* (commonly used for numbered steps and bibliographies, for example).

D paragraph spacing

To add space above or below a paragraph, enter the value in the **Before** or **After** spin boxes.

> **tip** Paragraph spacing isn't the same as line spacing. *Paragraph spacing* is the amount of space in between each of the paragraphs on a page; a paragraph is defined each time you press **enter.** *Line spacing* is the amount of space between each line in a paragraph.

E line spacing

To select the spacing for the lines within a paragraph, display the **Line spacing** drop-down list and specify either **Single, 1.5,** or **Double** spacing.

F word spacing

To set the spacing for the words on a page, enter the value in the **Word** spin box.

G preview

If you are unsure what an option does, check the **Preview** to see how the change affects the sample paragraphs.

steps Change Alignment

The *default alignment* for all text you type on a page is left alignment. If needed, you can change the alignment of the paragraphs on your page. You may, for instance, choose to center headings. For the date, you may want to use right alignment. For long paragraphs of text, you may want to *justify* the paragraph. With justified text, the text is spread evenly between the left and right margins, making it look neater, especially for text in columns.

> **tip** Keep in mind that if you are formatting text in a frame, the alignment applies only within that frame. For example, if you highlight the text in a frame and choose Center alignment, the highlighted text is centered within the frame, not the whole page. See Chapter 11, Divide A Page Into Frames.

1 select paragraphs

Select the paragraphs you want to change. To change a single word, paragraph, or heading, click within it. To change several paragraphs, select them first.

2 choose alignment

Click one of the following alignment buttons:

Align Left (a)	Text lined up on left margin (the default)
Center (b)	Text centered between left and right margin
Align Right (c)	Text lined up on right margin
Justified (d)	Text evenly spaced between left and right margins

FrontPage makes the change. To undo the change, select the same paragraphs and then select another alignment. You can't click the toolbar button again to undo the change (as you can for Bold, Italic, and Underline).

If you prefer to use the **Paragraph** dialog box to make alignment changes, select the paragraphs and then choose **Format▸Paragraph.** Choose the alignment you want from the **Alignment** drop-down list.

> **tip** FrontPage inserts a special *hard return* character each time you press **enter.** This character doesn't print, but you can view this and other hidden characters, such as spaces and tabs. To do so, click the **Show All** button (e). To hide the marks, click the **Show All** button again. This information is useful when formatting paragraphs, for instance, because you can clearly see the paragraph markers.

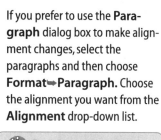

c align right

b center

d justified

1 select paragraphs

a align left

e show all

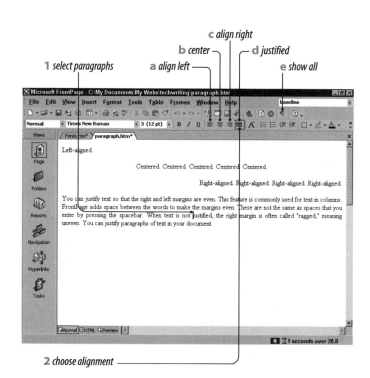

2 choose alignment

steps Indent Text

If you want to set off certain passages of text, you can use an *indent*. You might indent quotations for a source, for instance. You can use the **Increase Indent** and **Decrease Indent** features for regular-spaced indents. For a more exact position, you can stipulate a specific value for the indent in the **Paragraph** dialog box. You can also use this dialog box to set special first-line indents.

1 select paragraphs

Select the paragraphs you want to change. To change a single paragraph, click within it. To change several paragraphs, select them first.

2 choose paragraph

Choosing this command opens the **Paragraph** dialog box.

3 set indent

Do one of the following, entering all values in pixels:

To indent the text from the left margin, enter the amount to indent in the **Before text** spin box.

Check the preview area to see how the indented text will appear.

To indent the text from the right margin, enter the amount to indent in the **After text** spin box.

To set a *first-line* indent, enter the amount to indent in the **Indent first line** spin box.

To create a *hanging* indent, where the second line of text is indented under the first line, enter a negative amount in the **Indent first line** spin box and the same amount (but positive) in the **Before text** spin box.

4 click OK

FrontPage sets the indents exactly as you told it to.

> **tip** You can also indent text by clicking the **Increase Indent** button in the Formatting toolbar. To unindent the text, click the **Decrease Indent.** You can press **ctrl+M** to indent from the left and right margins. Press **ctrl+shift+M** to unindent the text.

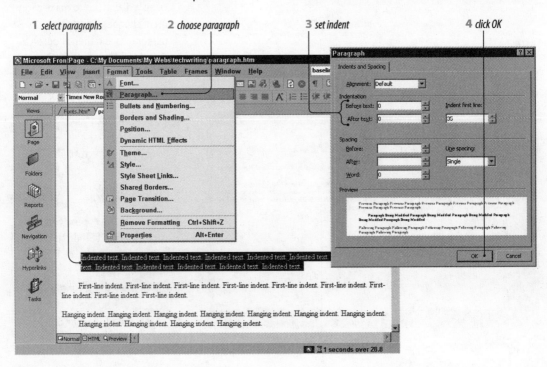

1 *select paragraphs* 2 *choose paragraph* 3 *set indent* 4 *click OK*

steps Change Spacing

To make your text easier to read and more effective, you may want to add space between paragraphs, between the lines in a paragraph, or between the words in a paragraph. As an example, you might add space after a document heading so that the heading and following text aren't so close, making the heading more visible. Or you might want to double-space between paragraphs to give your visitors a little breathing room while they read. Or you can space a word apart from the rest of the paragraph to highlight its special significance.

1 select paragraphs

Select the paragraphs you want to change. To change a single paragraph, click within it. To change several paragraphs, select them first. If you want to add space above or below a paragraph, select just that paragraph. You don't need to select the paragraph and its following paragraph to add space above or below. If you want to change the spacing of a paragraph (for instance, to double spacing), select just that paragraph.

2 choose paragraph

The **Paragraph** dialog box appears, allowing you to make many choices about the spacing of your text.

3 change paragraph spacing (optional)

If you want to add space above the selected paragraph, enter the amount in the **Before** spin box. To add space after the selected paragraph, enter the amount in the **After** spin box. Enter the value in pixels. The higher the value, the more space added.

4 change word spacing (optional)

To add spacing between the words in the selected paragraph, enter the amount in pixels in the **Word** spin box.

5 change line spacing (optional)

To change the line spacing, display the Line spacing drop-down list and choose **Single** (the default), **1.5**, or **Double.**

6 click OK

After you confirm your entries, FrontPage makes the changes.

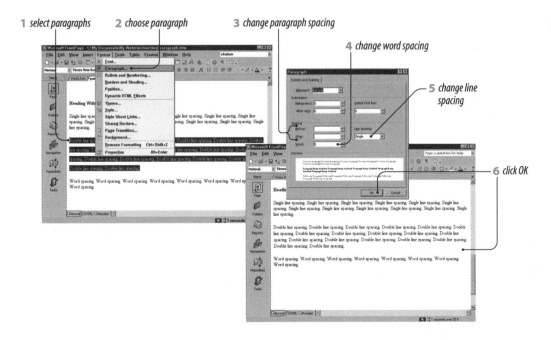

1 *select paragraphs* 2 *choose paragraph* 3 *change paragraph spacing* 4 *change word spacing* 5 *change line spacing* 6 *click OK*

The Bullets And Numbering Dialog Box

You can create bullet and numbering effects by highlighting text and clicking the **Bullets** or **Numbering** buttons in the Formatting toolbar; however, these buttons set your text with the default bullet and numbering styles.

If you want more control over the look of the bullets or numbers, use the options available on the various tabs in the **Bullets and Numbering** dialog box instead. Here you can specify a picture bullet, select from several other bullet styles, and finally, enter a starting number for numbered lists and select the numbering style. To display the dialog box, choose **Format→Bullets and Numbering.**

A picture bullets tab
On the **Picture Bullets** tab, FrontPage lets you use the picture from the current theme or specify a different image file to use as the bullet. You can type the file name or use the **Browse** button to locate and select the image to use. See Add Picture Bullets on page 88 for information on using pictures.

B plain bullets tab
Click the **Plain Bullets** tab and choose from the available bullet styles. You can change the formatting of the selected paragraph by clicking the **Style** button. See Chapter 9, Work With Styles, for more information on styles.

> (tip) You can create a *collapsible outline* which lets visitors show or hide sublevels in the outline. For information on collapsible outlines, see Create An Outline on page 90.

C numbers tab
Click the **Numbers** tab and then select one of the available number styles. You can use *Arabic numbering, Roman numerals* (upper- and lowercase), and *letters* (upper- and lowercase). To use a starting number other than 1, enter it in the **Start at** spin box.

> (tip) Most users prefer to type text and then go back and make formatting changes. You can, though, apply formatting as you type. As an example, you can turn on bullets or numbering and type the list. FrontPage inserts a bullet or number each time you press **enter** to start a new paragraph. To stop typing the list, press **enter** and then press **backspace** to delete the number or bullet and type regular text.

A *picture bullets tab*   B *plain bullets tab*   C *numbers tab*

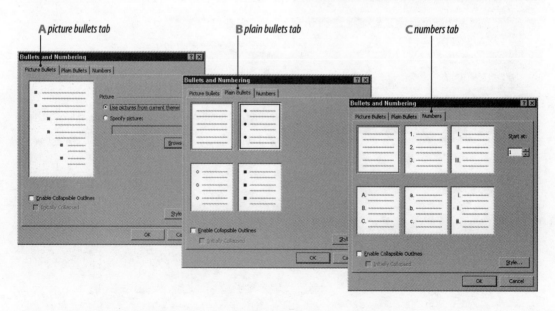

Add Bullets

To call attention to items in a series, such as agenda items or key points, consider using a *bulleted list*.

You can quickly apply a bulleted list using the **Bullets** button in the Formatting toolbar. If you want to select a different bullet character, you can use the **Format➡Bullets and Numbering** command. When you use either method, FrontPage adds the bullet character to the start of each paragraph and creates a hanging indent for the text.

For information on using a picture bullet, see Add Picture Bullets on page 88.

1 select paragraphs
Select the paragraphs you want to add bullets to.

2 click bullets button
To add the default bullet to the selected paragraphs, click the **Bullets** button. *Round* is the default style, but if you have applied a template, clicking the Bullets

button may yield a different style bullet. You can skip the remaining steps if you're happy with the bullet style.

> 💡 To remove the bullets, select the paragraphs again and click the **Bullets** button.

3 click bullet style (optional)
To use a different bullet style, choose **Format➡ Bullets and Numbering.** Click the **Plain Bullets** tab and then click the bullet style you want to use. Click **OK** to make FrontPage apply the bullets.

> 💡 As another option for creating a bulleted list, you can apply the Bulleted List style. Select the paragraph(s) and then display the Style drop-down list in the Formatting toolbar. Select Bulleted List. The formatting of the particular style varies depending on the theme you have selected.

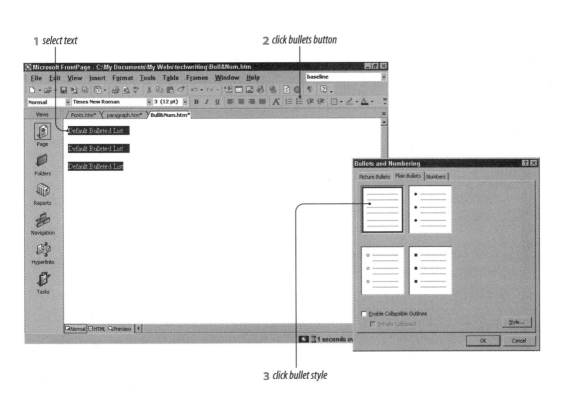

1 *select text*

2 *click bullets button*

3 *click bullet style*

Add Picture Bullets

You don't have to settle for plain old vanilla bullets for your bulleted lists! To add visual interest, consider using a graphic image as the bullet instead. If you have a small, somewhat bullet-shaped image, you can tell FrontPage to use this image as the bullet. You can also make clipart into bullets; FrontPage includes two categories of *Web bullets*, bullets designed specifically for use on Web pages. Many themes offer a picture bullet as the default bullet style.

> *tip* FrontPage inserts the graphic at its existing size. If your image is full-size, you need to resize or crop the image down to a manageable bullet size. A good size for bullets is 12 to 15 pixels square, although you could use a larger bullet if the text is larger. Chapter 6, Add & Edit Pictures, tells you more about resizing and cropping graphic files.

1 select paragraphs

Select the paragraphs you want to add bullets to.

2 choose bullets and numbering

Doing so opens the **List Properties** dialog box.

3 click picture bullets tab

This is where you get to tell FrontPage which graphic file you want to use as your picture bullet.

4 select picture

To use the picture from the current theme, click that radio button. The tab shows a preview of this bullet. (For more information on themes, see Apply A Theme on page 173.)

To use a different picture, click the **Specify picture** radio button and then either type the path and file name for the graphic or click the **Browse** button and then browse through the folders to find and select the image.

> *tip* To view a preview of the selected bullet, click the down arrow next to the **Views** button in the **Select Picture** dialog box and select **Preview.**

5 click OK

FrontPage uses the picture you selected for the bullets in the list. Ain't you got style?

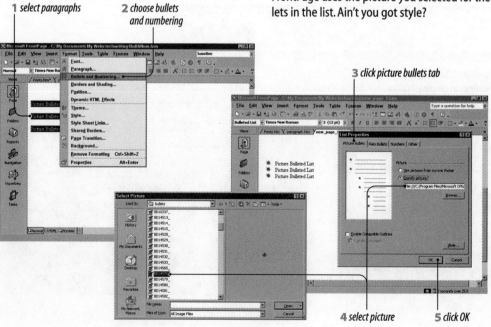

1 *select paragraphs*

2 *choose bullets and numbering*

3 *click picture bullets tab*

4 *select picture*

5 *click OK*

steps Number Paragraphs

A *numbered list* calls attention to items in a series, such as steps. You might use a numbered list to highlight steps on how to use a feature at your site. Or you might use a numbered list to rank the most popular or most visited links at a site. In any case, you can use the **Numbering** button or the **Format→ Bullets and Numbering** command to make your list. Use the button when you want simple Arabic numbers, numbered from 1 to whatever. The menu command comes in handy when you want to use an alternative numbering style, such as Roman numerals or letters, or when you want to start the numbering sequence with a number other than 1.

If you delete an entry or move entries in the list, FrontPage automatically adjusts the list for you. FrontPage also creates a hanging indent for the numbers so that the text is aligned to the left of the number.

> *tip* To turn off numbering, select the paragraph and click the **Numbering** button.

1 select paragraphs
Select the paragraphs you want to number.

2 add default numbers
To add regular Arabic numbers that start the numbering sequence at 1, click the **Numbering** button and skip the remaining steps.

3 select number style (optional)
To use a different number style, choose **Format→Bullets and Numbering.** Click the **Numbers** tab and then click the number style you want to use.

4 change starting number (optional)
Sometimes you may need to start your list with a number other than one; you may be continuing a previous list, for example. To change the starting number, type the number in the **Start at** spin box or use the spin arrows to increment the value. Click **OK** to have FrontPage create the numbered list.

> *tip* As another option for creating a numbered list, you can apply the Numbered List style. Select the paragraph(s) and then display the **Style** drop-down list in the Formatting toolbar. Choose **Numbered List.** The formatting of the particular style varies, depending on the theme you have selected.

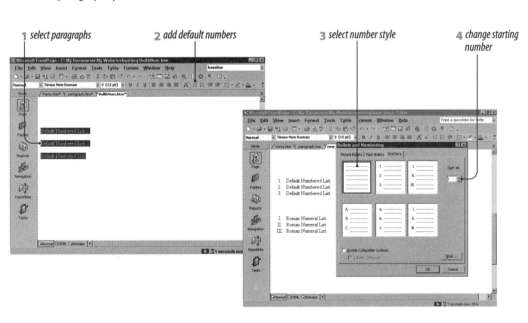

1 *select paragraphs*　　2 *add default numbers*　　3 *select number style*　　4 *change starting number*

🌀steps Create An Outline

Outlines aren't just for school anymore—an outline is also a great way to organize your Web's content.

An *outline* consists of a main numbered list and a series of nested numbered lists. To create an outline, you begin by typing the first or top level of the list, and then you type each of the nested levels. Next, you need to assign a numbering scheme for each level of the nested list—typically starting with uppercase Roman numerals, going down to uppercase Arabic letters, then to Arabic numbers, and finally to lowercase letters.

1 create main list
Type a numbered list containing the highest-level topics in the outline.

2 display list properties
Right-click the list and choose **List Properties** from the context-sensitive menu to display the **List Properties** dialog box.

3 change number style
Click the uppercase Roman numerals option. Then click **OK** or press **enter** to change the number style and close the dialog box.

4 insert next level
For each main heading, click after the heading and press **enter**. Type the list items for the next level down. Click the **Increase Indent** icon twice. Front-Page indents the insertion point and removes the bullet or number. Type the nested list, pressing **enter** after you finish each entry.

> *tip* Creating an outline in Front-Page is much like creating an outline in Microsoft Word or PowerPoint. You control the heading levels by indenting text and/or by assigning styles. You can have top-level headings, with subtopics, as well as nested topics within the subtopics.

5 display list properties
Right-click the nested list and choose the **List Properties** command to redisplay the **List Properties** dialog box.

6 set number type
Select the uppercase letters option and click **OK** or press **enter** to apply the new number type.

Continue to build the list and various levels by repeating steps 4 through 6.

> *tip* You can *collapse* an outline to show only the top-level list by activating the **Enable Collapsible Outlines** and **Initially Collapsed** checkboxes in the **List Properties** dialog box. Test the effect in Preview view. Note that a collapsed outline is only visible in the Internet Explorer browser window.
>
> Users viewing the outline with other browsers see the full outline.

1 *create main list* **2** *display list properties* **3** *change number style*

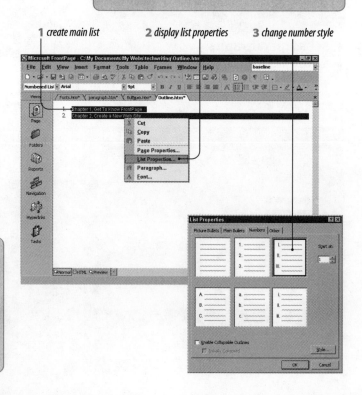

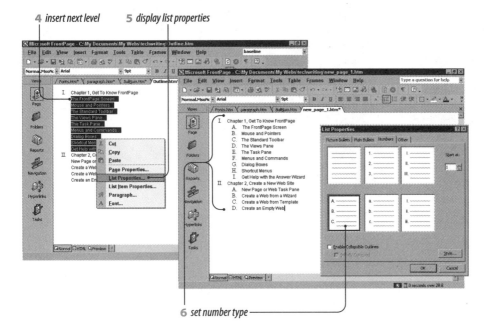

4 *insert next level*   **5** *display list properties*

6 *set number type*

Create A Definition List And HTML List Codes

Instead of the single list items found in ordered and unordered lists, *definition lists* are made up of pairs of items: terms and definitions. The most common type of definition list is a glossary. You can create a definition list by following these steps:

1. Click at the spot where you plan to enter the first term. Then choose

Defined Term from the **Style** drop-down list on the Formatting toolbar.

2. Type a term and press **enter** to start a new line. FrontPage automatically changes to the **Definition** style, which indents the insertion point.

3. Type a definition and press **enter** to start a new line. FrontPage

switches back to the **Defined Term** style. Continue to enter terms and definitions until you complete the list.

Occasionally, you may want to edit a list at the HTML level. The following table lists the elements used to create lists and list items.

HTML	Description	HTML	Description
OL	Numbered (ordered) list preceded by numbers	DL	Definition list, such as a glossary
UL	Bulleted (unordered) list preceded by bullets	DT	Definition or glossary term
LI	List item in numbered and bulleted lists	DD	Definition or glossary description
DIR	Simple (deprecated) list, such as a file directory	MENU	Simple (deprecated) list, such as a menu

The Borders Tab

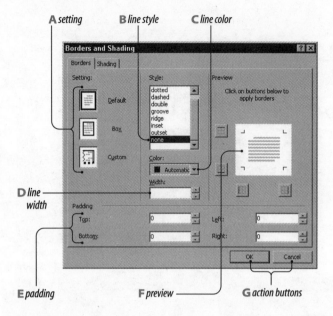

A setting   **B** line style   **C** line color

D line width

E padding   **F** preview   **G** action buttons

Borders add interest to a key paragraph or section of your page. You can highlight your text with pre-defined borders provided by FrontPage, or you can create a custom border. For both, you choose the style, color, and width of the border's line. You can also determine the *padding* (the amount of space between the border and the text). To add a border, display the **Borders and Shading** dialog box by choosing **Format➡Borders and Shading** and then clicking the **Borders** tab.

A setting

Choose from several predesigned borders, all listed in the **Setting** area. You can select the Default (no borders), a Box, or a Custom border. The Box setting uses the line style, color, and width you select for all sides. For Custom, you can specify different line styles, colors, and widths for each side.

B line style

Several line styles are at hand here, including dotted, dashed, and others. Click the style of your choice.

C line color

The default color is Automatic (usually black). Choose other colors by clicking the down arrow next to the

Color list box and clicking the color you want from the palette. See Select Web-Safe Colors on page 99 for more information on color choices.

D line width

Type the width, in pixels, for the border's line.

E padding

You can specify the amount of space between each of the border sides and the content. Enter the space, in pixels, for the top, bottom, left, and right edges of the border and its contents.

F preview

Check a preview of your choices here. When creating a custom border, use the preview area to select which sides are bordered. See Add A Custom Border on page 95.

G action buttons

The action buttons let you complete or cancel an action. Click **OK** or press **enter** to apply your changes to the border and close the dialog box. Click **Cancel** to close the dialog box without making any changes to the border.

The Shading Tab

Shading lets you fill a paragraph with a background color to emphasize that paragraph. As an even fancier effect, you can use a background picture for the shading. You can't manipulate shading using a toolbar button; you must do so on the **Shading** tab of the **Borders and Shading** dialog box. To select a shading, choose **Format➟Borders and Shading** and then click the **Shading** tab.

A background color   B foreground color

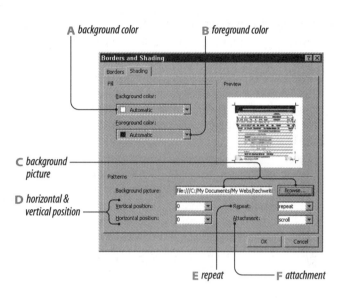

C *background picture*

D *horizontal & vertical position*

E *repeat*   F *attachment*

A background color

Display the **Background color** drop-down list and choose the color to use for the shading. The standard colors are listed, but you can click the **More Colors** option and pick a color from the color wheel.

B foreground color

For paragraphs that contain text, the *foreground color* sets the color of the text. Display this list and then choose a color. If the paragraph doesn't include text, the foreground color has no effect.

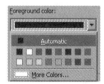

C background picture

If you want to use a picture as the shading, type the path and file name of the picture or click **Browse** and select the image to use.

D horizontal & vertical position

If you use a picture to create the shading, you can set the vertical and horizontal position of the image within the selected paragraphs. You can select top, center, or bottom for the vertical position and left, center, or right for the horizontal position.

E repeat

By default, the image is repeated within the paragraph. You can choose to repeat vertically (repeat *x*), repeat horizontally (repeat *y*), repeat both vertically and horizontally (*repeat*), or just include one image (*no repeat*).

F attachment

Choose an option from this drop-down list to determine whether the background picture scrolls (the *Scroll* option) as you scroll up or down the page or stays in place (the *Fixed* option). At present, this effect is available only for the Internet Explorer browser, so it's best to not use it—at least, not until other browser technologies catch up.

steps Add A Box Border

The most common border is to add a box to all the sides of a paragraph. Many people add a box border to a table of contents area to set it off, as an example. You can choose the style, color, and width of the box as well as the amount of space between the box and its contents. When you select multiple paragraphs, FrontPage adds the border around all of the paragraphs.

> **tip** The **Borders** button offers quick access to several common border styles, including a box, line above, line below, line to the right, line to the left, and others. Just select the text you want to "borderize," click the down arrow next to this button, and then select the border style you want.

1 select paragraphs
Select the paragraphs you want to border.

2 choose borders and shading
Choosing **Format➡Borders and Shading** displays the **Borders and Shading** dialog box.

3 select box
In the Setting area, click **Box.** When you select this option, borders are added to all sides of the paragraphs.

4 select line style
You can use different styles for different effects. For instance, for a 3D effect, try inset or outset.

5 select line color & width
Select a color for the line from the **Color** list and a width from the **Width** spin box.

> **tip** To add more or less space between the contents of the box and the box itself, change the padding. You can change the top, bottom, left, or right padding by entering the appropriate values in the boxes of the **Padding** area.

6 click OK
Click **OK** to add the borders.

1 *select paragraphs*   **2** *choose borders and shading*

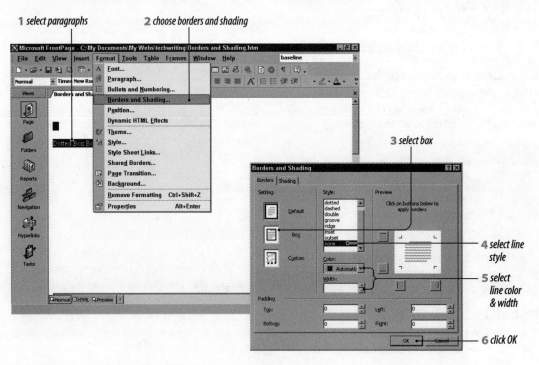

3 *select box*

4 *select line style*

5 *select line color & width*

6 *click OK*

94 ⑤ **Enhance Page Design:** Add A Box Border

steps Add A Custom Border

If you want to vary the look of the border's line, or if you don't want a border on all sides, you can create a *custom border*. For example, you might want to set off the headings on your page by adding a border below them, or you can add borders to the left and right of several paragraphs to make them stand out. You have many more choices when creating a custom border than you do with a simple box.

1 select paragraphs
Select the paragraphs you want to border.

2 choose borders and shading
The **Borders and Shading** dialog box appears to take your order.

3 select custom
In the Setting area, click **Custom.** You can now individually select the style, color, and width for each side of the border.

4 select line style, color, width
Select the line style, color, and width for the border.

5 add border
In the preview area, click the button that indicates where you want to place this border. You can click either top of paragraph(s) (a), bottom of paragraph(s) (b), left of paragraph(s) (c), or right of paragraph(s) (d).

> *tip* To turn off a border, don't click the line itself in the preview area. Instead, click the button that represents that side.

Do this for each side you want to add. You can select different styles, colors, and widths for each of the sides.

> *tip* To add more or less space between the contents of the box and the box itself, change the padding. You can change the top, bottom, left, or right padding.

6 click OK
FrontPage adds the border to the selected paragraph(s).

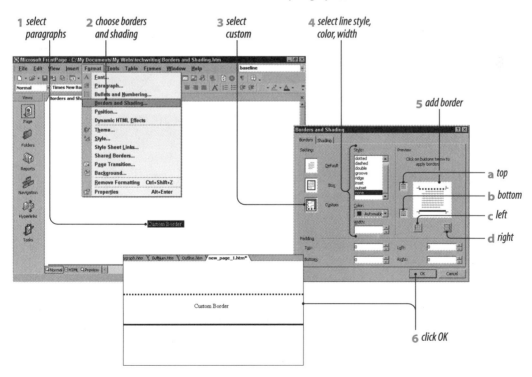

1 *select paragraphs*　2 *choose borders and shading*　3 *select custom*　4 *select line style, color, width*

5 *add border*

a *top*
b *bottom*
c *left*
d *right*

6 *click OK*

steps Add Background Or Foreground Color

Most often you create a border and optionally add shading. You can add shading without the borders, but it may not look as neat as you intend. When adding shading, you can select a background color, and if the paragraph(s) contain text, you can select a foreground color—that is, a color for the text. You might use shading to add emphasis to a section of a page or to page headings.

Be sure to use colors that complement the page. Also, keep in mind that colored text on a colored background may be difficult to read, so take care to preview the effect to make sure that the text is readable.

> **tip** One clever way to emphasize a selected paragraph is to reverse the default colors by changing the background color to black and the foreground color to white.

1 select paragraphs
Select the paragraphs you want to shade.

2 choose borders and shading
The **Borders and Shading** dialog box appears.

3 click shading tab
The Shading tab offers your options for adding shading.

4 select background color
Display the **Background** color drop-down list and select the color to use. Unlike word processing programs, you can't select fills such as patterns or gradients. You can only select colors.

5 select foreground color (optional)
To change the color of the text in the paragraph(s), display the **Foreground** color drop-down list and select a color.

6 click OK
Click **OK** to add the shading.

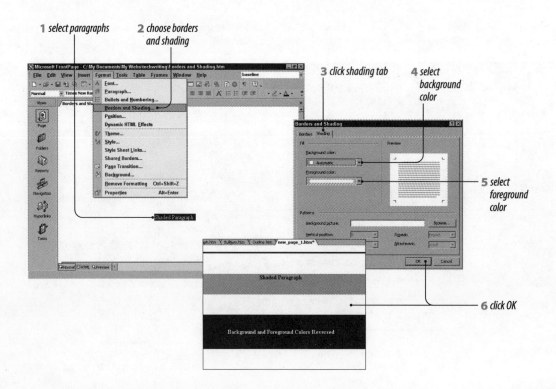

1 select paragraphs

2 choose borders and shading

3 click shading tab

4 select background color

5 select foreground color

6 click OK

Shade With A Picture

If you want an even fancier effect for shading, you can use an image for the background of selected paragraph(s). For instance, you might include a special section on a page and want it to stand out. You can make this section pop by using a background image as the shading. To use an image, it must be available as a file on your computer. It's a good idea to store all images within the images subfolder of the Web folder so that all files are stored within that one main folder.

> **tip** You can also use an image as the background for an entire page. See Add A Background Picture on page 100.

1 select paragraphs
Select the paragraphs you want to shade.

2 choose borders and shading
The **Borders and Shading** dialog box appears.

3 click shading tab
This is where you are going to tell FrontPage which picture to use and how to use it.

4 select image
Type the path and file name if you know it. If you don't, or if you prefer to click to select the file, click the **Browse** button. Then in the **Select Background Picture** dialog box, open the folder that contains the image, select it, and click **Open.**

5 select position
Display the **Vertical** position drop-down list and select top, center, or bottom. Display the **Horizontal** position drop-down list and select left, right, or center.

6 click OK
Click **OK** to add the picture shading.

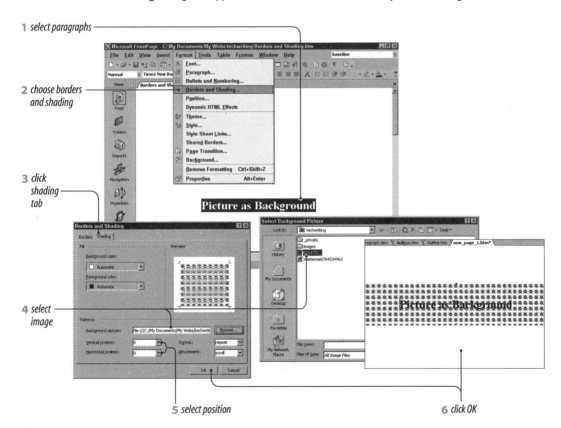

1 *select paragraphs*

2 *choose borders and shading*

3 *click shading tab*

4 *select image*

5 *select position*

6 *click OK*

steps Change The Colors On A Page

FrontPage automatically uses the *HTML default colors* for page elements; page backgrounds are white, text is black, unvisited links are blue, active links are red, and visited links are purple. The default colors are excellent choices because they are quite effective and will likely be familiar to your site's visitors. However, sometimes you may want to use different colors.

1 open page

To change the color properties for a page, the page must be open in Page view. The fastest way to open a page is to double-click its file icon in the **Folder List**.

2 choose properties

Or right-click and choose **Page Properties** from the shortcut menu. The **Page Properties** dialog box appears.

3 click background tab

Click the **Background** tab to display the **Background** section of the **Page Properties** dialog box.

4 select colors

Whether you choose to change the color of the page background, text, hyperlinks, visited hyperlinks, or active hyperlinks, the procedure is the same: display the drop-down list to open a color palette. Click the color you want and then click **OK.** The color palette closes and your new color selection appears in the dialog box.

5 click OK

Click **OK** to close the **Page Properties** dialog box and apply your changes.

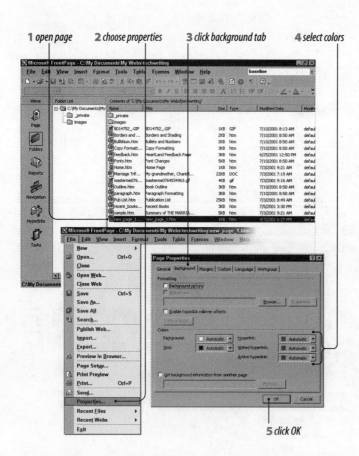

1 *open page* **2** *choose properties* **3** *click background tab* **4** *select colors*

5 *click OK*

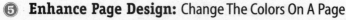

Select Web-Safe Colors

Various computers, operating systems, and video cards interpret and display colors differently. So, your best and safest choice is to select from a palette that contains colors recognized by most browsers and computers that run the Windows or Macintosh operating systems. For example, although GIF files can use 256 colors, only 216 colors are common to Windows and Macintosh systems. Each FrontPage color palette includes a small sampling of the 216 *Web-safe* colors. To access the whole lot, you need to open the **More Colors** dialog box.

1 open color palette

Display the color drop-down list. You can display this list for font, highlight, background, and default page colors.

2 click more colors

Click the **More Colors** option at the bottom of the palette to open the **More Colors** dialog box.

3 select color

Move the mouse pointer around the palette until you find a color that you want. Then, click the color to select it.

4 click OK

After you've selected a color, click **OK** or press **enter** to close the **More Colors** dialog box.

> *tip* You can go beyond the **More Colors** dialog box to select a custom color or a color from anywhere on screen. But, note that the color may not be Web-safe. To select a custom color, click the **Custom** button. In the **Color** dialog box that appears, either click a color or enter values in the textboxes in the lower-right corner to mix a color. Valid color values range from 0 to 255. Then, click **OK** or press **enter** to return to the **More Colors** dialog box.
>
> To select a color from the screen, click **Select** in the **More Colors** dialog box. The mouse pointer changes to an eyedropper. (To inactivate the eyedropper without selecting a color, press **esc**.) Move the eyedropper over a color on screen and click to select it.

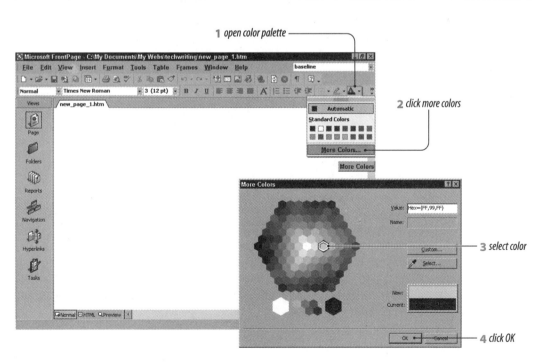

1 open color palette

2 click more colors

3 select color

4 click OK

steps Add A Background Picture

One way to make a certain page within a Web stand out is to use a picture or *watermark*—that is, an image that appears on the background of the page. You can include it as a watermark (a fixed element) or as a picture (image that scrolls with the text). In either case, the image is tiled over and over on the page to cover the entire page.

1 **open page**

Open the page to which you want to add the image. The fastest way to open a page is to double-click its file icon in the **Folder List**. See Open & Edit A Page on page 57 for help on opening pages. To display a page that's already open, click its tab.

2 **choose background**

You see the **Page Properties** dialog box.

3 **click background tab**

Click the **Background** tab to display the Formatting options for the page background.

4 **check background picture**

This tells FrontPage that you want to jazz up the background a bit.

5 **select picture**

When you do so, the other image options become available. Then type the path and file name if you know them. If you don't, or if you prefer to click to select the file, click the **Browse** button. Then in the **Select Background Picture** dialog box, open the folder that contains the image, select it, and click **Open**.

> *tip* If you want the image fixed on the page (not to scroll with text), check **Watermark**.

6 **click OK**

Click **OK** to add the picture background. The image is repeated (tiled) on the page.

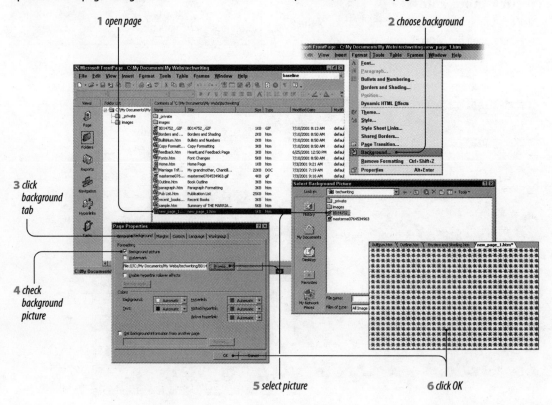

1 *open page*

2 *choose background*

3 *click background tab*

4 *check background picture*

5 *select picture*

6 *click OK*

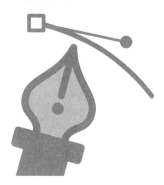

A Web would be pretty boring if it featured only text. Graphics lend life and visual interest to your page, and if you use them effectively, graphics can be as important to your site as text.

You can find graphics for your Web in many places. You might include pictures that you scan and save as a file or shoot and save with a digital camera. You might create your own illustrations using a drawing or illustration program. As another alternative, you can use *clipart,* which are prepackaged images that come with FrontPage and many other programs. We tell you how to add each of these kinds of graphics to your Web, and more.

You also learn how to manage the graphic files— how to store them with your Web as well as how to move, resize, and delete images. Finally, we tell you about image-editing tools that can help you make your graphics picture-perfect.

The Insert Clip Art Task Pane

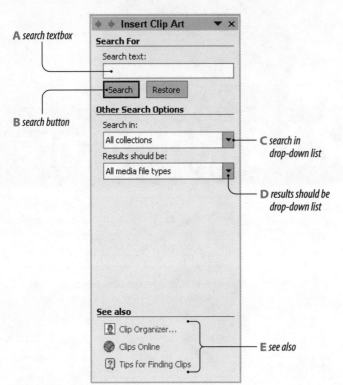

A *search textbox*

B *search button*

C *search in drop-down list*

D *results should be drop-down list*

E *see also*

B search button

To start the search, click the **Search** button. If you have searched previously and want to return to a previous search setting, click the **Restore** button.

C search in drop-down list

You may have several collections of clipart on your computer, supplied by FrontPage or other Office programs, such as My Collections, Office Collections, and Web Collections. This drop-down list helps you specify which collections of clipart are searched.

Any checked items in the list are searched. If you see a plus sign next to a collection, that means the collection includes other subcategories. You can expand the list to see these collections, checking the collections you want to search and unchecking those you want to exclude. To do so, click the plus sign. The plus sign changes to a minus sign, and you see the subcategories. You can continue to expand the subcategories within subcategories, fine-tuning which collections are searched.

Even if you aren't the world's greatest artist, you can still include drawn images in your Web by using *clipart,* or prepackaged artwork. FrontPage offers many sample clipart images which you can use in your Web, and many additional clipart images are available from other sources. You can purchase clipart collections at retail stores or find and download them online. For information on finding clipart online, see Find Clipart Online on page 108.

To view and insert clipart images in your page, you use the **Insert Clip Art** task pane, which you open by choosing **Insert➤Picture➤Clip Art**.

A search textbox

Searching helps you locate a particular image on your computer quickly. You can enter a keyword or phrase in this textbox, and FrontPage displays any matching images.

D results should be drop-down list

In addition to clipart images, you can insert other types of media, including photographs, movies, and sounds. Select the type of media to search for from this drop-down list.

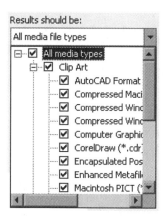

 For information on inserting movies and sounds, see Chapter 10, Apply Dynamic Effects.

Clipart files come in a variety of different formats. To choose which formats FrontPage searches for, click the plus sign next to the Clip Art category. Check the formats that FrontPage should look for, and uncheck any formats that you want FrontPage to ignore.

E see also

You can click any of the **See also** links to get more helpful information about clipart. Click **Clip Organizer** to display the Clip Organizer, which you use to categorize the clipart images on your computer (see The Microsoft Clip Organizer on page 106 for more information). To start Internet Explorer and go to Microsoft Design Gallery Live, click **Clips Online** (Find Clipart Online on page 108 tells you more about this option). To display online tips for finding clips, click **Tips for Finding Clips.**

Types Of Images

You can insert any of the following types of clipart media files on your page:

file type	extension
AutoCAD Format 2-D	DXF
Compressed Macintosh PICT	PCZ
Compressed Windows Metafile	WMZ
Computer Graphics Metafile	CGM
CorelDraw	CDR
Encapsulated PostScript	EPS
Enhanced Metafile	EMF
Macintosh PICT	PCT or PICT
Micrografx Designer/Draw	DRW
Print Shop Graphics (Row and Column)	PSG, PRG, PCG
Windows Metafile	WMF
WordPerfect Graphics	WPG

For photographs or other illustrations, you can use any of the following file formats:

file type	extension
FPX Format	FPX
Graphics Interchange Format	GIF
JPEG File Interchange Format	JPEG
Kodak Photo CD	PCD
PC Paintbrush	PCX
Picture It! Format	MIX
Portable Network Graphics	PNG
Tag Image File Format	TIF or TIFF
Windows Bitmap	BMP, DIB, RLE, BMZ

The most common types of Web files are JPEG and GIF. Why? Because they are supported by most browsers, they offer good quality, and they load pretty quickly.

(steps) Search Clipart Collections

If you need an image for your Web site on the fly, you may be happy to find out that your computer already has a whole bunch of clipart already on it. Usually this clipart comes packaged with any Office programs that you have installed on your computer. The clipart is organized into groups, or *collections,* that you can search by keyword using the **Insert Clip Art** task pane.

1 choose clip art

The **Insert Clip Art** task pane appears to help you find the perfect image for your page.

2 type search text

In the **Search** textbox, type a keyword or phrase that describes the clipart you want to find.

3 select search location

Display the **Search in** drop-down list and select which collections to search. Any items that are checked are searched. Uncheck any collections you want to exclude from the search.

> *tip* When searching for a particular type of image, make your keyword or phrase as specific as possible. If you type *art,* for instance, you may end up with too many matches. If you type *art palette,* however, you fine-tune the search to images that are close to what you have in mind. On the other hand, if you don't find any matches, try a broader word or phrase.

4 click search

FrontPage searches the selected collections and displays matching images in the task pane. Scroll through the list of images to see all of the matches.

You can expand the search by clicking the plus sign next to a collection and then checking or unchecking any of the subcategories. You can also limit the search to a particular file type using the **Results should be** drop-down list. See The Insert Clip Art Task Pane on page 102 for more information on limiting the search.

> *tip* To search again, click the **Modify** button, which returns you to the starting **Insert Clip Art** task pane and clears the results.

1 choose clip art

2 type search text

3 select search location

4 click search

Insert Clipart

To insert a clipart image, search the clipart collections on your computer as we describe in Search Clipart Collections on page 104. From the list of matches, you can then choose the image to insert on your page. The *clipart menu* also includes several other commands for working with the found image.

1 place insertion point

Click the insertion point at the location where you want to insert the image.

> **tip** You can move and resize the image as needed after you place it on the page. See Move, Resize, & Delete A Graphic on page 130 for more information.

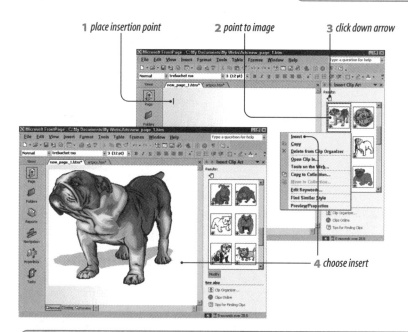

1 place insertion point

2 point to image

3 click down arrow

4 choose insert

2 point to image

When you point to the image you want to insert, a down arrow appears next to the image.

3 click down arrow

Click the down arrow next to the image to display the **clipart menu**.

4 choose insert

To insert the image, choose **Insert**. The image appears in the default size at the location of the cursor, and the **Insert Clip Art** task pane remains open. To close the task pane, click its **close** button.

The Clipart Menu

In addition to inserting the image, you can do any of the following from the clipart menu:

To copy the image (perhaps to place it in another program), choose **Copy**. Then move to the document where you want to place the copy and choose **Edit➥Paste**.

To remove the clip from the Clip Organizer, choose **Delete from Clip Organizer**. See The Microsoft Clip Organizer on page 106 for more information on this feature.

To open the clipart in the default viewing program, choose **Open Clip in**.

To view the available Office Media Resources, choose **Tools on the Web**. From here you can access Design Gallery Live, Tools on the Web, and Picture It!

To copy the image to another collection, choose **Copy to Collection**. Then select the collection in the Copy to Collection dialog box. Likewise, you can use **Move to Collection** to move the image to another collection.

To edit the keywords associated with this image, choose **Edit Keywords**. You see a list of the keywords for the selected image. Add new words, modify words, or delete words using the appropriate buttons.

To find images similar in style (not content), choose **Find Similar Style**.

To preview the image and view its properties, including its name, file type, resolution, size, orientation, default program, and keywords, choose **Preview/Properties**.

The Microsoft Clip Organizer

A *collection list*   **B** *preview pane*

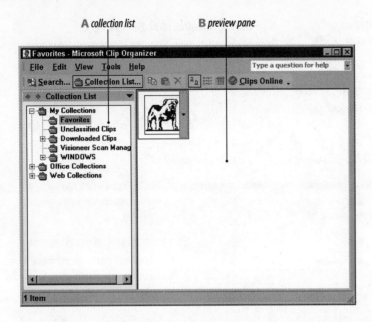

If you have more than one set of clipart on your computer, you can use the **Clip Organizer** to categorize and organize the clipart images. Doing so helps you quickly find and insert the images you use most often. The images included with Front-Page are already organized into collections, and you can use the Clip Organizer to view these collections. To display the Clip Organizer, choose **Insert➡Picture➡Clip Art** to display the **Insert Clip Art** task pane and then click **Clip Organizer.**

A collection list

The **collection list** displays all of the collections, including subcategories. You most likely have My Collections, Office Collections (if you have Microsoft Office), and Web Collections. If you have set up other collections, they appear in the list as well.

To expand a list to see its subcategories, click the plus sign next to the collection or category. For example, you can click the plus sign next to Web Collections and then Design Gallery Live to view all of the subcategories.

To display the images in a particular category, click the folder icon in the Collections List.

B preview pane

The **preview pane** displays the images in the selected folder or subcategory. You can browse through the various collections to get an idea of the many available images.

> *tip* By default the images in the preview pane are displayed in *Thumbnail* view. You can change to another view by choosing **View➡List or View➡Details.** Use List to display the images by name. Use Details to see the name, size, type, caption, keyword, and creation date for each image. You can also change the views by clicking any of the view buttons (E).

You can select any of the images that are displayed. To select a single image, click it. To select multiple images, **ctrl+click** each image you want to select. To select all images, choose **Edit➡Select All** or press **ctrl+A.** Selected images have a box around them.

You can also display the clipart menu for any of the images. To do so, point to the image to display its down arrow. Then click the down arrow. The menu choices are the same ones that appear when you select an image in the **Insert Clip Art** task pane. See The Clipart Menu on page 105 for more information.

> 💡 To view the keywords for a particular image, select the image and then choose **Edit➡ Keywords.** For images that aren't part of a preset collection, you can add, modify, and delete keywords. You can also scroll through the images by clicking the **Previous** and **Next** buttons in the Keywords dialog box.

C search button/collection list

To search for a particular set of images, click the **Search** button. You see the **Search** task pane on the left side of the Clip Organizer window. This task pane contains the same items as the **Insert Clip Art** task pane and works the same. See The Insert Clip Art Task Pane on pages 102-103 and Search Clipart Collections on page 104 for more information.

To return to the collection list after you have searched, click the **Collection List** button.

D copy, paste, delete buttons

You can use the **Copy** button to copy an image from the Clip Organizer to the Clipboard. You can then paste it into any receiving program. Likewise, you can copy an image from another source and paste it to the collection using the **Paste** button. To delete an image from the collection, select it and then click the **Delete** button. Note that you can't delete items from some of the predefined collections.

> 💡 To copy and paste a clip from one collection to another, select the clip and then click **Copy.** Open the collection in which you want to paste the clip and then click **Paste.**

E view buttons

You can change how the images are displayed by clicking any of the view buttons: Thumbnails, List, or Details.

F clips online

To go online to find and copy clips, click **Clips Online.** See Find Clipart Online on pages 108-109.

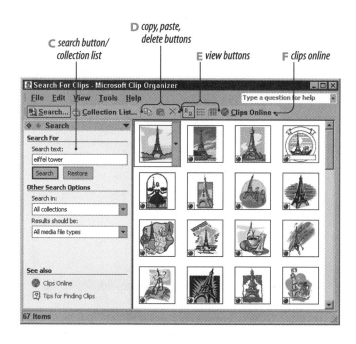

C *search button/ collection list*

D *copy, paste, delete buttons*

E *view buttons*

F *clips online*

Find Clipart Online

In addition to images provided with FrontPage or other Microsoft programs (including Office), you can also go online to find clipart images for your pages. When you use the **Clips Online** link in the **Insert Clip Art** task pane or the **Clips Online** button in the Clip Organizer, FrontPage starts Internet Explorer and then goes to the **Microsoft Design Gallery Live** site. From this site, you can find and download images.

1 click clips online

To go to the **Microsoft Design Gallery Live** site, click **Clips Online** in the **Insert Clip Art** task pane or the

Clips Online button in the Microsoft Clip Organizer. You see the **Design Gallery Live** Web site.

> **tip** To take advantage of **Clips Online**, you must have an Internet connection, and you must be connected. If you aren't connected, FrontPage prompts you to make a connection.

2 browse links

You can browse any of the collections by clicking the appropriate link. The site is updated frequently, so the clips you see in these figures may differ from the ones you see when you go online. As an example, in July 2001, you can click Summer to view several summer-related images.

1 *click clips online*   **2** *browse links*

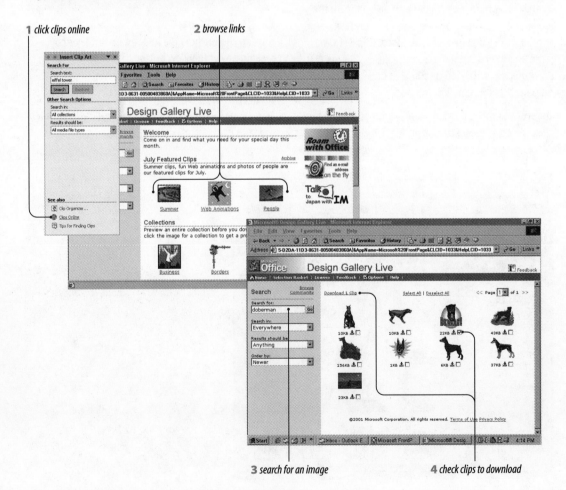

3 *search for an image*   **4** *check clips to download*

> *tip* To view archived images from previous months, click **Archive.**

3 search for an image

If you can't find an image you like by browsing, you can search for one using the search pane on the left side of the page. Type a keyword that matches the image you want in the **Search for** textbox. You can select which category to search from the **Search in** drop-down list. To select a particular media type (clip art, photos, sound, or motion, for example), use the **Results should be** drop-down list. To specify the order in which the images are displayed, use the **Order by** drop-down list. You can arrange the images by newest first, by file size, or by media type. After you enter your search criteria, click the **Go** button to search.

The search results are displayed in the order you selected. If the results run more than one page, use the scroll links to scroll forward and backward through the matching images. The top of the page lists the current page number and total pages.

4 check clips to download

When you find a clip that you want to download, check the checkbox under the image. You can check as many images as you want. The top of the page lists the number of images selected. The file size is listed under the image.

5 click download now

Once you have selected the image(s) you want to download, click the download link. You see the **download page** which lists the total number of clips selected, the total file size, the estimated download time, and the format type. Click the **Download Now** button to download.

6 view & insert clip (optional)

The clip(s) is placed in the relevant category folder (here, Signs) in the **Downloaded**

Clips folder in My Collections. The image also appears in the Microsoft Clip Organizer. To insert the clip immediately after downloading, click the down arrow next to the clip and then click **Copy.** Then return to FrontPage and open the page in which you want to paste the clip. Select the location for the clip and then choose **Edit➡Paste.**

> *tip* You can download most of the images at the Microsoft site for free. If there is a charge involved, you will be alerted before downloading. For additional clipart, visit www.clipart.com, a popular online clipart source.

5 *click download now*

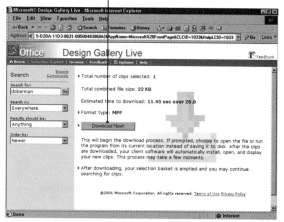

6 *view & insert clip*

The Picture Dialog Box

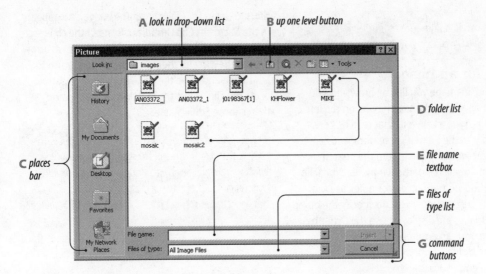

A *look in drop-down list*   B *up one level button*

C *places bar*

D *folder list*

E *file name textbox*

F *files of type list*

G *command buttons*

Clipart is not the only type of image you can add to your Web pages. You can also insert images stored as files on your computer. These might be a picture from a digital camera, a scanned image, or an illustration you created with a drawing program. You can insert any of the common graphic file types (see the sidebar on page 103). To insert a picture, use the **Picture** dialog box, which you can open by choosing **Insert➞Picture➞From File**.

A look in drop-down list

This list displays the current folder name. To select another folder or file, click the down arrow next to this list.

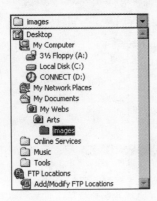

B up one level button

To insert a picture, you need to navigate to and open the folder in which the image is stored. You can move up one level in the folder structure using this button.

C places bar

The **places bar** displays icons for commonly-used folders. You can click any of these icons to open that particular folder. For instance, to open the **My Documents** folder, click that icon. **History** displays a list of recently-opened files and folders. **Desktop** displays the contents of your desktop folder. **Favorites** displays folders and files you have added to this folder. And finally, **My Network Places** opens up a folder of network sites, if you're connected to a network.

D folder list

The main area of the dialog box is the **folder list.** This area displays the subfolders and files within the current folder. Find the file you want to insert in the folder list so that you can select it.

You can change how the contents of the folder are displayed in the folder list. To do so, click the down arrow next to the **View** button and choose the view you want.

Large Icons — Displays contents as large icons

Small Icons — Displays contents as small icons

List — Displays contents as a list

Details — Displays contents in a detailed list with name, size, and date

Properties — Displays the contents on one half of the folder list and the file properties for the selected item in the second half

Preview — Displays the contents of the folder on one half of the folder list and a preview of the selected item in the other half

Thumbnails — Displays contents as small pictures

E file name textbox

When you select a file, its name is listed here. You can also type the name of a file here to open it.

F files of type list

By default, FrontPage lists all image files. You can limit the list to just a particular file type by clicking the down arrow and selecting the file type. You can display GIF and JGP files, Bitmap files, TIF files, Windows Metafiles, SUN Raster files, PostScript files, PCX files, PCD files, or Targa files.

G command buttons

To insert a selected picture, click the **Insert** button. To close the dialog box without inserting an image, click **Cancel**.

Search For An Image

If you can't find an image by browsing through the folders, you can search for it using the **Search** command in the **Picture** dialog box. To do so, follow these steps:

1. Click the down arrow next to the **Tools** button and click **Search.**

2. In the **Search** dialog box, type the search text. Use a unique word or phrase.

3. If needed, display the **Search in** drop-down list and select the drives or folders you want to search. To select a drive or folder, check the item's checkbox. Uncheck items to exclude them from the search. You can expand the listed items, selecting or deselecting folders within, by clicking the plus sign next to the item. For instance, click the plus sign next to My Computer to display all of the drives and system folders on your computer.

4. To limit the search to a particular file type, display the **Results should be** drop-down list and then check the type of files to match.

5. Click the **Search** button to search. The matching results are displayed in the Results area of the dialog box. You can double-click one of the matches to return to the **Picture** dialog box and enter that file's path and name in the **File name** textbox.

steps Insert A Picture From A File

Use the method we tell you about here to insert pictures you have created in drawing or illustration programs, images you have scanned, digital photographs you have transferred from the camera to your PC, and other picture files such as screen captures or images that you have downloaded from the Web.

1 place insertion point

Click the insertion point at the location where you want to insert the picture.

> *tip* You can click within current text to place the graphic. You can also place a graphic within a table (tables are covered in Chapter 8) or within a frame (frames are covered in Chapter 11).

2 choose from file

The **Picture** dialog box appears.

3 locate image

Change to the folder and drive that contain the image. See The Picture Dialog Box on pages 110-111 for help on changing to the drive and folder.

4 select picture

Select the picture you want to insert by clicking on it.

5 click insert

The picture appears on the page, in its original size, where you placed the insertion point. If you want to move or resize the image, see Move, Resize, & Delete A Graphic on page 130.

> *tip* When you save the page, FrontPage prompts you to save the image in the Web folders. See Save An Image on page 114.

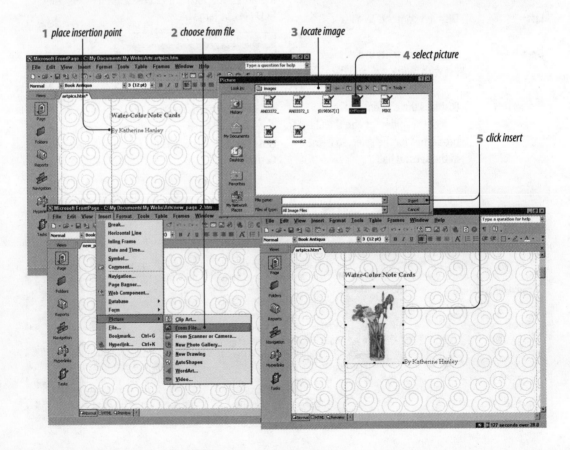

1 *place insertion point*   2 *choose from file*   3 *locate image*   4 *select picture*   5 *click insert*

steps Insert A Picture From A Scanner Or Camera

If you have a scanner and want to scan in an image and then insert it on your page, you can use the **Insert→Picture→From Scanner or Camera** command to do so. Likewise, if you have a digital camera and you want to access images stored in the camera's memory and then download an image from the camera to the page, you can do so with the same command.

If only one device is connected to your computer, you see the options for that device. If both devices are connected, you can select which device to use. You can also choose the resolution for the image.

> *tip* Every camera and scanner operates a little differently. This task gives you the general steps; for more detailed instructions, consult the documentation or online help for your camera or scanner.

1 place insertion point
Click the insertion point at the location where you want to insert the picture.

2 choose from scanner or camera
As you might expect, the **Insert Picture from Scanner or Camera** dialog box appears.

3 select device & resolution
Select the device from which you want to get the picture. Then select a resolution (if applicable).

4 click insert or custom insert
Click **Insert** or **Custom Insert** (depending on the device).

5 scan or transfer image
Then follow the instructions for your particular device to either scan the image or to transfer the image from a camera to the PC. For instance, if you select scanner, your scanner software opens, and you can use this software to scan in the image you want to insert. The image is then scanned and added to the page.

> *tip* You have much more control over the image (scan quality, sizing, and other options) if you first scan and then edit the image with the scanning software. After polishing the scanned image, save it as a file and then insert it using the Insert→Picture→From File command.

1 *place insertion point*   **2** *choose from scanner or camera*   **3** *select device & resolution*

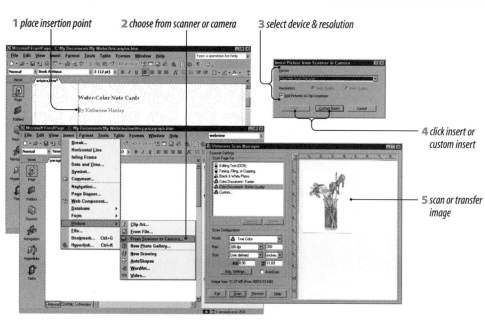

4 *click insert or custom insert*

5 *scan or transfer image*

Save An Image

After you add an image to a page, you are prompted to save the image when you save the page. You can enter a new name for the image, select the folder where you want the image stored, and change any of the picture options, such as the file type.

tip If you draw an object or add WordArt, these are saved as part of the page. See Draw An Object on page 127 and Add WordArt on page 128. You don't need to save these as separate graphic files.

1 *choose save*　　　　**2** *rename file*　　　　**3** *locate folder*　　　　**4** *change file options*

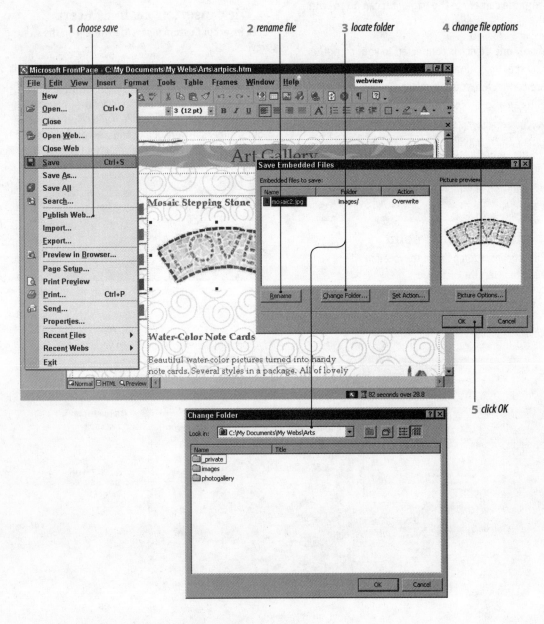

5 *click OK*

1 choose save

When you choose this command after adding a graphic to a page, the **Save Embedded Files** dialog box appears listing any of the images on the page that haven't been saved.

2 rename file (optional)

If you want to use a more descriptive name for the file, click **Rename** and then type a new name and press **enter.**

Renaming is most often used for clipart images, which can have sequential names that don't always identify the file. For instance, you might have a clipart file with a name like AN03372_1.GIF. You can rename this file to something like *Bulldog* to better identify the image.

3 locate folder (optional)

By default, images are stored within the Images folder, a subfolder of the Web folder. Using this location keeps all the images stored together in one main folder, making the images easy to upload to the Web server and to manage. If needed, you can click **Change Folder** and then select another folder in the **Change Folder** dialog box in which to save the image. For example, for complex Webs, you may have several subfolders for images. You can change to the appropriate folder and save the image. In the **Change Folder** dialog box, select the folder and click **OK.**

> *tip* To create a new folder, move to the folder in which you want to create the new folder. Then click the **New Folder** button, type the folder name, and click **OK.**

4 change file options (optional)

You can save the file as a JPEG or GIF file, the two most common graphic file types. JPEG is best for photos and GIF is best for line art and computer-generated drawings. Click **Picture Options** in the **Save Embedded Files** dialog box and then choose the image type in the **Picture Options** dialog box.

Make any changes to the settings for the selected file type. Then click **OK.**

5 click OK

Click **OK** to save the image with the name you entered and to the location you selected.

> *tip* If you don't want to be prompted to save an image every time you add one to a page, click **Set Action** in the **Save Embedded Files** dialog box, select **Don't Save,** and then click **OK.** If you edit the image using any of the features described later in this chapter, click the **Save** button to save the page. In addition to saving the page, you are prompted to save the image. The same dialog box shown in this task appears. Click **OK** to save the edited image with the same file name and in the same folder in which you originally saved it.

4 change file options

Picture Options

Original file: mosaic2.jpg   Original size: 18.32 KB
Changed file: Changed size:

○ **JPEG**
  Best for photos. Accurate color and small file size. Bad for line art and computer-generated drawings.

  Quality: 90
  Lowering the Quality reduces the file size of the picture.

  Progressive passes: 0
  Quickly displays a low-quality version of the picture and gradually increases the quality.

○ **GIF**
  Best for line art and computer-generated drawings. Only 256 colors. Insufficient color for many photos.

  ☐ Interlaced
  Paints the picture in bands rather than from top to bottom.

  ☐ Transparent
  One color in the image is drawn transparently. Turn transparency off here or use the Set Transparent Color button in the Picture toolbar to select a new transparent color.

  OK   Cancel

The Pictures Toolbar

When you add a picture (a clipart image, an image from a file, or a graphic from a scanner) to your page, you can use the **Pictures** toolbar to modify the picture. You can change its orientation, adjust the brightness, crop the picture, and make other changes. The **Pictures** toolbar should be displayed by default when you select a picture. If it isn't, choose **View➛Toolbars➛Pictures** to make it appear.

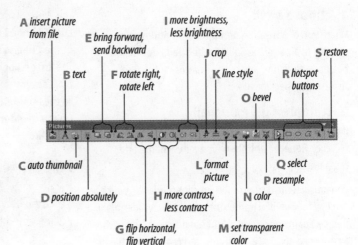

A *insert picture from file*
B *text*
C *auto thumbnail*
D *position absolutely*
E *bring forward, send backward*
F *rotate right, rotate left*
G *flip horizontal, flip vertical*
H *more contrast, less contrast*
I *more brightness, less brightness*
J *crop*
K *line style*
L *format picture*
M *set transparent color*
N *color*
O *bevel*
P *resample*
Q *select*
R *hotspot buttons*
S *restore*

A insert picture from file

Click this button to insert another picture from a file. See Insert A Picture From A File on page 112.

B text

You can overlay text on a picture by clicking the **Text** button. Doing so adds a textbox to the image. You can type text and resize the textbox as needed.

C auto thumbnail

To resize the selected image, click the **Auto Thumbnail** button. The image is resized to a small thumbnail of the image.

D position absolutely

If you want to lock a selected picture into place (so that you can't move it), click the **Position Absolutely** button. To turn off this feature, select the image and click the button again.

E bring forward, send backward

You can layer graphics on top of each other—for example, when you add text to a picture. To control the placement of the layers, use the **Bring Forward** and **Send Backward** buttons.

F rotate right, rotate left

To rotate a selected picture, click **Rotate Right** or **Rotate Left**.

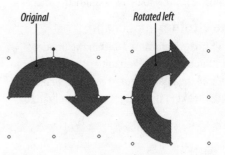

Original   *Rotated left*

G flip horizontal, flip vertical

To flip a selected picture, click **Flip Horizontal** or **Flip Vertical**.

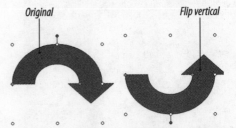

Original   *Flip vertical*

H more contrast, less contrast

To change the contrast among the colors in a selected image, click **More Contrast** or **Less Contrast**.

I more brightness, less brightness

To change the brightness of a selected picture, click **More Brightness** or **Less Brightness**.

J crop

If you want to use just part of an image, you can crop the image by clicking the **Crop** button. A cropping box appears on the picture; resize and move the cropping box until the portion of the picture you want to keep is selected. Then click the Crop button again.

Original

Cropped

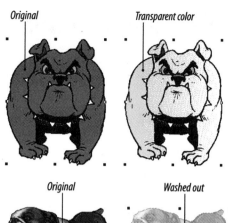
Original   Transparent color

Original

Washed out

> *tip* If you make a change and want to undo it, click the **Undo** button. If you have made several changes and want to redo them all, click the **Restore** button (S).

K line style

The **Line Style** button gives you access to many different line styles. Click the button to display a palette of choices and then click a line style. Use this button to change the line style of drawn objects or to change the line style of a picture's border.

L format picture

To display the **Format Picture** dialog box and make other changes to the image, click the **Format Picture** button. You can use this button to modify drawn objects or images with borders. You can change the style and color of the line, change the size of the drawn image, and make other modifications. See Set Picture Properties on page 121.

M set transparent color

Change the colors of a selected image to create a special effect by clicking the **Transparent Color** button. Click the button and then click the color in the graphic that you want to make transparent.

N color

To select the color for the image, click the **Color** button. You can select Automatic, Grayscale, Black & White, or Wash Out.

O bevel

To add a beveled edge to the border of a selected picture, click the **Bevel** button.

P resample

If you want to make a picture larger or smaller, you can resample it by clicking the **Resample** button. See Move, Resize, & Delete A Graphic on page 130 for more information.

Q select

Use the **Select** button to select the image or part of the image you want to work with.

R hotspot buttons

You can create an *image map,* making parts of the image into hyperlinks to other documents or Web sites. To assign a hyperlink to part of the image, draw a rectangular, circular, or polygonal *hotspot* on the portion of the graphic you want to assign a link. Use the **Highlight Hotspots** button to hide the image and display just the assigned hotspots. See Create An Image Map on pages 118 and 119 for the details.

S restore

If you make several changes to a graphic and need to undo them, you can click **Restore.** This undoes all changes you have made to the graphic since you last saved the page.

Create An Image Map

Many sites include an *image map*, which visually represents the site or the links at a site. You can assign *hotspots* to parts of the image; clicking the hotspots takes you to other pages in the Web or to other sites.

You begin creating an image map by adding the image you want to use to the page. Then you can define the hot spots as covered here.

1 **click image**

Click the image to open it for editing. The **Pictures** toolbar should be displayed. If it isn't, choose **View→Toolbars→Pictures** to make it appear.

2 **click hotspot button**

Click the hotspot button in the **Pictures** toolbar that most closely matches the shape of the part of the image you want to use as the hotspot. For instance, click **Rectangular Hotspot** to create a rectangular or square hotspot on the graphic. Click **Oval Hotspot** to

draw a circular or oval hotspot on the graphic. Use the **Polygonal Hotspot** for irregularly shaped hotspots.

3 **draw hotspot**

Draw the hotspot on the image.

To draw an oval, click and draw the circle from the center out.

To draw a rectangle, click and draw the rectangle from the center out.

To draw an irregular shape, click the **Polygonal Hotspot** button. Point to where you want to start the first line and click the mouse button. Drag to draw that line. When the line is the length you want, click the mouse button again. Draw the next line and end it by clicking the mouse button. You can draw as many lines at the angles needed to create the many-sided polygon. When all the sides are complete, double-click the mouse button to end the drawing.

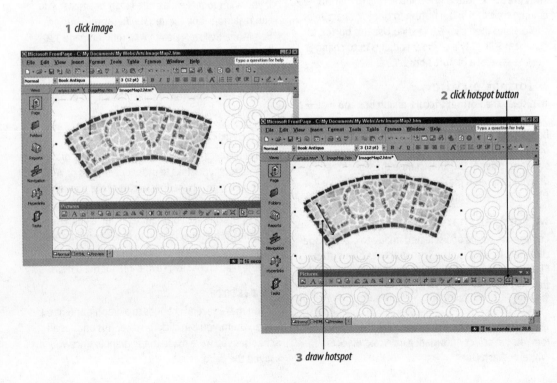

1 *click image*

2 *click hotspot button*

3 *draw hotspot*

> *tip* To draw a circle or square, hold down the **shift** key as you draw using the Oval Hotspot or Rectangular Hotspot tools, respectively.

4 assign hyperlink

When you finish drawing the hotspot, the **Edit Hyperlink** dialog box appears. Using this dialog box, you can assign a link to the selected part of the image. You can create a link to an existing file within the Web by selecting the file in the contents pane. You can link to another Web site by typing the address in the Address textbox. You can also create other types of links, including an e-mail link or a link to a bookmarked section on the page. For complete information on all hyperlink options, see Chapter 7.

5 create screentip

A *ScreenTip* appears in the status bar when you hover the pointer over a hotspot in a graphic. Adding a

ScreenTip helps your visitor understand what site or page is linked to each part of the image map. To create the ScreenTip, click **ScreenTip,** type the text to use, and click **OK.**

6 click OK

Click **OK** to add the hyperlink to the designated hotspot on the graphic. Follow steps 2 through 6 to add hotspots to other parts of the image, if you wish. Remember to click the **Save** button to save the page with the linked image map.

> *tip* To view just the hotspots on the image, click the **Highlight Hotspots** button. Doing so lets you see the placement of each of the hotspots. Click **Highlight Hotspots** again to return to the view of the actual picture.
>
>

4 *assign hyperlink*   5 *create screentip*

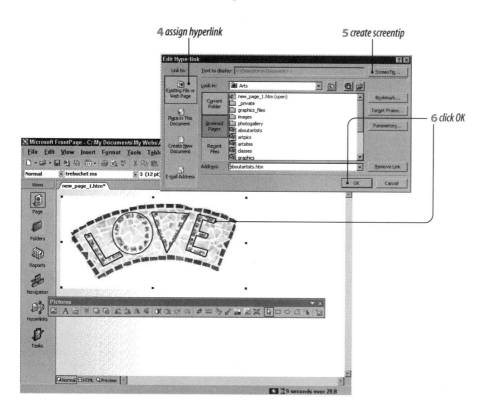

6 *click OK*

The Picture Properties Dialog Box

A *wrapping style*

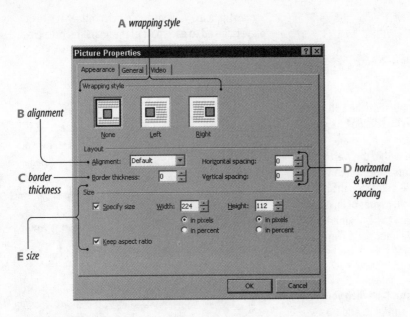

B *alignment*

C *border thickness*

D *horizontal & vertical spacing*

E *size*

To control text wrapping, size, borders, and other options for a picture, you use the **Picture Properties** dialog box. To display this dialog box, double-click the picture you want to modify, or select the picture and then choose **Format→Properties**.

A wrapping style

You can control how text wraps around a picture. If you select None, the picture is treated as a character and moves with the text. If you select Left, the picture is placed to the left of the text, and text wraps around the graphic. If you select Right, the picture is placed to the right of the text. For both Left and Right, you can move the picture by dragging. See Move, Resize, & Delete A Graphic on page 130.

B alignment

You can select an alignment for the picture by displaying the **Alignment** drop-down list and then choosing Left, Right, Top, Texttop, Middle, Absmiddle, Baseline, Absbottom, or Center.

C border thickness

To add a border around the image, change the border thickness to something other than 0. You can type a value in pixels or use the spin arrows to increment the value.

D horizontal & vertical spacing

To control the amount of space used as a buffer between the image and the text, increment the **Horizontal spacing** and **Vertical spacing** spin boxes.

E size

You can use the default size for a graphic, resize the image by dragging the selection handles (see Move, Resize, & Delete A Graphic on page 130), or set a specific size for the image. Use a specific size when you have an exact measurement. Check **Specify size** and then type the width and height either in pixels or as a percent of the window size.

> *tip* To maintain the *aspect ratio* (the ratio of the width to the height) when resizing a graphic, check **Keep aspect ratio**. If you want to distort the image, uncheck this checkbox. You can then change the width or the height independently.

Set Picture Properties

When you add a graphic, it appears on the page in the default size and at the location of the insertion point as a character. Part of creating the page is aligning all of the elements, including graphics, on the page. Therefore, you often need to adjust the size and placement of the picture. You can drag to change the size or location of the image as covered in Move, Resize, & Delete A Graphic on page 130. Or you can use the **Picture Properties** dialog box. Double-click the picture you want to modify to display the **Picture Properties** dialog box, or select the picture and then choose **Format→Properties**.

1 choose wrapping style

By default, the graphic is inserted as an inline character and moves with the text. This is the most difficult of the placements to work with because you drag it as if it were a single character. To change the graphic to another wrapping style, choose Left or Right.

tip You can use the **Position Absolutely** button to move the graphic anywhere on the page, but you lose all the wrapping and padding capabilities. If you want wrapping and padding, the image must be an inline element. See The Pictures Toolbar on page 116 for information on the **Position Absolutely** button.

2 choose alignment

You can also display the **Alignment** drop-down list and select an alignment. If you select an alignment for Left or Right (see the previous step), the choice overwrites the left/right option. Use the alignment options for selecting a position for a picture whose Text wrapping style is none.

tip To fix the graphic on an absolute position on the page, select it and then click the **Position Absolutely** button in the Pictures toolbar.

3 add buffer space

To add more or less space in between the text and the graphic, enter new values in the **Horizontal spacing** and **Vertical spacing** spin boxes.

4 add border

If you want the picture to have a border, or if it has a border and you want to change the thickness of that border, enter the appropriate value in the **Border thickness** textbox. Type a value in pixels or use the spin arrows to increment the value.

tip You can also type an exact measurement for the size of the graphic, but it's easier to resize visually by dragging. See Move, Resize, & Delete A Graphic on page 130.

5 click OK

The graphic is formatted with the options you selected.

1 choose wrapping style

2 choose alignment

3 add buffer space

4 add border

5 click OK

The Drawing Toolbar

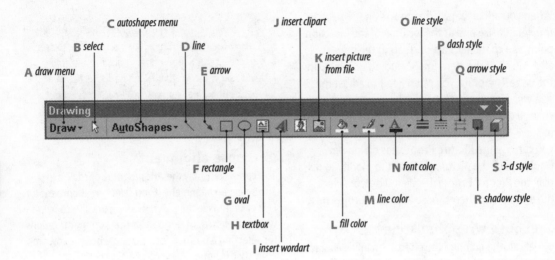

C autoshapes menu

B select

A draw menu

D line

E arrow

J insert clipart

K insert picture from file

O line style

P dash style

Q arrow style

F rectangle

G oval

H textbox

I insert wordart

L fill color

M line color

N font color

R shadow style

S 3-d style

With the tools in the Drawing toolbar, you can create simple shapes (ovals, rectangles, lines, and so on) or basic drawings to add special interest to the page. For example, you can use the toolbar to draw an arrow to point out an important point on the page. You can also create textboxes to position text at a specific location on the page. To display the Drawing toolbar, click the **Drawing** button.

> (tip) You can move the Drawing toolbar to any location on the screen. Click a blank area of the toolbar and drag to move the whole toolbar. If you move the toolbar next to a window border, it is *docked*. You can make it a *floating palette* by moving it away from the edge. A floating palette can be placed anywhere on the page.

A draw menu

After you draw an image, you can select it and make modifications with the commands in the **Draw** menu. If this menu is dimmed, you haven't drawn an object or the object isn't selected.

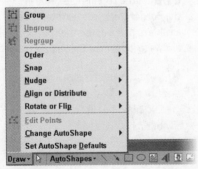

B select

To select an image, click the **Select Objects** button and then click the image.

C autoshapes menu

You can draw some predefined shapes using the **Auto-Shapes** menu. See Add An AutoShape on page 126.

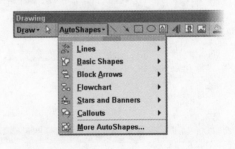

D line

To draw a line, click the **Line** tool. Then click within the page, hold down the mouse pointer, and drag to draw the line. To draw a straight line, hold down the **Shift** key as you draw.

lines

> **tip** You draw all shapes using the same technique: click the tool, click where you want to start the object, hold down the mouse button, and then drag to draw the object.

E arrow

To draw an arrow, click the **Arrow** tool. You can change the style of the arrow using the **Arrow Style** tool (Q).

Arrows

F rectangle

To draw a rectangle or square, click the **Rectangle** tool. To draw a square, hold down the **shift** key as you drag to draw. You can fill the object with color or make it shadowed or 3-D. See the callouts for these tools later in this part.

Rectangles

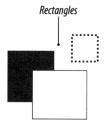

G oval

To draw an oval or circle, click the **Oval** tool. To draw a circle, hold down the **shift** key as you drag to draw. You can fill the object with color or make it shadowed or 3-D. See the callouts for these tools later in this part.

Ovals

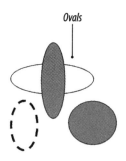

H textbox

You can draw a textbox and then type text into that box. This tool is handy for placing text at a specific location on the page. Rather than mess with margins, indents, or other paragraph settings, you can draw the textbox, type the text, and then position the textbox anywhere on the page by dragging.

To draw a textbox, click the **Textbox** tool. Then click on the page and drag to draw the textbox. Type the text and you're done.

Textboxes

I insert wordart

You can insert special effect text, called *WordArt*. To do so, use the **Insert WordArt** tool. See Add WordArt on page 128.

J insert clipart

You can insert clipart using this tool. See Insert Clipart on page 105.

K insert picture from file

You can insert a picture stored as a file using the menu command or this tool in the Drawing toolbar. See Insert A Picture From A File on page 112.

L fill color

If you have created a rectangle, square, oval, or circle, you can fill it with color using this tool. Select the object to fill, click the down arrow next to the tool, and then click the color. See Select Web-Safe Colors on page 99 for information on picking colors.

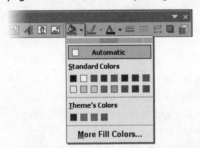

> *tip* If the **Fill Color** button is dimmed, you have selected an object that can't be filled. You can't, for instance, fill a line with color (although you can change the line color).

M line color

You can change the color used for the lines of any drawn object. You can do so before you draw the object or after. To do so first, click the down arrow next to this button, click the color, and then draw the object. Any objects you draw use this line color until you change it. To change the line color after drawing the object, select the object and then click the down arrow next to the **Line Color** button. Click the color you want to use from the palette that appears.

N font color

For textboxes, you can change the color of the text using this tool. Click the textbox to change, click the down arrow next to this button, and then click the color you want.

O line style

Click this button to display a palette of different line styles. Click the line style you want to use.

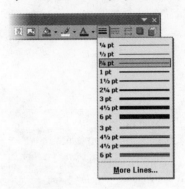

P dash style

For dashed lines in an object, select the object to modify, click this button, and then click the dash style to use from the palette.

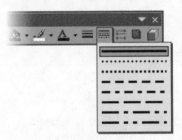

Q arrow style

If you have drawn an arrow, you can change the look of the arrow. Just click the arrow, click this button, and then select the style from the palette.

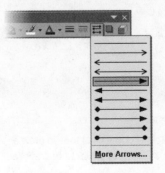

R shadow style

To apply a shadow to an object, select it, click this button, and then click the style to add.

S 3-D style

To apply a 3-D effect to an object, select it, click this button, and then click the 3-D style to add.

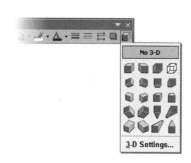

Draw Menu Commands

In addition to the toolbar buttons, you can use the commands in the **Draw** menu to modify an object. Select the object or objects. (Some commands—for instance, Group—require more than one object to be selected.) Then do any of the following.

You can create a drawing using several shapes. You can group the various shapes into one object so that it's easier to move and resize all of the objects together. Select all of the objects to group as one and then choose **Group.** (To select objects, hold down the **ctrl** key and click each object to select.) After you have grouped an object, you can ungroup it, if needed, to modify the individual shapes. Select the grouped object and choose **Ungroup.** Use **Regroup** to regroup a drawing that's been grouped and then ungrouped.

If you have layered objects on top of each other (by drawing objects on top of each other or by moving objects on top of each other), you can change the order in which they are placed on the page. To do so, select the object, choose **Order,** and then click an order: Bring to Front, Send to Back, Bring Forward, or Send Backward.

To snap objects to the underlying drawing grid, select the object and choose **Snap➡To Grid.** To snap objects to the shape, choose **Snap➡To Shape.**

You can move an object by dragging it to another position on the page. Sometimes you need to move the object just a hair, which is hard to do by dragging. In stead of dragging, you can nudge the object. Select the object and then choose **Nudge.** You can nudge up, down, left, or right by choosing the appropriate command.

If you want to change the alignment for several objects, select them. Then choose **Align or Distribute.** You can align left, center, right, top, middle, or bottom. You can also distribute the selected objects evenly using Distribute Horizontally or Distribute Vertically.

To change the orientation of an object (flip or rotate it), select it, and then choose **Rotate or Flip.** You can rotate left or right or flip horizontal or vertical. To drag to rotate, choose **Free Rotate** and then drag the rotation handle on the object.

You can select an AutoShape and then change it to a different one using **Change AutoShape.** You can also set the defaults for AutoShapes by selecting an object that has the line color, line style, and other object properties defined. Then choose **Draw➡Set AutoShape Defaults.**

steps Add An AutoShape

If you aren't much of an artist, you can easily add simple shapes to your pages with the **AutoShapes** button. You can build images using different lines, basic shapes, block arrows, flow chart symbols, stars and banners, callouts, and other graphic elements. The menu that appears when you click the button lists the categories of graphic elements, and then once you select the category, you see a mini-picture of the available AutoShapes.

1 click autoshapes

In the Drawing toolbar, click **AutoShapes** to display the AutoShapes menu.

> *tip* If the Drawing toolbar isn't displayed, click the **Drawing** button on the Standard toolbar.

2 select category

Click the category of the shape you want to add. When you click a category, you see the shapes available in that category.

The categories include lines, basic shapes (squares, circles, cylinders, happy face, heart, and others), block arrows (often used in flow charts or to indicate movement), flow chart (additional charting images, not necessarily related to flow charts, including pie graphs, triangles, cylinders, and diamonds), stars and banners (different star and banner shapes), and callouts (lines with attached dialog bubbles in circular and rectangular shapes).

> *tip* You can add text to autoshapes. For instance, add text to a banner or a callout by layering a text box over an autoshape.

For additional autoshapes, click **More AutoShapes**. You see the Insert Clip Art task pane which displays additional autoshapes from your clipart collection.

3 draw autoshape

Move the mouse pointer (which looks like a crosshair) to the page and to the position on that page where you want to draw the shape. Click, hold down the mouse button, and drag to draw the shape on the page.

You can now use any of the buttons on the Drawing toolbar to modify the shape. For example, you can change the line color, add a fill color, change the line style, and make other changes. See The Drawing Toolbar on page 122 for help on the various changes you can make.

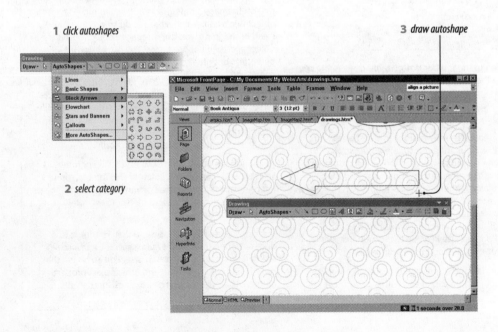

1 *click autoshapes*

2 *select category*

3 *draw autoshape*

🌀steps Draw An Object

Try your hand at being a graphic designer by creating simple illustrations using the **Drawing** toolbar. You can draw objects, including lines, arrows, circles, squares, and rectangles; if you're really fancy, you can combine a couple of simple drawings into a more complex shape.

1 click tool

Click the tool for the object you want to draw. For instance, to draw an arrow, click the **Arrow** tool.

See The Drawing Toolbar on pages 122-125 for an overview of the available tools.

2 draw object

Move the mouse pointer (which looks like a crosshair) to the page and to the position on that page where you want to draw the object. Click, hold down the mouse button, and drag to draw the object. The object is added to the page.

Use any of the buttons on the Drawing toolbar to modify the object. You can change the line color, add a fill color, change the line style, and make other changes. See The Drawing Toolbar on pages 122-125 for help on the various changes you can make.

> 💡 *tip* To draw a straight line, a circle, or a square, click the appropriate tool (the line, oval, or rectangle, respectively). Then hold down the **shift** key as you draw.

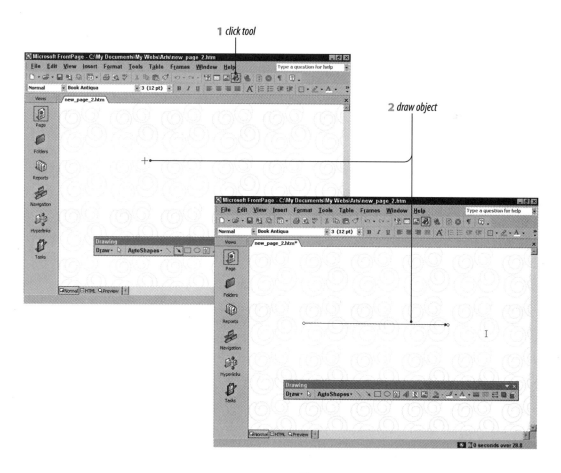

1 *click tool*

2 *draw object*

steps Add WordArt

WordArt is graphical text. It's great for use as headings because you can type as much text as you want and then use one of the many different WordArt styles to create text that really pops out of the page. WordArt is an object, so you can move it around on the page, resize it as needed, and make other object-related changes. To begin, display the page to which you want to add the WordArt.

1 choose wordart
The **WordArt Gallery** dialog box opens.

2 select wordart style
Click any of the WordArt styles. Don't worry about the sample text used for each of the styles; you replace this text with your own. Click **OK** after you select the style.

3 type text
When you click OK, you see the **Edit WordArt Text** dialog box. Now type the text you want as your WordArt.

4 make formatting changes (optional)
You can change the font and size of the text, and make the text bold or italic by clicking any of the buttons in the dialog box. When you are done typing and formatting the text, click **OK.**

> *tip* Note that you can't press **enter** to close the dialog box and insert the text. If you do so, you enter a paragraph break as part of the WordArt text.

The text is added to the page. You can move or resize the text as needed. See Move, Resize, & Delete A Graphic on page 130.

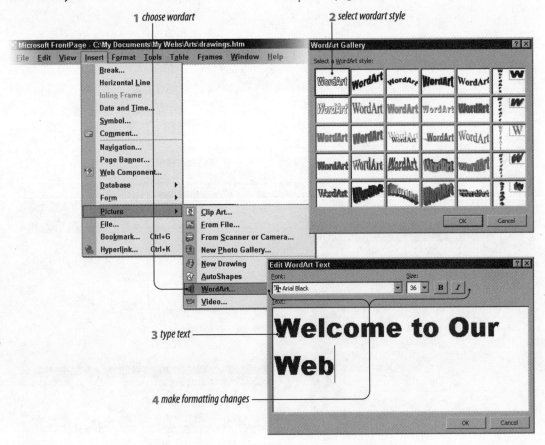

1 *choose wordart*

2 *select wordart style*

3 *type text*

4 *make formatting changes*

Edit & Format WordArt

After you add WordArt to a page, you can use the **WordArt** toolbar to edit the text if needed. You can also modify the appearance of the text. Start by clicking the WordArt object; the WordArt toolbar appears.

1 edit text

If you want to make a change to the text, click the **Edit Text** button. You see the **Edit WordArt Text** dialog box which allows you to edit or replace any text. Click **OK** when you are finished.

> *tip* For even more control over the appearance of your WordArt, click the **Format WordArt** button. In the **Format WordArt** dialog box that appears, you can select the color of the fill and lines, select a size, change the layout, and make other changes. Make your selections and then click **OK.**

2 change style

If you want to change the style of the WordArt, click the **WordArt Gallery** button. You see the same WordArt Gallery you used when you created the object. Select a new style and click **OK.**

3 change shape

If you want to use a different shape or slant for the WordArt object, click the **WordArt Shape** button and then select one of the available shapes from the palette of choices. Click **OK** to confirm your choice. To make all of the letters the same height, click the **WordArt Same Letter Heights** button.

> *tip* To change the spacing of the characters, click the **WordArt Character Spacing** button and then click Very Tight, Tight, Normal, Loose, Very Loose, or Custom (a certain percentage).

4 change alignment

To change the alignment of the WordArt object, click **WordArt Alignment** and then choose Left Align, Center, Right Align, Word Justify, or Stretch Justify.

> *tip* You can also make the text vertical by clicking the **WordArt Vertical Text** button.

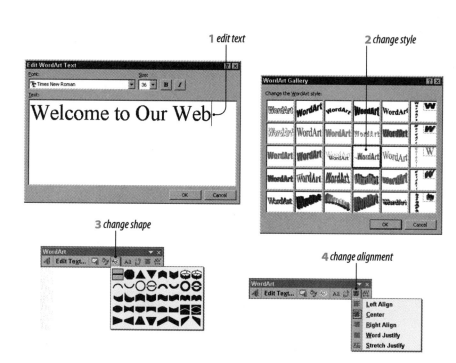

1 *edit text*

2 *change style*

3 *change shape*

4 *change alignment*

Move, Resize, & Delete A Graphic

Part of making a graphic work on a page is making sure it's in the right position so that it doesn't crowd or overwhelm the text. You also may need to adjust the size, again, so that the graphic doesn't detract from the text. And if you add a graphic you no longer need, FrontPage lets you delete the graphic from the page without charging you a dime.

You use these same methods to work with any type of graphic: clipart images; pictures inserted from a file, scanner, or camera; or objects you have drawn, including WordArt and AutoShapes.

1 select graphic
Click the graphic once to select it. You see selection handles around the sides of the graphic.

2 drag handle to resize
To change the size of the graphic, put the mouse pointer on one of the selection handles and drag.

> **tip** By default, FrontPage keeps the *aspect ratio* (ratio of height and width) of pictures the same. To change this or to resize by typing in exact measurements, see Set Picture Properties on page 121.

3 drag to move
To change the placement of the graphic on the page, put the pointer within the graphic and then drag to move the graphic to the new location.

> **tip** You can also change the position of the graphic using the **Format Picture** dialog box. See Set Picture Properties on page 121.

To delete a graphic, press the **delete** key.

> **tip** When you delete a picture that you have saved with the page to one of your Web folders, the picture file is not removed from that folder. You can delete the picture file to keep the files from getting cluttered with images you are not using in the Web. Click **Folders** to change to folder view. Then in the Folder List, open the folder that contains the image (usually the images folder). When you open this folder, you see the folder's contents in the contents pane. Right-click the picture you want to delete and then choose **Delete.** Confirm the deletion by clicking **Yes.**

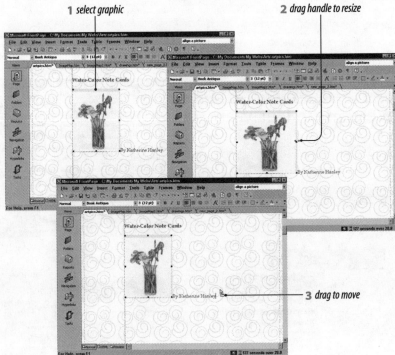

1 select graphic

2 drag handle to resize

3 drag to move

chapter 7

Create Hyperlinks

Part of creating an interesting Web is including links, also called *hyperlinks*. Links are what make a Web so exciting; links help your visitors navigate through your site and beyond. Clicking a link, which usually appears as blue, underlined text or as a *hotspot* on an image, takes you to another page, to another section in the Web, or to another Web entirely. As you construct your Web, part of that construction involves planning and adding your links.

You can create links by simply typing them on a page, but that doesn't give you much control over the wording or appearance of the links. Enter the **Insert Hyperlink** dialog box to give you all the control over your links that you need. This handy dialog box helps you build each of the different types of hyperlinks, including ones that go to a bookmark, to another page, to another Web, and to an e-mail address. In this chapter, you learn all about the various types of links and how to put them to use in your Web.

The Insert Hyperlink Dialog Box

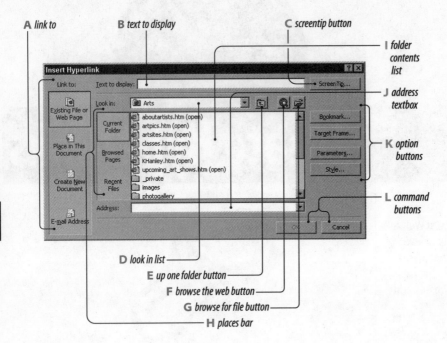

A *link to*

B *text to display*

C *screentip button*

I *folder contents list*

J *address textbox*

K *option buttons*

L *command buttons*

D *look in list*

E *up one folder button*

F *browse the web button*

G *browse for file button*

H *places bar*

You can insert a typed hyperlink directly into a document, but this method doesn't allow you to add a *ScreenTip,* to select what text is displayed when the cursor hovers over the link, or other options. For the easiest and most feature-rich way to add a hyperlink, use the **Insert Hyperlink** dialog box. To open this dialog box, choose **Insert→Hyperlink.**

> **tip** You can also click the **Insert Hyperlink** button on the Standard toolbar or use the keyboard shortcut (**ctrl+K**) to open the Insert Hyperlink dialog box.

A link to

In the **Link to** area, you choose the type of link you want to create. You can link to an existing file or Web page, to a place in a document you are currently working on (the place must be *bookmarked* as covered in Insert A Bookmark on page 138), to a new document, or to an e-mail address. When you click one of these options in the Link to area, the folder contents

list (I) changes to show options relevant to your choice. Here we show the options that appear when **Existing File or Web Page** is selected. Keep reading this chapter for help on linking to a place in the document, to a new document, or to an e-mail address.

B text to display

Here you type the text that makes up your hyperlink. This text can be anything you want—it doesn't necessarily have to be a plain old address. For example, suppose that you want to add a link from your site to the online bookstore, Amazon.com (www.amazon.com). Rather than use the address as the text in the document, you can type something like "Amazon, the World's Largest Bookstore" in the **Text to display** text box. That more descriptive text appears on the page as the hyperlink.

C screentip button

The *ScreenTip* is the text that appears in the status bar when the mouse pointer is hovered over the link. You can use the actual address or a more descriptive name. For instance, you might include information such as "click this link to go to the online bookstore."

D look in list

If you want to link to a document on your hard disk, you can select the appropriate folder and drive from this drop-down list. When you select a folder or drive, the contents appear in the folder contents list (I).

The Look in drop-down list box only appears when browsing for a file. If you choose to link to a place in the document, to a new document, or to an e-mail address, you don't see the Look in list. If you choose Existing File or Web Page and click Browsed Pages or Recent Files in the Places bar, the Look in drop-down list box is hidden.

E up one folder button

If you link to a document on your hard drive, you need to first navigate to that folder or drive. You can move up one level in the folder structure by clicking this button. The contents of the current folder are displayed in the folder contents list (I).

F browse the web button

If you want to link to another Web address, you can type the address or browse to the Web and select the page. Browse when you don't know the exact address or when the address is complex and you could easily make a mistake when typing it. Clicking this button opens Internet Explorer. You can then go to the site to which you want to link. When you go back to Front-Page, the address of the last page you visited is inserted in the Address textbox (J).

G browse for file button

If you are linking to another document on your hard disk and want to browse for the file rather than navigate to the file using the Look in drop down list (A) and Up One Folder button (E), click **Browse for File** to open the **Link to File** dialog box. You can then select the file to link to using the options in the dialog box.

H places bar

The buttons in the **Places bar** help you navigate to the locations you want to link to. To display the current folder, click **Current Folder;** use this button when linking to a file. To see a list of recently browsed pages, click **Browsed Pages;** use this button when linking to a Web site. To view a list of recently opened files, click **Recent Files;** use this button when linking to a file.

I folder contents list

The **folder contents list** displays files or pages available for linking. This list is updated if you change to another drive or folder using the Look in drop-down list (D) or Up One Folder button (E). If you view a list of browsed pages or recent files, the folder contents list changes to show the applicable list.

> **tip** You can open a folder and display its contents by double-clicking any folder icon in the folder contents list.

J address textbox

Browse to select a file or Web site or type the address here. For a file, type the path and document name. For a Web site, type the *URL,* or address, to that site. To go to a particular page (other than the home page), type the address, path, and page name. For example, you can go to the White House home page by typing www.whitehouse.gov.

K option buttons

The option buttons help you further fine-tune the link. Click **Bookmark** to display a list of bookmarks in the current page. To set the *target frame* for frames pages, click the **Target Frame** button. (See Frames & Links on page 137 for more information.) To use a *database query string,* click the **Parameters** button. (Get a computer geek friend to help you with this option; it's way outside the parameters of this book.) To set the style for the link, click the **Style** button. See Chapter 9, Work With Styles, for information on styles.

L command buttons

You get the standard choices here. Click the **OK** button to insert the hyperlink. Click **Cancel** to close the dialog box without inserting the link.

Link To A File Or Page

To help visitors navigate from one page to another at your Web site, you need to add links to each of the pages. Linking pages is especially important if your Web site includes many pages; links make it easy for your visitors to get from one page to another, encouraging people to view all the many pages at your site.

> **tip** A *table of contents* is another tool to help navigate among the pages at your Web. For information on this navigation feature, see Create A Table Of Contents on page 226.

1 select text
Select the text you want to use for the link. To use an image as the link, select the image by clicking it.

2 choose hyperlink
The **Insert Hyperlink** dialog box appears to do your bidding.

> **tip** You can also press **ctrl+K** or click the **Insert Hyperlink** button to summon the Insert Hyperlink dialog box.

3 click existing file or web page
If Existing File or Web Page isn't already selected, click it. You should see the Look in drop-down list and the contents of the current folder displayed in the folder contents list.

4 select file
Change to the folder or drive that contains the file to which you want to link. You can use the Look in drop-down list to change to another drive or folder. You can also click the Up One Level button to move up a level in the folder structure. As another option, you can double-click any of the folders listed in the folder contents list to open that folder. After you find the file, click it to select it.

> **tip** If you haven't created the document you want to link to, you can still create the link. Click **Create New Document** in the Link to area. Then type the name of the new document. Choose to edit the new document later or now. Click **OK** to add the new page. If you choose to edit the document now, the page appears. If you choose to edit later, the current page appears. In either case, the link is added from the current page to this new page.

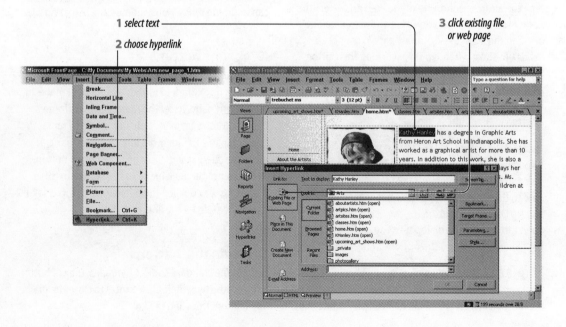

1 select text
2 choose hyperlink
3 click existing file or web page

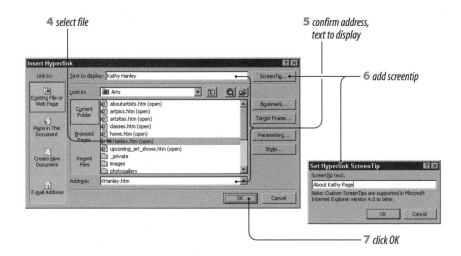

4 *select file*

5 *confirm address,
text to display*

6 *add screentip*

7 *click OK*

5 confirm address, text to display

The name of the file appears in the Address text box. You see the text you selected in step 1 in the Text to display textbox. Edit this text if needed. If you type something different, keep in mind that this new text will appear on the page. If you selected an image for step 1, you don't need to type anything in the Text to display textbox.

> *tip* You can type the address directly in the box rather than selecting the file, but selecting the file is easier and less error-prone.

6 add screentip

The *ScreenTip* appears in the status bar when the mouse pointer is hovered over this link. The ScreenTip tells the reader a little about where the link goes and helps them decide if they want to click the link. Click the **ScreenTip** button, type the entry you want, and click **OK.**

7 click OK

Click **OK** to insert the hyperlink. The link is added to the page, and it appears underlined and in the default link color. When a visitor looks at the page, he or she simply clicks the link to visit the associated page or file.

> *tip* To test the link when editing in FrontPage, hold down the **ctrl** key and click the link. You should see the Web page or file that you linked to.

Edit & Delete Hyperlinks

As your site grows and changes, you may find that you need to change some of the links on your site or delete them altogether. Although this isn't the most fun part of maintaining a Web, it's a necessary evil if you want to have a site that functions well and is easy for visitors to use. There's nothing more frustrating than clicking a link that doesn't go anywhere or goes to the wrong place! Don't let that happen on your site!

To edit a link, click within the link and then choose Insert➡Hyperlink. The **Edit Hyperlink** dialog box appears, which, except for the name, is the same as the Insert Hyperlink dialog box. Make any changes you want; for example, you can amend the text to display, the link itself, or the ScreenTip, as needed.

To remove a link, first select the link, open the Edit Hyperlink dialog box, and then click the **Remove Link** button. The text remains in the document, but the link is removed.

See Fix Broken Links on page 144 for more information on keeping your links up-to-date.

steps Link To A Web Site

Your Web won't be interactive if the site is a dead-end—that is, if you don't include links beyond your own site. To make your Web as entertaining and useful as possible, you should add links to other appropriate sites. For example, if you are creating a business site, including links to news or financial sites relating to your business makes your page that much more powerful and useful to visitors. For personal pages, you may include a list of your favorite sites to give a more in-depth view of your tastes. In either case, make sure to consider the usefulness and relevance of any links you add to your site; both too few and too many links can annoy visitors. Finally, be sure that the linked site is still active. Don't include links to sites that are no longer up and running.

> **tip** To check the validity of your links, see Hyperlinks Reports on page 142.

1 select text
Select the text you want to use as the link. You can select existing text, or click a place where new text

(the text you type to create the link) will be entered. To use an image as the link, select the image by clicking it. If you use an image as your hyperlink, you don't need to type any text to display (step 5).

> **tip** For information on selecting text, see Select & Edit Text on page 47. Note that you can also create an image map, as covered in Create An Image Map on page 118.

2 choose hyperlink
The **Insert Hyperlink** dialog box appears to do your bidding.

> **tip** You can also press **ctrl+K** or click the **Insert Hyperlink** button to summon the Insert Hyperlink dialog box.

3 click existing file or web page
If Existing File or Web Page isn't already selected, click it.

4 type address
Type the address to the page you want to use as the link. If you don't know the address, click the **Browse**

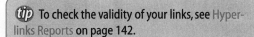

1 select text

2 choose hyperlink

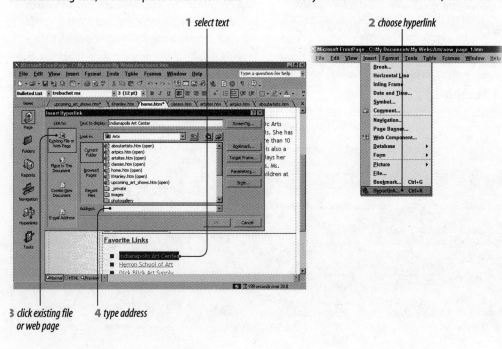

3 click existing file or web page

4 type address

the Web button. FrontPage opens your browser. Surf to the page to which you want to link and then use the taskbar button to switch back to FrontPage. When you return to FrontPage, the page address is listed in the Address textbox.

> *tip* To view a list of pages you have recently visited and choose one of these pages for the link, click **Browsed Pages** in the Places bar. Then click the page you want to use.

5 confirm text to display

If you selected text for step 1, the Text to display lists this text. If you didn't select any text, the address is inserted as the Text to display. Edit this entry if you wish. Remember that anything you type in this box will appear on the Web page.

6 add screentip

The *ScreenTip* appears in the status bar when the mouse pointer is hovered over this link. The ScreenTip tells the reader a little about where the link goes and helps them decide if they want to click the

link. Click the **ScreenTip** button, type the entry you want, and click **OK.**

7 click OK

The link appears on the page, underlined and in the default link color. People can now click this link and be taken to the associated Web site. If you want to change the colors on a page, see Change Colors On A Page on page 98.

> *tip* To test the link when editing in FrontPage, hold down the **ctrl** key and click the link. The Web page to which you linked should appear.

5 confirm text to display   *6 add screentip*

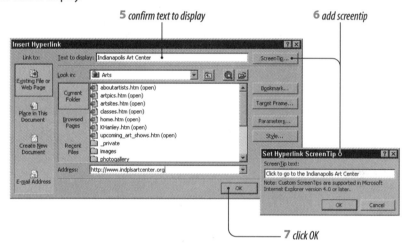

7 click OK

(Chapter 11, Divide A Page Into Frames, tells you how to create

Frames & Links

If you have divided a document into *frames,* you need to set up links to documents for each frame on the page. (Chapter 11, Divide A Page Into Frames, tells you how to create and use frames in a Web.) On a frames page, links work like this: When you click a link in one frame, the linked page appears in the *target frame* on that same page. If you

use a template to create a frames page, the target frame is already set up; however, you can change the target frame if you want to.

To change the target frame, select the hyperlink and choose **Insert➡Hyperlink.** Then click the **Target Frame** button. The **Target Frame** dialog box displays a visual representation of the frames in the Cur-

rent frames page area and a list of common target frame settings understood by all browsers. Choose the correct target frame from the Current frames page or the Common targets and then click **OK.** Now when you click a link within the frames page, the linked page appears in the target frame you selected.

⦿steps Insert A Bookmark

If your Web page is long, *bookmarks* give visitors a
quick way to move from topic to topic on the page.
Each main topic is bookmarked, and then a list of
topics is linked to each bookmark; when a visitor
clicks a bookmark, the page automatically jumps to
the topic on the page that is associated with the
bookmark. To use this type of link, you have to start
by creating the bookmarks for each section you
want to link to. Then you actually establish the
links; see Link To A Bookmark on page 139 for information on how to do that.

1 select bookmark location

Click the location where you want to insert the bookmark. If you want to use existing text, select that text.
Bookmarked text is underlined with a dotted line in
FrontPage. If you want to use an image as a bookmark, click the image to select it. If you don't select
text, FrontPage inserts a little flag icon to indicate the
bookmark location.

2 choose bookmark

You see the **Bookmark** dialog box.

3 name
bookmark
(optional)
If you selected text in
step 1, this text is sug-
gested as the book-
mark's name. Type or
edit the bookmark
name as needed. This
name appears in the
list of bookmarks,
either when going to
a bookmark or when
creating a link to a
bookmark.

> *tip* The shortcut
> key for displaying
> the Bookmark dia-
> log box is **ctrl+G.**

4 click OK

The bookmark is now available for linking. Bookmarked text is underlined with a dotted line in Front-
Page. Follow steps 1-3 for each section you want to
bookmark. For example, many people create bookmarks for each of the major headings on a page to
make it easier to navigate among the main topics on
the page.

> *tip* To delete a bookmark, select it and then
> choose **Insert⮞Bookmark.** Then in the Bookmark
> dialog box, click **Clear.** To go to a particular book-
> mark, choose **Insert⮞Bookmark,** select the book-
> mark you want to go to, and then click **Goto.**
>
> Note that you can't clear a bookmark unless you
> have selected it. If you select one of the listed
> bookmarks (not the current one) and click **Clear** in
> the Bookmark dialog box, the current bookmark is
> deleted, not the one you select from the list. First
> select the bookmark and then clear it. Or display
> the list, go to that bookmark, and then clear it.

1 *select bookmark location*

2 *choose bookmark*

3 *name bookmark*

4 *click OK*

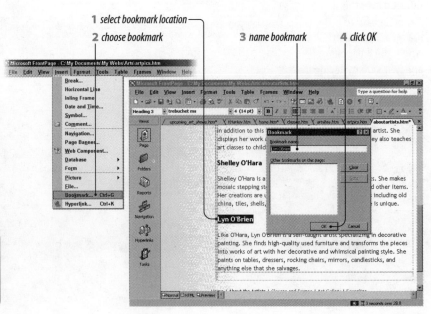

Link To A Bookmark

To create a link to a bookmarked section on the page, first add the bookmark as covered in Insert A Bookmark on the preceding page. Then you can actually create the link, which we tell you how to do here.

1 select destination text

Select the text to use as the link. This is the link to the bookmarked section. When a visitor clicks this link, he or she will jump to the bookmark (which you set up in step 4).

> **tip** Often the destination text and the bookmarked text are the same. For instance, you may set up a list of the main sections of a page, at the top of the page. Then a visitor can quickly jump to the topic of interest. This type of example is shown here.

2 choose bookmark

You see the **Insert Hyperlink** dialog box.

3 click place in this document

Click **Place in This Document** in the Link to area. The folder contents list displays the available bookmarks.

> **tip** You can also click the **Bookmark** button to display the **Select Place in Document** dialog box; the contents of this dialog box and the folder contents list after clicking Place in This Document are the same.

4 select bookmark

Click the bookmark to which you want to link.

5 add screentip

The *ScreenTip* appears in the status bar when the mouse pointer is hovered over this link. The ScreenTip tells the reader a little about where the link goes and helps them decide if they want to click the link. Click the **ScreenTip** button, type the entry you want, and click **OK**.

6 click OK

The link is added to the bookmarked section, and it appears underlined and in the default link color.

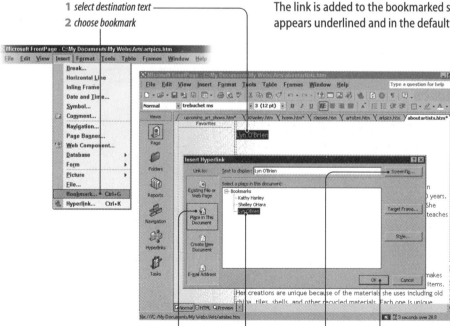

1 *select destination text*
2 *choose bookmark*

3 *click place in this document*
4 *select bookmark*
5 *add screentip*
6 *click OK*

steps Create An E-Mail Link

If you want your visitors to be able to send e-mail to someone, you can create an *e-mail link*. When a visitor clicks an e-mail link, a pre-addressed e-mail message appears, ready for the visitor to type and send a message. For instance, you may include a link to your site's web master for suggestions or feedback for the Web. If you are providing a service, you may include your e-mail address so that visitors can send requests for more information.

> **tip** Keep in mind that if you post your e-mail address, anyone who visits the site has that address. Consider creating a separate mail account for mail from the Web site, separate from your other personal or business e-mail.

1 **select text**

Select the text that you want the visitor to click in order to call up the e-mail message form. If you don't select any text, what you enter for the text to display is entered into the document and used as the link.

2 **choose hyperlink**

The **Insert Hyperlink** dialog box opens for you.

3 **click e-mail address**

Click **E-mail address** in the Link to area. The folder contents list displays textboxes for e-mail entries.

4 **type e-mail address**

Type the e-mail address you want to use for the link. When you start typing, FrontPage automatically inserts mailto: before the e-mail address, indicating that this is a *mailto link*. You can also select an address from the list of Recently used e-mail addresses.

5 **type subject** (optional)

If you want to include a subject on all e-mail messages that originate from the site, type your tag into the Subject line.

6 **click OK**

FrontPage creates the e-mail link, and you are in business. When a visitor clicks this link, a mail window opens with the address and subject already entered. The visitor just has to type the message and click **Send** to send a message to your address.

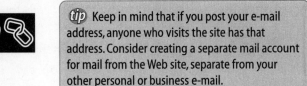

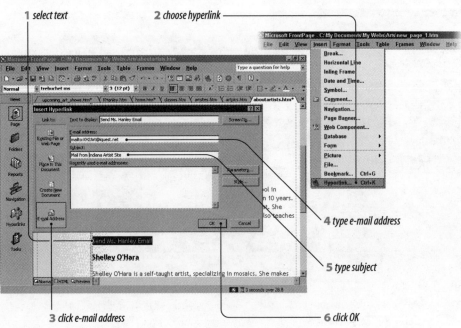

1 *select text*
2 *choose hyperlink*
4 *type e-mail address*
5 *type subject*
3 *click e-mail address*
6 *click OK*

140 ⑦ **Create Hyperlinks:** Create An E-Mail Link

Hyperlinks View

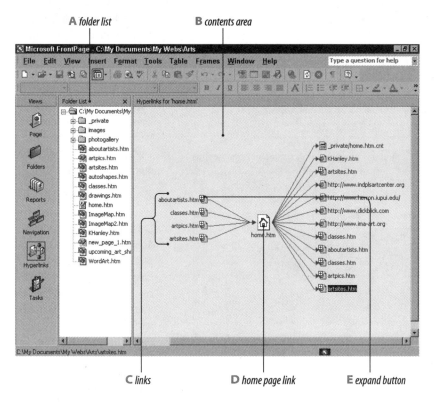

A *folder list*

B *contents area*

C *links*   D *home page link*   E *expand button*

B contents area

The **contents pane** displays the links for the selected page. The selected page appears at the center of the contents page, with tracer lines showing links to other pages and sites.

C links

Links are indicated with a page icon. These include links to other pages, documents, Web sites, or e-mail addresses. Bookmark links don't appear here.

D home page link

The home page is indicated with a

special **home page icon.** You can see how the current page is linked to the home page. If the home page is the page you are displaying, its icon appears in the center of the contents area.

E expand button

If any of the linked pages also contain links, you see a plus sign on the page icon. You can click this plus sign to expand the view and show the links on that particular page.

When a link is expanded, the button changes to a minus sign. Collapse, or hide, the links for that page by clicking the minus sign.

To get an overview of the links at your Web, you can change to **Hyperlinks** view. This view lets you see all the links embedded in your site—links within your own Web and links to other sites. You can expand or collapse the links for each page to get an overall sense of the flow of the Web from page to page and from site to site. To change to Hyperlinks view, click the **Hyperlinks** view button.

A folder list

The **Folder List** is displayed by default in Hyperlinks view. You can select any of the listed pages to display the links for that page. When you click a page, the contents area (B) displays the links for that page. If you want more space to display the contents pane, you can close the Folders List by clicking its **close** button.

Hyperlinks Reports

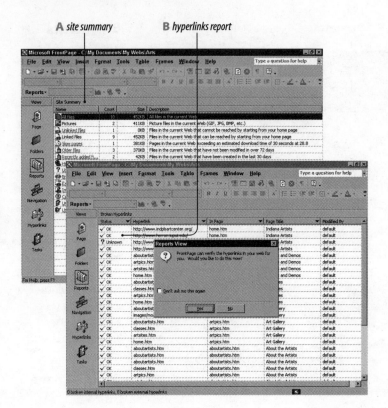

A site summary **B** hyperlinks report

size of the report, and a description.

FrontPage includes several reports for hyperlinks including Hyperlinks, Unverified Hyperlinks, Broken Hyperlinks, External Hyperlinks, and Internal Hyperlinks. To view any of these reports, click the link for that report.

B hyperlinks report

When you click the **Hyperlinks report** link in the Site Summary (A), you are prompted to verify all the links in your Web. Click **Yes** to do so; click **No** to skip the verification. You see the status of each link (broken, unknown, or OK), the hyperlink, the page that link is contained in, the page title, and the modification information.

Hyperlink reports let you verify all the links at your site and view any *broken links* (links that aren't verified). You can then fix any links if needed, ensuring that all links at your site are current and applicable.

To view the list of FrontPage reports, click the **Reports** view button in the Views pane. For information on other reports, see Chapter 15, Manage A Web.

A site summary

When you first click the Reports view button, you see the **Site Summary.** (If you have displayed other reports, you see the last report you viewed. To go back to the site summary, choose **View➡Reports➡Site Summary.**)

The Site Summary lists each report and displays the number of items that match the listed report type, the

C unverified hyperlinks report

To view a list of hyperlinks that point to unconfirmed target files, click the **Unverified hyperlinks report** link in the Site Summary (A). You are prompted to first let FrontPage verify the sites. If you click Yes, all links are verified and only those that can't be confirmed are listed.

> *tip* To sort the report, click the appropriate column heading. For instance, to sort by page title, click the Page Title column heading. To filter the report (show only matching entries), click the down arrow next to the column which you want to filter. For example, to filter the report to show just broken links, click the down arrow next to Status. Then select the entry to match. The drop-down list displays all of the options for that particular column. To return to all of the listings, click the down arrow again and select (All).

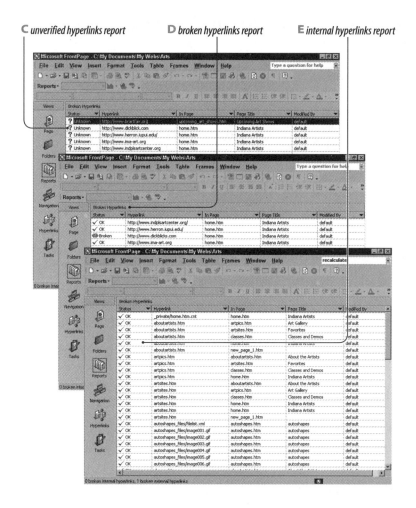

tip When you view most reports, you are prompted to let FrontPage verify the links. You can do so then, or you can also *recalculate* the links at any time, in any view. To do so, choose **Tools→Recalculate Hyperlinks**. The **Recalculate Hyperlinks** dialog box displays a message stating what happens when you recalculate. Click **Yes.** Instead of just verifying the links exist, *recalculating* repairs the links, updates information for shared components, and synchronizes Web data.

D broken hyperlinks report

To view a list of hyperlinks that were verified and found not correct, click **Broken hyperlinks** in the Site Summary (A). You are prompted to first let FrontPage verify the sites. If you click Yes, all links are verified and only those that can't be confirmed are listed. You see a broken link, and the word "Broken" appears in the Status column of the report.

E internal hyperlinks report

To view links to pages within the Web, click the **Internal hyperlinks** report link. This view helps you when you want an overview of all the links within the Web.

Fix Broken Links

If you find a *broken link* in any of the reports (if a link is broken, it appears in several of the hyperlink reports), you can fix the link. You may have a broken link if you typed the Web address incorrectly or if the address has changed. When you fix the link, FrontPage gives you the option of updating the hyperlink in all of the pages in the Web, saving you from having to manually find and correct all the incorrect links.

> *tip* You can follow these same steps to edit a link. For instance, suppose that you linked to the home page at a site and would rather direct your visitors to a particular page within that site. You can edit the link, replacing it with the appropriate link to the page you want.

1 double-click link

Double-click the link you want to edit from any of the reports (see Hyperlinks Reports on page 142). The report doesn't matter, and you can double-click any link type (not just broken or unverified links).

You see the **Edit Hyperlink** dialog box, listing the link and page.

2 type new link

Type the correct link to use for the selected link. You can click the Browse button to display the main Edit Hyperlink dialog box (the one that's the same as the Insert Hyperlink dialog box, except for the name). From this dialog box, use any of the links or buttons to select the correct link. See The Insert Hyperlink Dialog Box on page 132.

3 select replacement option

You can update the link in all places it's used or in just the selected pages (the pages are listed below these options). To select the pages, click **Change in selected pages** and then **ctrl+click** each page that contains the link to be updated.

4 click replace

FrontPage makes the replacements, fixing the broken link. If the link is still not correct, you see Broken again in the report you started from in step 1. If it's correct, the status is changed to OK.

1 double-click link   *2 type new link*

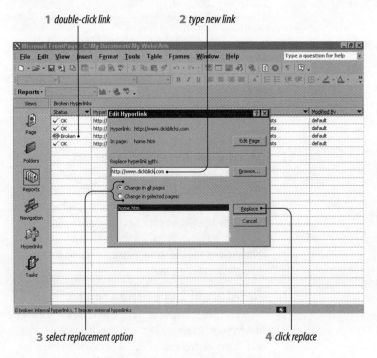

3 select replacement option   *4 click replace*

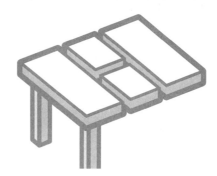

chapter 8

Insert Tables

Tables, composed of rows and columns of cells into which you can place text and graphics, are a common feature of Web pages, used to present information—such as timetables, rates, pricing information, and so on—in a grid-like format.

In addition to presenting information on a Web page, using tables can also help you lay out the page itself. Simply create a table and place your text and graphics within it to create a well-ordered, eye-pleasing page. And, of course, tables offer you the same flexibility when it comes to formatting your text and graphics as non-table pages do.

In this chapter, you learn how to use tables to both display information within a page, and to lay out the page itself.

145

The Insert Table Dialog Box

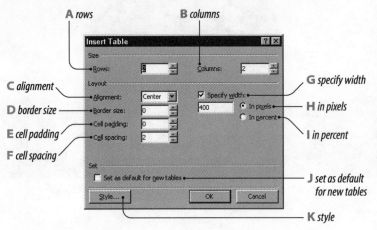

A rows
B columns
C alignment
D border size
E cell padding
F cell spacing
G specify width
H in pixels
I in percent
J set as default for new tables
K style

F cell spacing

Cell spacing refers to the space between cells in a table. Type a number to determine the cell spacing in pixels.

G specify width

By default, FrontPage sets the table width automatically based on cell contents. If, however, you prefer to give the table width either in pixels or as a percentage of the browser window's width, check this checkbox.

H in pixels

To specify the table width in pixels, select this radio button and type a number in the accompanying textbox to indicate how many pixels wide the table should be.

> **tip** If you give the table width in pixels, that width is constant. That is, regardless of how large or small the viewer's Web browser window is, the table remains the same size.

I in percent

To dictate the table width as a percentage of the Web browser window's width, select this radio button and type a number in the accompanying textbox to indicate what percentage of the browser window's width the table width should be.

J set as default for new tables

Check this checkbox to instruct FrontPage to change the default table settings to the ones you specify.

K style

Click this button to open the **Modify Style** dialog box and apply style-sheet formatting.

> **tip** *Style-sheet formatting* lets you more precisely control spacing, alignment, fonts, and colors than is possible with basic HTML. (You can find out more about styles in Chapter 9, Work With Styles.)

Before you can use a table to display information or lay out a page, you must first insert a table on the page. The **Insert Table** dialog box offers several sizing and layout options. To open this dialog box, choose **Table➥Insert➥Table.**

A rows

Type a number to specify how many rows the table should contain.

B columns

Type a number to specify how many columns the table should contain.

C alignment

Choose **Default, Left, Right,** or **Center** to specify the table's position on the page.

D border size

Type a number to specify the size of the border, in pixels, to surround the table. Set the border size to 0 if you want no border.

E cell padding

Cell padding refers to the space between the contents of the cell and the cell's border. Type a number to tell FrontPage the cell padding in pixels.

The Tables Toolbar

Use the **Tables** toolbar to format your table's rows, columns, alignment, and more. The toolbar opens automatically when you create a table using the **Insert Table** dialog box; alternatively, you can open it by choosing **Table➥Draw Table.**

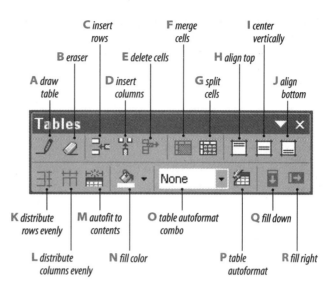

A draw table
Draw a table by hand. (See Other Ways To Add A Table on page 149.

B eraser
To erase unwanted lines within a table, click and drag down toward the line you want to erase until the line turns red. When it does, release your mouse button.

C insert rows
Insert a row into your table.

D insert columns
Insert a column into your table.

E delete cells
Delete the selected cell, row, or column.

F merge cells
Merge two cells into a single cell.

G split cells
Split a single cell into two cells.

H align top
Align the table along the top of the page.

I center vertically
Place the table in the middle of the page.

J align bottom
Align the table along the bottom of the page.

K distribute rows evenly
Evenly distribute the rows in the table.

L distribute columns evenly
Evenly distribute the columns in the table. (See Change Column Width & Row Height on page 161.)

M autofit to contents
Cells are sized to fit their contents.

N fill color
Fill the selected cells with color.

> **tip** To change the color, click the **Fill Color** button's down-arrow. Then choose a color from the palette that appears or click **More Fill Colors** at the bottom of the palette for more options.

O table autoformat combo
Choose from among several pre-designed table formats.

P table autoformat
Open the **Table AutoFormat** dialog box, where you can choose from several pre-designed table formats and customize the format you choose.

Q fill down
Copy content from one cell to others in the same column.

R fill right
Copy content from one cell to others in the same row.

Add A Table To A Page

You use the **Insert Table** dialog box to establish the sizing and layout settings for your table and to place the table on your Web page. After you place the table on the page, you finish up by adding text and formatting to your table.

1 set table location
Click the spot on the Web page you are creating where you want to insert the table.

2 choose table
To open the **Insert Table** dialog box, choose **Table➤Insert➤Table.**

3 set rows
Type a number in the **Rows** textbox to specify the number of rows in the table.

4 set columns
Type a number in the **Columns** textbox to determine the number of columns in the table.

5 set alignment
Open the **Alignment** drop-down list and choose **Center**, **Left**, **Right**, or **Default** to tell FrontPage how the table should be positioned on the page.

6 set border
Type the width of the border surrounding the table, in pixels, in the **Border size** textbox. Type 0 if you don't want a border around your table.

7 set cell padding
Specify how many pixels should separate the contents and borders of the table's cells by typing a number in the **Cell padding** field.

8 set cell spacing
Specify how many pixels of space should exist between each cell by typing a number in the **Cell spacing** field.

9 set table width
Check the **Specify width** checkbox and then select **In pixels** or **In percent.** Type a number in the accompanying field to represent the width of the table in pixels or a percentage of the width of the browser window, respectively.

10 click OK
Clicking **OK** closes the **Insert Table** dialog box and inserts the new table on the page. The Tables toolbar also appears (see The Tables Toolbar on page 147).

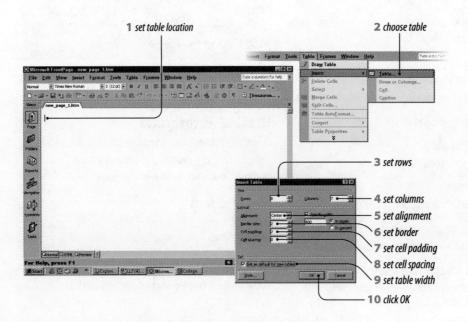

1 *set table location* **2** *choose table*

3 *set rows*
4 *set columns*
5 *set alignment*
6 *set border*
7 *set cell padding*
8 *set cell spacing*
9 *set table width*
10 *click OK*

Sunday	Monday	Tuesday	Wednesday	Thursday	Friday	Saturday
Heidi	Heidi	Wilma	Heidi	Heidi	Wilma	
Wilma	Wilma	Evelyn	Evelyn	Evelyn	Evelyn	
Lloyd	Lloyd	Lloyd	Sue	Lloyd	Sue	
Sue	Sue	Ian	Caitlin	Ian	Caitlin	
Ian	Ian	Caitlin	John	Caitlin	John	
John	Jay	John	Jay	Jay	Jay	
Jay	Rae	Rae	Rae	Rae	Rae	

11 *add text*

Sunday	Monday	Tuesday	Wednesday	Thursday	Friday	Saturday
Heidi	Heidi	Wilma	Heidi	Heidi	Wilma	
Wilma	Wilma	Evelyn	Evelyn	Evelyn	Evelyn	
Lloyd	Lloyd	Lloyd	Sue	Lloyd	Sue	
Sue	Sue	Ian	Caitlin	Ian	Caitlin	
Ian	Ian	Caitlin	John	Caitlin	John	
John	Jay	John	Jay	Jay	Jay	
Jay	Rae	Rae	Rae	Rae	Rae	

12 *format text*

11 add text

Click in a cell where you want to add text and then type your text. Repeat until all cells in the table contain the text you want.

When you type in a cell, it expands to accommodate the text at the expense of the width of other cells in the table. If all the cells in a row contain text that consumes more space than is available, the text in each cell wraps to make room.

12 format text

You format the text in your table just as you would any other text on the page; use the buttons in the **Formatting** toolbar and other formatting resources to change the look of the text. For more formatting basics, read Chapter 5, Enhance Page Design, which starts on page 74.

Other Ways To Add A Table

FrontPage offers multiple methods for adding tables to your pages.

The Insert Table toolbar button

Begin by clicking on the Web page in the spot where you want the table to appear. Then, click the **Insert Table** button. Drag down and to the right until you select the number of rows and columns you want your table to contain (as many as five rows and five columns). The table appears on the page ready for you to add text to it.

4 by 5 Table

Draw a table

If you prefer to draw the table directly on your page, choose **Table➥Draw Table**. The **Tables** toolbar opens (see page 147). Click the **Draw Table** button; then, on your page, click and drag from the upper-left corner to the lower-right corner to draw the table's border. Click and drag within the table to draw vertical and horizontal lines (use the **Eraser** tool to erase unwanted lines). When you're finished, click the **Draw Table** button on the **Tables** toolbar a second time to deselect it.

draw table button   eraser button

Convert text to a table

You can also convert existing text into a table. Before you can do so, you must insert *separator characters*, such as commas or paragraph marks, to indicate where the text should be divided into rows and columns (avoid using tab characters; they aren't supported by HTML). For example, the following text

Last Name, First Name, Middle Name

Shoup, Katherine, Elizabeth

will convert to a table that looks like this:

Last Name	First Name	Middle Name
Shoup	Katherine	Elizabeth

Once you've delimited the text you want to convert, select it, place the cursor on your Web page where you want the table to appear, and then choose **Table➥ Convert➥Text To Table**. The **Convert Text to Table** dialog box opens; specify the separator character you used to separate columns (it's assumed you used the paragraph mark to indicate the end of a row) and click **OK**.

Add & Delete Rows & Columns

Use the **Tables** toolbar to quickly add or delete rows or columns in your table. If the Tables toolbar isn't currently open in your FrontPage window, choose **Table➥Draw Table** to open it.

1 place insertion point
Click a cell in the table.

2 click insert rows
Click the **Insert Rows** button to add a new row to the table above the cell you clicked.

> *tip* To add a single cell to a row, click the cell to the right of where you want the new cell to appear. Choose **Table➥Insert➥Cell**. A new cell is added to the row, and all cells to its right shift one position to make room.

3 place insertion point
Click a cell in the table.

4 click insert columns
Click the **Insert Columns** button to add a new column to the table to the left of the cell you clicked.

> *tip* If you're adding multiple rows or columns, open the **Insert Rows or Columns** dialog box (click a cell in the table and then choose **Table➥Insert➥Rows or Columns**). Specify the number of rows or columns you want to add, and where the new rows or columns should be located.

5 select cells
Select two or more adjacent cells. (You can select an entire row or column if desired.)

6 click delete cells
Click the **Delete Cells** button on the **Tables** toolbar; the selected cells are deleted.

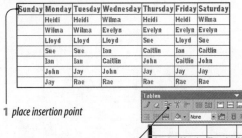

1 *place insertion point*

2 *click insert rows*

3 *place insertion point*

4 *click insert columns*

5 *select cells*

6 *click delete cells*

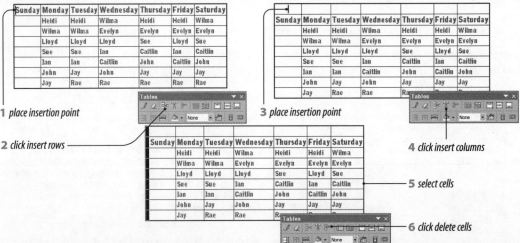

Select Cells

FrontPage offers you several ways to select cells within a table. You can click inside the table, column, row, or cell you want to select, choose **Table➥Select** and pick **Table, Column, Row,** or **Cell** from the submenu that appears. You can also drag to select multiple adjacent cells, or **ctrl+click** to select multiple non-adjacent cells.

Alternatively, hover your mouse pointer over the left-most table border and, when the pointer turns into a right arrow, click to select the entire row. Selecting a column is similar: Hover your mouse pointer over the top-most table border until it turns into a down arrow and then click to select the column.

ⓢⓣⓔⓟⓢ Merge & Split Cells

You can use the **Tables** toolbar to merge or split cells. (If the **Tables** toolbar isn't currently open, choose **Table▸Draw Table** to open it.) By merging two or more cells, you join them; the line between them disappears. Splitting a cell—creates two cells where before there was only one. Merging and splitting cells is especially handy if you are using a table to lay out your Web page, because doing so lets you fit myriad content into different-sized spaces.

1 select cells

Select two or more cells that you would like to merge. (See Select Cells on page 150 for more information about selecting cells.)

2 click merge cells

The selected cells are merged into one.

3 click cell

Click a cell that you would like to split.

> 🄣🄘🄟 You can select more than one cell when performing a splitting operation (they can be adjacent or non-adjacent). If you do, each of the selected cells is split in two.

4 click split cells

When you click this button, the **Split Cells** dialog box opens.

5 set split parameters

In the **Split Cells** dialog box, specify whether the selected cell should be split into columns or rows, and the number of rows or columns the split cell should contain.

6 click OK

Click the **OK** button to close the Split Cells dialog box and split the selected cell.

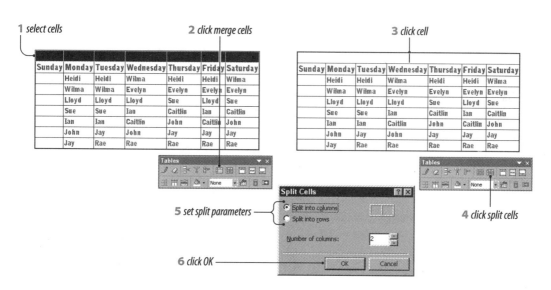

1 select cells   *2 click merge cells*   *3 click cell*

5 set split parameters

6 click OK

4 click split cells

Insert A Table In A Cell

At some point, you may need to add a table within a table—that is, to insert a table into a single cell of a larger table. Doing so is simple; click the cell into which you want to place a table, and then insert a table using the method you prefer (see Add A Table To A Page on page 148 to investigate your options).

The Table AutoFormat Dialog Box

FrontPage features several pre-designed templates that you can use to format your table. In addition, you can tweak these formats to suit your taste by enabling or disabling certain formatting features. Choose **Table➡ AutoFormat** to open this dialog box.

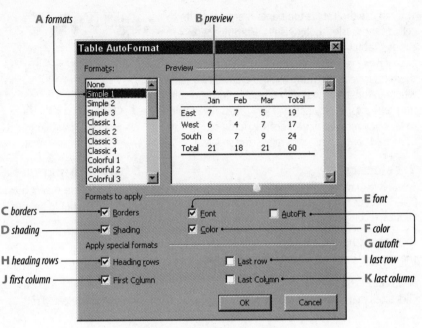

A *formats*   **B** *preview*

C *borders* **D** *shading* **H** *heading rows* **J** *first column*

E *font* **F** *color* **G** *autofit* **I** *last row* **K** *last column*

A formats
Select a format from this list of pre-designed templates.

B preview
View the selected format in the **Preview** window.

C borders
Check this checkbox if you want the format you selected to be applied to your table's borders.

D shading
Check here if you want the shading feature of the format you selected to be applied to your table.

E font
Check this box to apply the selected format's font to the text in your table.

F color
Check here if you want the selected format's colors to be applied to your table.

G autofit
If you want the table to be automatically sized to fit its contents, check this box.

H heading rows
Many formats apply special features, such as bold font, special borders, shaded backgrounds, or other attributes, to the heading rows in your table. If you want these features, check this checkbox; if the format you select in the **Formats** list (A) supports the use of a special format for heading rows, it appears in the Preview area (B).

I last row
Some formats apply special features, like the ones mentioned above, to the last row in your table. To apply these features, check this checkbox.

J first column
Some formats apply special features, like the ones mentioned above, to the first column in your table. If you want these features in your table, check here.

K last column
Some formats apply special features, like the ones described above, to the last column in your table. Check this box to apply these features.

AutoFormat A Table

After you insert a table on your page, you can *Auto-Format* it—that is, apply a predefined format (a *format* in this context is a set of fonts, borders, and more). FrontPage 2002 has several predefined formats that you can choose from.

> **tip** Using FrontPage's AutoFormat feature is only one way to format your table. For more information on table-formatting options, see Table & Cell Properties Dialog Boxes on page 154.

1 choose table autoformat

Click anywhere in the table you want to format and then choose **Table⮕Table AutoFormat** to open the **Table AutoFormat** dialog box.

2 select format

Click in the **Formats** list until you find a format you like, previewing each selected format in the **Preview** window.

3 apply formats

Decide which formats you want to apply. Experiment by checking and unchecking the **Borders**, **Shading**, **Font**, **Color**, and **AutoFit** boxes under **Formats to apply** to see how each one affects the image in the **Preview** window.

4 apply special formats

Check and uncheck the **Heading rows**, **Last row**, **First Column**, and **Last Column** boxes under **Apply special formats** until you find a combination you like. To help you make your decision, check the Preview window to see how each setting affects the image.

5 click OK

Clicking **OK** closes the **Table AutoFormat** dialog box and applies the formatting changes.

> **tip** Readability is key. Avoid table formats that make the text in your table difficult to read.

1 choose table autoformat

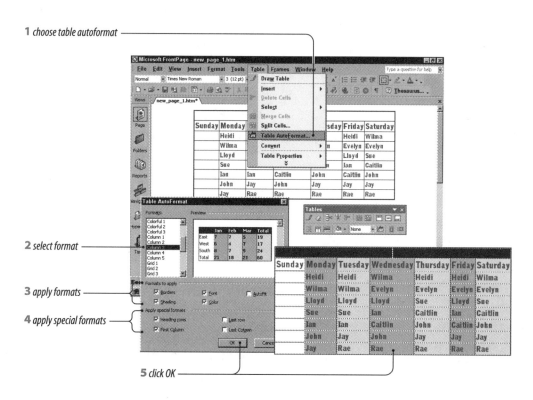

2 select format

3 apply formats

4 apply special formats

5 click OK

Table & Cell Properties Dialog Boxes

You may prefer the flexibility of using FrontPage's **Table** and **Cell Properties** dialog boxes to format your tables instead of AutoFormatting them. To open these dialog boxes, choose **Table→Table Properties** and then **Table** or **Cell**.

A *alignment*
B *float*
C *cell padding*
D *cell spacing*

G *(border) size*
H *(border) color*

M *use background picture*

P *style*

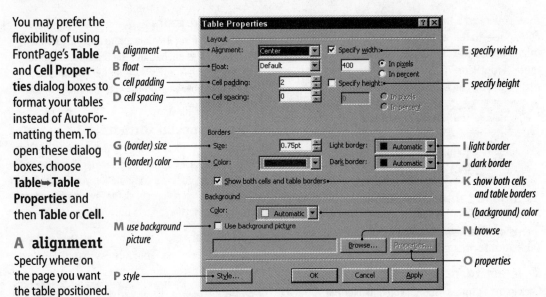

E *specify width*
F *specify height*

I *light border*
J *dark border*
K *show both cells and table borders*
L *(background) color*
N *browse*
O *properties*

A alignment
Specify where on the page you want the table positioned.

B float
Specify how you want text outside the table to flow around the table.

C cell padding
Type a number to specify the cell padding in pixels. (*Cell padding* refers to the space between the contents of the cell and the cell's border.)

D cell spacing
Type a number to specify the cell spacing in pixels. (*Cell spacing* refers to the space between cells in a table.)

E specify width
Check this checkbox and specify the table width either in pixels or as a percentage of the browser window's width. Choose **In pixels** or **In percent** to identify the unit of measure you prefer.

> *tip* If you give the table width in pixels, that width is constant. That is, regardless of how large or small the viewer's Web browser window is, the table stays the same size.

F specify height
Check this checkbox and specify the table height either in pixels or as a percentage of the browser window's height.

G (border) size
Type a number to specify the size of the border, in pixels, to surround the table. Set the border size to 0 if you want no border.

H (border) color
Choose a color for the table border.

I light border
You can apply a two-colored border; doing so creates a three-dimensional effect. Select the lighter of the two colors here.

J dark border
If you want to apply the two-colored border to create a three-dimensional effect, select the darker of the two colors (for the top and left sides) here.

K show both cells and table borders
Add a border to the table and to each of the cells within it.

L (background) color
Choose a color for the table's background.

M use background picture

Place a background picture in the table. Then, in the accompanying text field, type the path and file name of the picture you want to use.

N browse

Don't know the path and filename of the background picture you want to use? Click the **Browse** button to locate it.

O properties

View the properties for the background picture, such as its path and filename or URL, the file type (GIF or JPEG), and so on.

> *tip* If the **Properties** button is grayed out, close the **Table Properties** dialog box and then reopen it.

P style

Click this button to open the **Modify Style** dialog box and apply style-sheet formatting. (You learn more about styles in Chapter 9, Work With Styles.)

Q horizontal alignment

Specify the *horizontal alignment* for cell contents— that is, whether text in the cell should be aligned left-aligned (**Left** or **Default**), right-aligned (**Right**), centered (**Center**), or justified (**Justify**).

R vertical alignment

Specify the *vertical alignment* for cell contents—that is, whether text should appear along the top of the cell (**Top**), in the middle of the cell (**Middle, Baseline**, or **Default**), or along the bottom of the cell (**Bottom**).

S rows spanned

Specify the number of rows spanned by the cell.

T columns spanned

Specify the number of columns spanned by the cell.

U width & height settings

Specify the cell width and height either in pixels or as a percentage of the table's width or height.

V header cell

Designate the selected cell (or cells) as a *table header*. Text in the selected cells is formatted bold and centered by default.

W no wrap

Prevent Web browsers from wrapping text inside the selected cell.

X border settings

Cell border settings work much like their table-border counterparts (refer to G, H, I, J, and K), except that you can't specify the border size. You can, however, select border colors (regular, light, and dark).

Y background settings

Set a background color or image for a cell or group of cells. These settings mimic their table-properties counterparts (refer to letters L and M).

Z style

Click this button to open the **Modify Style** dialog box and apply style-sheet formatting to cells. (See Chapter 9, Work With Styles, for more information about style-sheet formatting.)

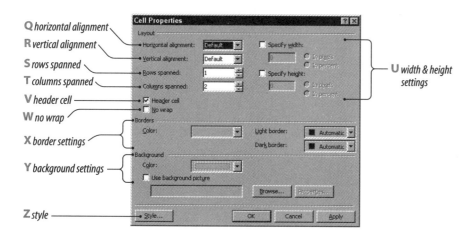

Set Table Layout

Although you probably specified how to lay out your table when you first added it to your page, you might need to make a few changes as you work. For example, once you see how the table and text flow together, you might need to change the alignment or how the text wraps around the table (called *float*). Follow these steps to make these and other changes to your table's layout.

1 choose table

Click the table you want to amend to select it, and then choose **Table➡Table Properties➡Table** to open the **Table Properties** dialog box.

2 set alignment

Open the **Alignment** drop-down list to specify where on the page you want the table positioned. Your options are **Default** (left), **Left, Right,** and **Center.**

1 choose table

2 set alignment

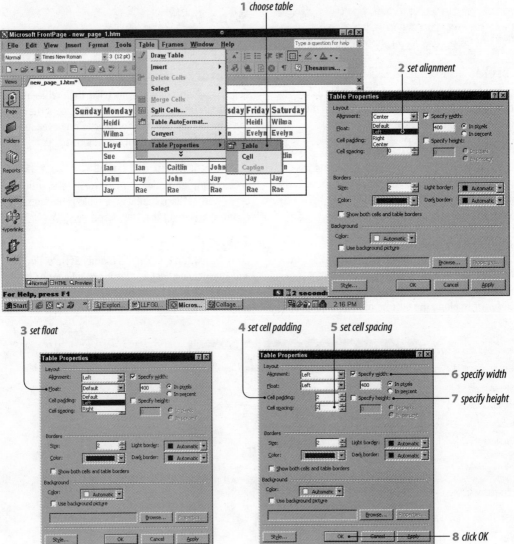

3 set float

4 set cell padding

5 set cell spacing

6 specify width

7 specify height

8 click OK

3 set float

Open the **Float** drop-down list to specify how you want text outside the table to flow around the table. Options are **Default** (left), **Left,** and **Right.**

4 set cell padding

Type a number in the **Cell padding** box to specify the *cell padding* (the space between the contents of the cell and the cell's border). Type 0 if you want no cell padding.

5 set cell spacing

Type a number in the **Cell spacing** spin box to specify the *cell spacing* (the space between cells in the table). Type 0 if you want no cell padding.

6 specify width

Check the **Specify width** checkbox and then select either the **In pixels** or **In percent** radio button. In the accompanying textbox, type a number to represent the number of pixels wide you want the table to be, or the percentage of the browser window's width, depending on which radio button you chose.

7 specify height

The **Specify height** section acts like the **Specify width** section. Check the **Specify height** checkbox, choose **In pixels** or **In percent**, and type a value in the textbox.

8 click OK

Click **OK** to apply the settings.

Tables As Page Layout

Using a table to lay out your page can help you create an ordered, eye-pleasing page. At the same time, tables offer you tremendous flexibility. You're not limited to a grid with a set number of rows and columns; you can split and merge cells, set cell padding and cell spacing, and more to create a page with an interesting layout.

Page size

If you want your table to completely fill the viewer's browser window, no matter how big or small that window is, check the **Specify width** and **Specify height** checkboxes in the **Table Properties** window, choose **In percent**, and type 100 in the accompanying textbox. Note, however, that doing so may significantly alter the layout of your page depending on the size of the viewer's browser window. If you prefer your table size (and, as a result, layout) to remain constant, specify the size in pixels instead of as a percentage.

Merging & splitting cells

After that, consider how you want your page to be laid out. Do you want a column of buttons along the left side? If so, you might decide to split the cells in the left-hand column, and place a button in each cell. Do you want a large graphic in the center of the page? Then you might decide to merge several cells to create a large block of space. Do you want a large header area, advertising the title of your page or the name of your site? Again, you might want to merge cells to create space. (Refer to the section Merge & Split Cells on page 151.)

Cell padding & spacing

To prevent the content in one cell from crowding the content in adjacent cells, it's a good idea to apply cell padding and cell spacing settings. (*Cell padding* refers to the space between the contents of the cell and the cell's border; *cell spacing*

is the space between cells in the table.) Try starting with a setting of 2 to 5 for each, and experiment as needed.

Borders

You can apply borders to tables being used for page-layout purposes, but they may make the page appear less seamless than you might like. Unless you have a good reason for using borders, avoid them. (See Set Table Borders on the next page for more information about borders.)

Add background

Background colors and images, discussed in Add Background Color (page 159) and Insert A Picture Into A Table (160), can greatly enhance your page layout. Rules of good design apply, however: Avoid using a background color or image that makes your page's text unreadable.

Set Table Borders

Accentuate your table by surrounding it with a border. FrontPage lets you customize the border in many ways, including changing the thickness and color.

1 choose table

After you click in the table whose borders you want to set, choose **Table→Table Properties→Table** to open the **Table Properties** dialog box.

2 set border size

Type a number in the **Size** spin box to specify the size of the border in pixels. (If you don't want a border around your table, type 0.)

3 set border color

Open the **Color** drop-down list to choose a color for the table border.

4 set light border color (optional)

Create a three-dimensional effect by applying a two-colored border; begin by selecting the lighter of the two border colors here.

5 set dark border color (optional)

Select the darker of the two colors (for the top and left sides) in the two-colored border here.

6 show cell and table borders (optional)

Click here to display borders around the cells in your table.

To format the borders of individual cells, you must first click inside the cell whose borders you want to change and then choose **Tables→Table Properties→Cell**. Then, in the **Cell Properties** dialog box, select a border color, or choose a light color and a dark color.

7 click OK

Click **OK** to close the **Table Properties** dialog box and apply your changes.

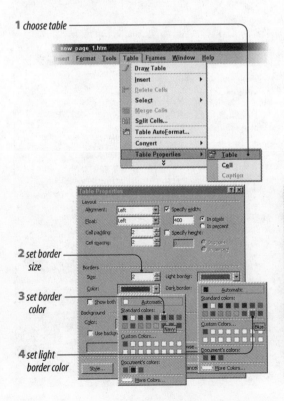

1 *choose table*

2 *set border size*

3 *set border color*

4 *set light border color*

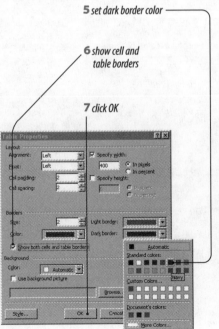

5 *set dark border color*

6 *show cell and table borders*

7 *click OK*

Add Background Color

To add a bit of color to an otherwise drab table, apply a *background color*. You can add a background color to an entire table, or to selected cells.

1 choose cell

To apply a background color to selected cells, choose **Table➠Table Properties➠Cell**.

2 choose color

Open the **Color** drop-down list in the **Background** area and select a color.

3 click OK

Click **OK** to apply the color to the selected cells and close the **Cell Properties** dialog box.

4 choose table

To apply a background color to an entire table, choose **Table➠Table Properties➠Table**.

5 choose color

Open the **Color** drop-down list in the **Background** area and select a color.

> *tip* Be careful when selecting a background color; you don't want it to obscure the text in the table. If you use dark text, a light-colored background looks best, and vice versa.

6 click OK

Click **OK** to apply the color to the table's background and close the **Table Properties** dialog box.

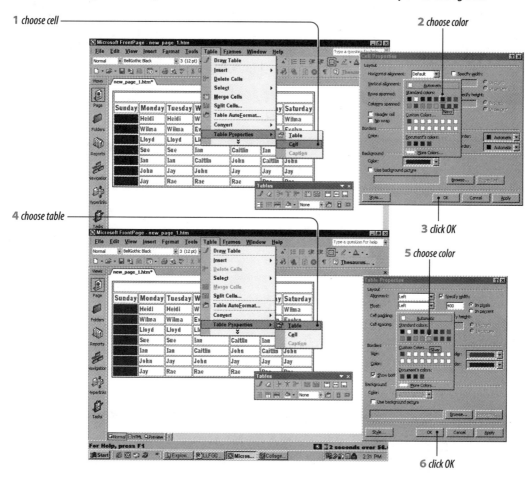

1 *choose cell*

2 *choose color*

4 *choose table*

3 *click OK*

5 *choose color*

6 *click OK*

Insert A Picture Into A Table

You can easily add an image to your entire table, or to selected cells. Before you do so, however, you must first size the image using your favorite image-editing program. For example, if you want an image to fill a table that's 200 by 200 pixels, you must size the image to those measurements before placing it in the table. If you add the image to multiple selected cells, a small version of the image appears in each cell. If you want a single image to span several cells, you must first merge those cells. (For help merging cells, refer to page 151, Merge & Split Cells.)

> **tip** Netscape Navigator doesn't support background images in Web pages. If the **Use background picture** option is disabled, FrontPage has been instructed to create pages that are compatible with the Netscape browser.

1 choose cell

Choose **Table➡Table Properties➡Cell** to open the **Cell Properties** dialog box.

2 click use background picture

Specify that you want to place a background image in the selected cells.

3 click browse

Click **Browse** to open the **Select Background Picture** dialog box.

4 select image

Navigate to the folder containing the picture you want to use, click to select it, and click **Open.**

5 click OK

Click **OK.** The image appears in your table.

> **tip** If you want your background image to span the entire table rather than selected cells within the table, simply choose **Table➡Table Properties➡Table**. From there, the process is identical to the one outlined in steps 2-5 above.

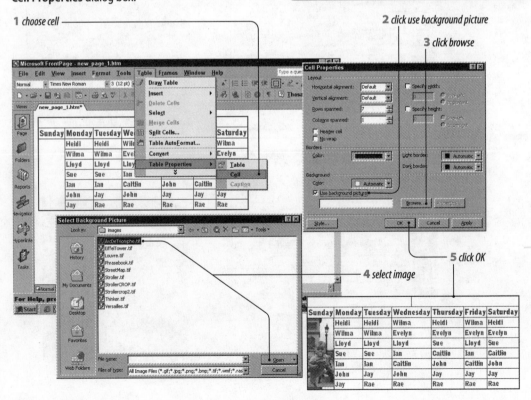

1 *choose cell*

2 *click use background picture*

3 *click browse*

4 *select image*

5 *click OK*

Change Column Width & Row Height

You may need to change the width of a few columns or the height of a few rows in your table.

1 select cell within row
Click a cell within the row you want to resize.

2 choose cell
Choose **Table**➡**Table Properties**➡**Cell** to open the **Cell Properties** dialog box.

3 specify height
Click the **Specify height** checkbox and choose **In pixels** (to set the height in pixels) or **In percent** (to set the height as a percentage of the table height). Type the desired height in the accompanying textbox.

4 click OK
Click **OK** to close the **Cell Properties** dialog box and apply the row-height settings.

5 select column
Click a cell within the column you want to resize.

6 choose cell
Choose **Table**➡**Table Properties**➡**Cell** to open the **Cell Properties** dialog box.

7 specify width
Click the **Specify width** checkbox and choose **In pixels** or **In percent**. Type the desired width in the accompanying textbox.

8 click OK
Click **OK** to close the **Cell Properties** dialog box and apply the column-width settings.

> *tip* If you're having trouble changing the column width, it may be because you've set the table width in pixels, and the other columns in your table are too wide to let you widen the selected column.

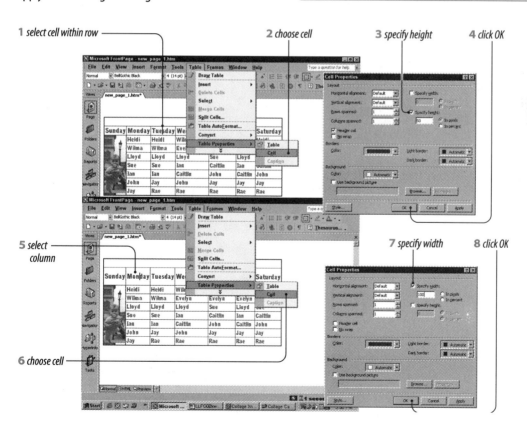

1 *select cell within row* **2** *choose cell* **3** *specify height* **4** *click OK*

5 *select column* **6** *choose cell* **7** *specify width* **8** *click OK*

steps **Add Headers & Captions**

You can designate certain cells in your table as *header* cells. FrontPage makes text in these cells bold and centered to add emphasis to the cells. In addition, you can add a *table caption* to label or summarize the table.

1 select cells

Select the cells that you want to use as *headers*.

2 choose cell

Choose **Table➡Table Properties➡Cell** to open the **Cell Properties** dialog box.

3 select header cell

Click to select the **Header cell** checkbox.

4 click OK

Click **OK** to close the **Cell Properties** dialog box and apply the header-cell setting.

5 click table

Click in the table to which you want to add a caption.

6 choose caption

Choose **Table➡Insert➡Caption**.

7 type & format caption

A space for the caption appears at the top of the table. Type and format text to label or summarize your table.

---

tip To move the caption to the bottom of the table, choose **Table➡Table Properties➡Caption** to open the **Caption Properties** dialog box. Select the **Bottom of Table** radio button and then click **OK**.

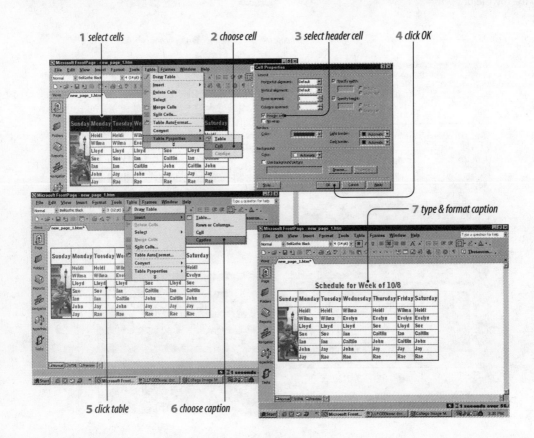

1 *select cells*   2 *choose cell*   3 *select header cell*   4 *click OK*

7 *type & format caption*

5 *click table*   6 *choose caption*

Work With Styles

Using styles, cascading style sheets, or themes, you can simultaneously format numerous page elements, including text, graphics, tables, and more.

FrontPage offers several pre-defined styles (that is, sets of formatting characteristics) called *built-in styles*; in addition, you can create your own styles (called *user-defined styles*) either by modifying built-in styles or by starting from scratch.

To apply consistent style information across multiple Web pages, you use a *cascading style sheet* (CSS). A CSS is a document that contains style information that can be referenced by multiple Web pages.

Another way to quickly format several pages is to use a *theme,* which is a set of design elements and color schemes that you can apply to your Web pages. FrontPage includes several pre-defined themes, or you can create your own.

steps Apply A Style

FrontPage supports two main types of styles: paragraph-level styles and character-level styles. *Paragraph-level styles* combine character and formatting settings (font, style, background color, and so on) and can be applied to entire blocks of page elements, including text, images, tables, and more. *Character-level styles* also combine character and formatting settings, but apply to text only.

The names of built-in paragraph styles are preceded by a small paragraph symbol; no symbol or icon precedes user-defined paragraph styles. The names of character styles, on the other hand, are preceded by a small underlined letter *a*.

1 select text

To apply a style to an entire paragraph, click anywhere within that paragraph. To apply a style to selected words, drag to select the text.

2 choose style

Open the **Style** menu in the Standard toolbox and choose a style. FrontPage applies the style immediately after you make your choice.

> *tip* If you don't find a style that works for you, fear not; to create and modify styles to better suit your needs, read Create A New Style on page 166.

1 *select text*

2 *choose style*

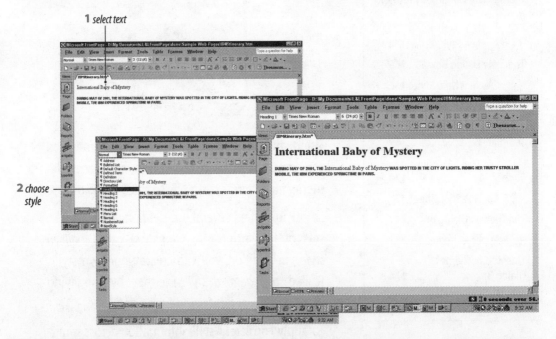

Page-Element Styles

A third type of style, a *page-element style*, is specific to certain types of page elements, such as tables, form fields, and so on. In most cases, if a page element supports this option, its **Properties** dialog box features a **Style** button. A detailed discussion of applying page-elements styles is beyond the scope of this book; for more information, open FrontPage Help and type **style** in the **Index** tab. From the list of topics that appears, choose **Apply a style**; in the **Apply a Style** Help page, click the **Apply a style to other page elements** link.

The Style Dialog Box

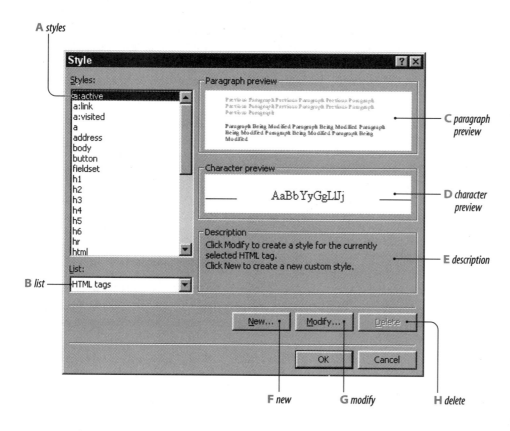

A *styles*

B *list*

C *paragraph preview*

D *character preview*

E *description*

F *new*   **G** *modify*   **H** *delete*

Using the **Style** dialog box, you can view pre-defined and user-defined styles, create new styles, modify existing styles, and delete styles. To open the Style dialog box, choose **Format➞Style.**

A styles
Click in the **Styles** list to preview a style in the **Paragraph preview** (C) and **Character preview** (D) areas.

B list
Select whether you want the **Styles** list to show a list of all HTML tags or all user-defined style tags.

C paragraph preview
View the paragraph-level style of the selected style.

D character preview
View the character-level style of the selected style.

E description
Read a description of the selected style.

F new
Click the **New** button to open the **New Style** dialog box, where you can create a new, user-defined style.

G modify
Click the **Modify** button to open the **Modify Style** dialog box, where you can modify an existing style.

H delete
Click the **Delete** button to delete the selected user-defined style.

> *tip* If the **Delete** button is grayed out, it's because a built-in style is selected. Although you can delete user-defined styles, you can't delete built-in styles.

Create A New Style

Your formatting needs may outgrow FrontPage's built-in styles. If so, you can easily create your own styles (called *user-defined* styles) and apply them to your pages just as you would a built-in style.

1 choose style

With a page open in Page view, open the **Style** dialog box by choosing **Format➡Style.**

2 click new

Click the **New** button to open the **New Style** dialog box.

3 name style

Type a name for the new style in the **Name (selector)** textbox. Don't include spaces in the style name.

> *tip* Try to think of a descriptive name for the new style to make the style easier to find and use. For example, you might incorporate information about your Web page with a description of the style's function.

4 set style type

Set the style type by choosing **Paragraph** or **Character** from the **Style type** drop-down list. (Refer to Apply A Style on page 164 for more information about character and paragraph styles.)

5 open font dialog box

Click the **Format** button and choose **Font** from the drop-down list to open the **Font** window.

6 apply font settings

Choose a font, font style, font size, font color, and any desired effects. View the settings in the Preview window; when you find the desired combination, click **OK.** (See The Font Dialog Box on page 76 for more information about applying font settings.)

7 open paragraph dialog box

Click the **Format** button and choose **Paragraph** from the drop-down list to open the **Paragraph** dialog box.

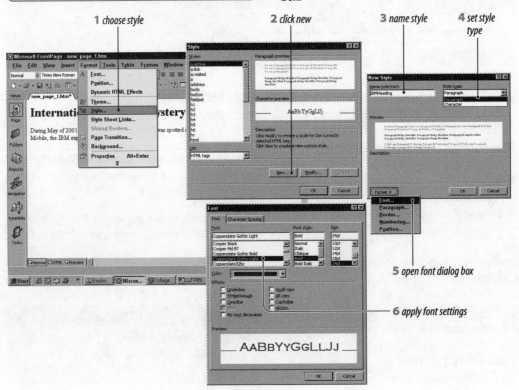

1 *choose style*
2 *click new*
3 *name style*
4 *set style type*
5 *open font dialog box*
6 *apply font settings*

8 apply paragraph settings

Specify the desired paragraph alignment, as well as any settings in the **Indentation** and **Spacing** areas, and click **OK**. (Refer to The Paragraph Dialog Box on page 82 for more information.

> **tip** To apply bullets and numbering to your style, click the **Format** button in the **New Style** dialog box and choose **Numbering**. The **Bullets and Numbering** dialog box opens; for information about using it, refer to The Bullets And Numbering Dialog Box on page 86.

9 open borders and shading dialog box

Click the **Format** button and choose **Border** from the drop-down list.

10 set borders & shading

Specify whether border or shading should be incorporated into the new style and click **OK**. (Refer to The Borders Tab and The Shading Tab starting on page 92 for more information.)

> **tip** Depending on what type of style you create, you may need to set *positioning properties*. These help you specify wrapping style, element location, and more. To do so, click the **Format** button in the **New Style** dialog box and choose **Position**.

11 click OK

Click the **OK** button in the **New Style** dialog box.

12 click OK

The style you created appears in the list of user-defined styles. Click **OK** to close the **Style** window. To apply your new style, refer to Apply A Style on page 164.

7 *open paragraph dialog box*

8 *apply paragraph settings*

9 *open borders and shading dialog box*

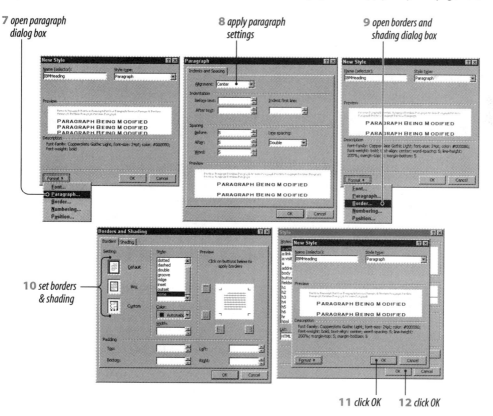

10 *set borders & shading*

11 *click OK* 12 *click OK*

Modify A Style

Suppose one of FrontPage's built-in styles nearly meets your formatting needs, but would be perfect if you could tweak it a bit. In such a case, it's easier to modify a built-in style than to create a new style from scratch. You can also modify styles you have created yourself.

1 choose style

To open the **Style** dialog box, choose **Format➡Style**.

2 select style

Within the **Styles** list, click the style you want to modify.

3 click modify

The **Modify Style** dialog box opens.

4 name style

Type a name for the new, modified style in the **Name (selector)** textbox. Don't include spaces in the style name.

5 set style type

Set the style type by choosing **Paragraph** or **Character** from the **Style type** drop-down list. (Refer to Apply A Style on page 164 for more information about character and paragraph styles.)

6 apply format settings

Click the **Format** button and choose Font, Paragraph, Border, Numbering, or Position to modify the style's settings. (Create A New Style on page 166 covers these format options in greater detail.)

7 click OK

Click **OK** to close the **Modify Style** dialog box.

8 click OK

The modified style is added to the list of user-defined styles. Click **OK** to close the **Style** dialog box.

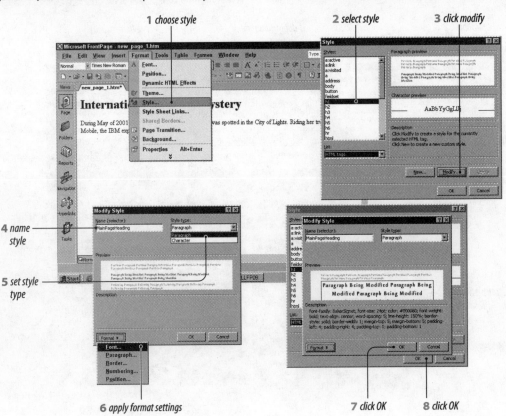

1 *choose style* **2** *select style* **3** *click modify*

4 *name style* **5** *set style type* **6** *apply format settings* **7** *click OK* **8** *click OK*

The Cascading Style Sheet Templates

Cascading style sheets (CSSs) are documents that contain style information. If you've applied a user-defined style to a single page element, or created or modified a style for use on a single page, you've already worked with two types of CSSs—*inline* and *embedded,* respectively. A third type, however, is even more useful: *external.* These can be linked to multiple Web pages, allowing you to quickly apply styles across an entire Web. FrontPage offers several CSS templates, which you can use to create your own external style sheets. To access these templates, choose **File➡New➡Page or Web** and, in the New Page or Web task pane, click the Page Templates link. Finally, in the Page Templates window, click the **Style Sheets** tab. (Although some browsers don't support CSS technology, MS Internet Explorer 4 and later and Netscape Navigator 4.0 and later do.)

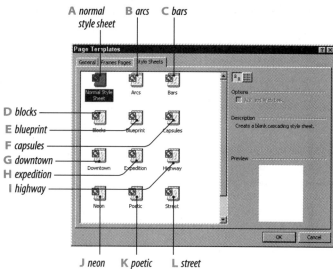

A *normal style sheet* B *arcs* C *bars*
D *blocks*
E *blueprint*
F *capsules*
G *downtown*
H *expedition*
I *highway*
J *neon* K *poetic* L *street*

A normal style sheet

Create a blank cascading style sheet, which you can then modify to suit your needs.

B arcs

Features brown Verdana text, brown Times New Roman headers, and a pale yellow background.

C bars

Features Arial text, Times New Roman headers, and a light olive background.

D blocks

Features Bookman Old Style text and headers, red hyperlinks, and a light silver background.

E blueprint

Features Century Gothic text and headers, purple hyperlinks, and a bright yellow background.

F capsules

Features Arial text and headers, reddish-orange hyperlinks, and a light green background.

G downtown

Features yellow Garamond text, Verdana headers, orange hyperlinks, and a royal blue background.

H expedition

Features Book Antiqua text and headers, and a peach background.

I highway

Features white Verdana text, Verdana headers, orange hyperlinks, and a black background.

J neon

Features neon-green Verdana text and headers, chartreuse hyperlinks, and a black background.

K poetic

Features purple Book Antiqua text, Book Antiqua headers, and a white background.

L street

Features navy Verdana text, Comic Sans MS headers, and a light cyan background.

M (not shown) **sweets**

Features dark-blue Arial text, Arial Rounded MT Bold headers, and a pale yellow background.

steps Create A Cascading Style Sheet

You can use the Normal Style Sheet template to create a new external cascading style sheet. This template is blank; you fill the blank sheet with the styles you want to create a CSS.

1 choose page or web

Choosing **File➛New➛Page or Web** opens the **New Page or Web** task pane.

2 click page templates

Click **Page Templates** in the New from template area to open the **Page Templates** dialog box.

3 click style sheets tab

You see a list of the available style sheet templates.

4 click normal style sheet

Click **Normal Style Sheet** to select it and then click **OK**. A blank CSS template opens on your desktop.

5 choose style

To add styles to the blank sheet, open the **Style** dialog box by choosing **Format➛Style**.

6 add styles

Click the **New** button and then follow the steps in Create A New Style (page 166) and Modify A Style (page 168) to add styles to the CSS. When you're finished, click **OK** in the **Style** dialog box.

7 choose save as

Choose **File➛Save As** to save your new CSS.

8 name .css file

Locate the folder in which you want to save the CSS file (if you're working with a Web, rather than a single page, place the CSS in the Web's main folder; save the CSS anywhere you like), name the file, and click **Save**.

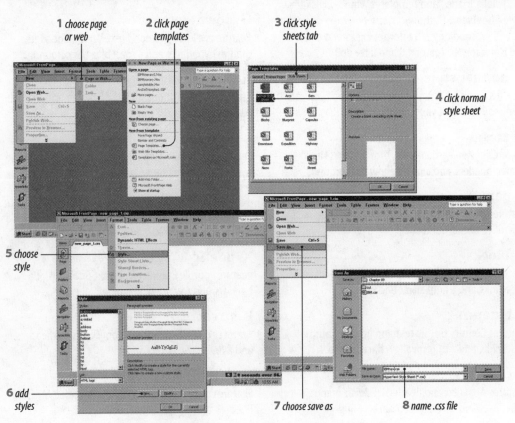

1 *choose page or web*

2 *click page templates*

3 *click style sheets tab*

4 *click normal style sheet*

5 *choose style*

6 *add styles*

7 *choose save as*

8 *name .css file*

After you create a CSS, linking it to your Web pages is a snap. You can link it to a single page, selected pages, or to all the pages in a Web (described here). Once the style sheet is linked to your Web, you can quickly apply the styles contained in the CSS to the site's pages.

1 open web

Open the Web to which you want to apply a CSS.

2 choose style sheet links

Choose **Format→Style Sheet Links** to open the **Link Style Sheet** dialog box.

3 click add

Click **Add** to begin linking the CSS to the Web.

4 locate .css file

Locate the cascading style sheet file that you want to apply and click the **Select File** dialog box's **OK** button.

> *tip* If the CSS file is not stored in the folder for the Web to which you are linking it, click the button featuring a magnifying glass over a folder in the lower-right corner of the **Select Style Sheet** dialog box to locate the file.

5 select file

The selected file appears in the **URL** list. Click it to select it and then click **OK** to apply it to the open Web.

6 apply header style

Open any page in the Web, and click in its header text. Then, open the **Style** menu in the Formatting toolbar and choose a header style from the CSS.

7 apply body style

Select the page's body text, open the **Style** menu, and choose the body style from the CSS.

> *tip* If you want to link your style sheet to a selected page or pages in your Web rather than to the entire Web, simply open any pages to which you want to link the CSS, open the **Link Style Sheet** dialog box, and choose the **Selected Files** radio button; then follow steps 3-7 on this page.

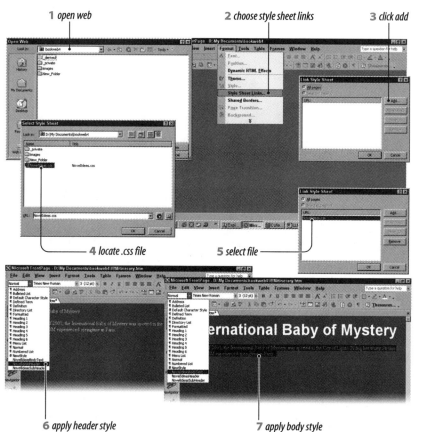

1 open web

2 choose style sheet links

3 click add

4 locate .css file

5 select file

6 apply header style

7 apply body style

The Themes Dialog Box

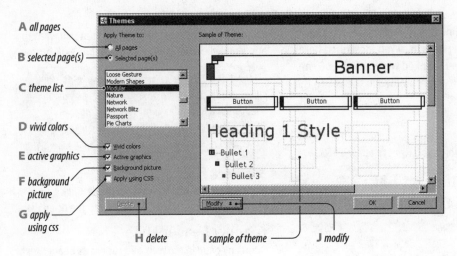

A *all pages*

B *selected page(s)*

C *theme list*

D *vivid colors*

E *active graphics*

F *background picture*

G *apply using css*

H *delete*   **I** *sample of theme*   **J** *modify*

A *theme* is similar to a CSS, in that it can be applied to all pages in a Web; themes, however, can affect more aspects of a page's appearance, including its colors, graphics, styles, and more. You apply a theme using the **Themes** dialog box, which you open by choosing **Format➡Theme**.

A all pages

Apply a theme to all pages in a Web.

B selected page(s)

Apply a theme to selected pages only.

C theme list

Choose from among several pre-defined themes here.

> *tip* You can install additional FrontPage themes by clicking the **Install Additional Themes** option in the theme list. You must have your FrontPage 2002 CD-ROM in order to do so.

D vivid colors

Themes offer two sets of colors, one vivid, the other more muted. If you prefer a vivid color set, check this checkbox.

E active graphics

FrontPage themes offer two sets of graphics (banners, buttons, bullets, and so on). *Active graphics,* the more

elaborate and lively set, are specified by default. Uncheck this checkbox to use the normal graphics. (Not all theme elements support active graphics. In such cases, the **Active graphics** checkbox isn't available.)

F background picture

A background picture is applied to each theme by default. To remove it, uncheck this checkbox.

G apply using css

When you apply a theme, it changes the HTML of the page itself. If you'd rather link the theme's settings information to the page as a cascading style sheet, you can do so by checking this checkbox.

> *tip* Not all browsers support CSS formatting. For this reason, it's probably best to leave this box unchecked.

H delete

Delete the selected theme. You can't delete built-in themes, but you can delete any themes you create. For more information, see Modify A Theme on page 176.

I sample of theme

View a sample of the theme you selected.

J modify

Reveal a panel of buttons that let you modify the selected theme.

🎯 steps Apply A Theme

By using themes, you can instantly apply a color scheme, fonts, banner art, button art, and other formatting options to your Web rather than making several individual changes to achieve the same result. As with a CSS, you can apply themes to a single page, to multiple pages, or to all the pages in a Web (outlined here). If you apply a theme to all pages in a Web, it becomes the Web's *default theme.* Any new pages you create in that Web use the theme.

1 open web
Open the Web to which you want to apply a theme.

2 choose theme
Choose **Format→Theme** to open the **Themes** dialog box.

3 select theme
Click a theme in the list on the left side of the **Themes** dialog box and view it in the **Sample of Theme** area. Continue clicking themes until you find one you like.

4 select vivid colors
(optional)
Click this checkbox to view the theme's alternate color scheme.

> 💡 **tip** The **Active graphics** and **Background picture** checkboxes are checked by default. For more information about these options, refer to The Themes Dialog Box on page 172.

5 click OK
Click **OK** to close the dialog box and apply the theme to your Web.

> 💡 **tip** If you want to apply a theme to a selected page or pages in your Web rather than to the entire Web, simply open any pages to which you want to apply the theme, open the **Link Style Sheet** dialog box, and choose the **Selected Files** radio button; then follow steps 2-5 on this page.

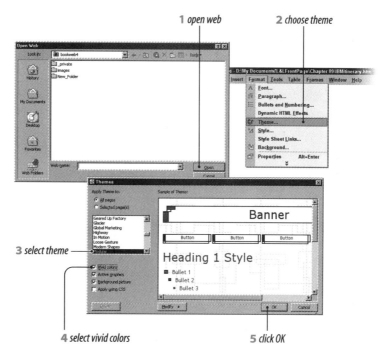

1 *open web*

2 *choose theme*

3 *select theme*

4 *select vivid colors*

5 *click OK*

Remove A Theme

If you apply a theme to your Web or to pages in your Web but later decide you don't like it, you can easily remove it. To do so, you follow the exact same steps you took to apply the theme, but you choose the **(No Theme)** option in the list of themes in the **Themes** dialog box.

The Modify Themes Dialog Boxes

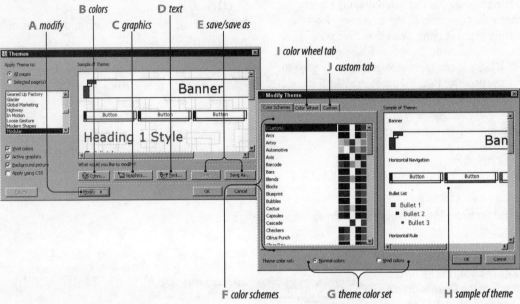

A modify   **B** colors   **C** graphics   **D** text   **E** save/save as

I color wheel tab   **J** custom tab

F color schemes   **G** theme color set   **H** sample of theme

To modify a theme to better suit your needs, you use any of three **Modify Themes** dialog boxes. To access these dialog boxes, click the **Modify** button in the **Themes** dialog box and choose **Colors**, **Graphics**, or **Text**.

A modify

Click this button to reveal the **Colors**, **Graphics**, and **Text** buttons, which let you modify the selected theme.

B colors

Click this button to open a **Modify Theme** dialog box for colors.

C graphics

Click this button to open a **Modify Theme** dialog box for graphics.

D text

Click this button to open a **Modify Theme** dialog box for text.

E save/save as

Click these buttons to save the changes you've made to the theme.

F color schemes

This area shows the color schemes of each pre-defined FrontPage theme, allowing you to apply a new, pre-designed scheme to the selected theme.

G theme color set

Specify whether you want to view *normal* colors or *vivid* colors by selecting the corresponding radio button.

H sample of theme

View the selected theme here.

I color wheel tab

Click the **Color Wheel** tab to create a new, custom color scheme.

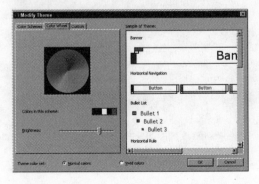

J custom tab

Click the **Custom** tab to apply different colors, existing or custom, to specific theme elements.

K item

Open this drop-down list to select the graphical element you want to modify.

L picture tab

This tab lets you select a new image to be associated with the graphical element you chose in the **Item** drop-down list. If you know the image's path and filename, type it in the textbox.

M browse

Click this button to locate the image you want to use if you don't know its path and filename.

N theme graphic set

Specify whether you want to view normal graphics or active graphics by clicking the corresponding radio button.

O sample of theme

View the selected theme here.

P font tab

Click the **Font** tab to change the font, font style, font size, or alignment of the selected graphical item.

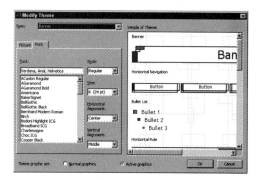

Q item

Open this drop-down list to select the text element you want to modify.

R font

Select a font for the text item you chose in the **Item** drop-down list.

S more text styles

Click this button to open the **Style** dialog box, containing several styles that you can apply to the text item you chose in the **Item** drop-down list.

T sample of theme

View the selected theme here.

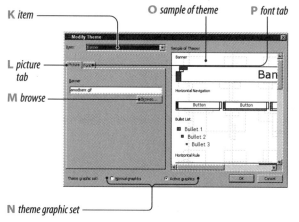

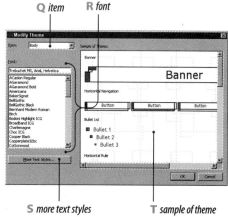

steps Modify A Theme

You can modify a theme by changing its colors, graphical elements (such as banners, buttons, and so on), and text.

1 choose theme

Choose **Format➞Theme** to open the **Themes** dialog box.

2 select theme to modify

Click the name of the theme you want to modify.

3 click modify

Click the **Modify** button to reveal a panel of buttons that enable you to modify the selected theme.

4 click colors (optional)

If you want to modify the theme's colors, click **Colors.** Otherwise, skip to step 12.

5 choose color scheme

Click options in the list of color schemes until you find one you like (preview the selected scheme in the **Sample of Theme** window).

6 click color wheel tab (optional)

If none of the pre-defined color schemes interest you, click the **Color Wheel** tab to create your own scheme.

7 choose new color family

Click in the color wheel to choose a different color family. When you find a color family you like, adjust the **Brightness** slider to brighten or darken the colors in the family.

8 click custom tab (optional)

To change the color of a specific theme element, click the **Custom** tab.

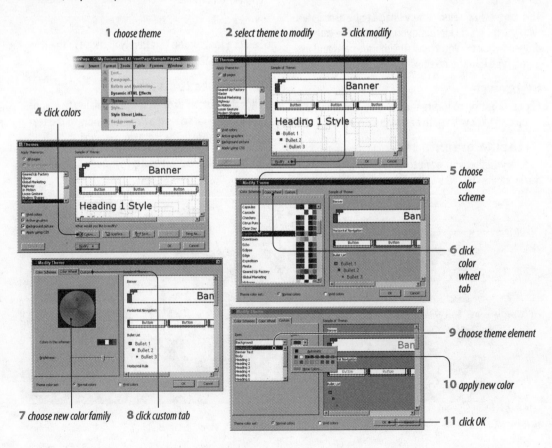

1 choose theme *2 select theme to modify* *3 click modify*

4 click colors

5 choose color scheme

6 click color wheel tab

7 choose new color family *8 click custom tab*

9 choose theme element

10 apply new color

11 click OK

9 choose theme element

Choose the theme element you want to change in the **Item** drop-down list.

10 apply new color

Choose a new color for the selected theme element in the **Color** drop-down list.

11 click OK

Click **OK** in the **Modify Style** dialog box to close it.

12 click graphics (optional)

If you want to modify the theme's graphics, click **Graphics**. Otherwise, skip to step 19.

13 choose theme element

Choose the theme element whose graphic you want to change in the **Item** drop-down list.

14 click browse (optional)

Click **Browse** to locate the graphic you want to use to replace the one the theme uses by default.

> **tip** The number of textboxes in the Picture tab may change depending on which theme element you've chosen. That means you need to repeat steps 14 and 15 for each textbox on the page.

15 locate graphic

When you find the graphic, click it to select it and then click the **Open** button. (You may only apply GIF and JPEG images to theme elements.)

16 click font tab (optional)

To change the font of a specific graphical element, such as a button or banner, select the element in the Item list, and then click the **Font** tab.

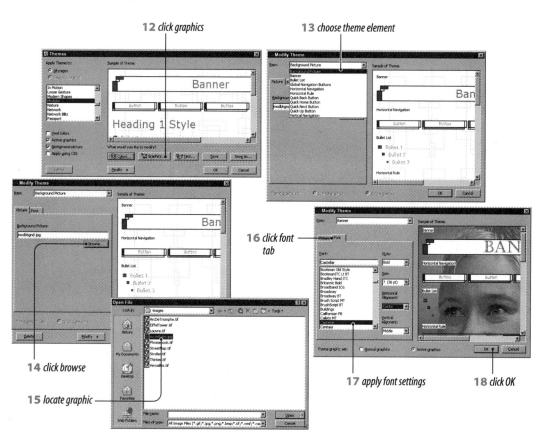

12 *click graphics*

13 *choose theme element*

16 *click font tab*

14 *click browse*

15 *locate graphic*

17 *apply font settings*

18 *click OK*

17 apply font settings

Choose the new font, font style, font size, and font alignment for the selected graphical element.

18 click OK

Click **OK** to close the dialog box and apply your changes to the theme.

19 click text (optional)

To modify the theme's text properties, such as the font used in its body text or header text, click **Text.**

20 choose theme element

Choose the theme element whose text properties you want to change in the **Item** drop-down list.

21 choose font

Select a font for the text item you chose in the **Item** drop-down list.

> *tip* Click the **More Text Styles** button to open the **Style** window, containing several styles that you can apply to the text item you chose in the **Item** drop-down list.

22 click OK

Click **OK** in the **Modify Style** dialog box to close it and apply your changes to the theme.

> *tip* After you modify a pre-set theme, you must save your changes as a new theme.

23 click save as

Click the **Save As** button in the **Themes** dialog box to save the new theme.

24 name theme

Type a descriptive name for the new theme in the **Save Theme** dialog box and click **OK.** The new theme is added to the list in the **Themes** dialog box.

> *tip* If you've gone a little crazy, creating a zillion themes you'll never use, you can easily delete them from the list in the **Themes** dialog box. To do so, select the theme you want to delete and click the **Delete** button. (You can't delete pre-defined themes, only modified themes.)

19 *click text*　　**20** *choose theme element*

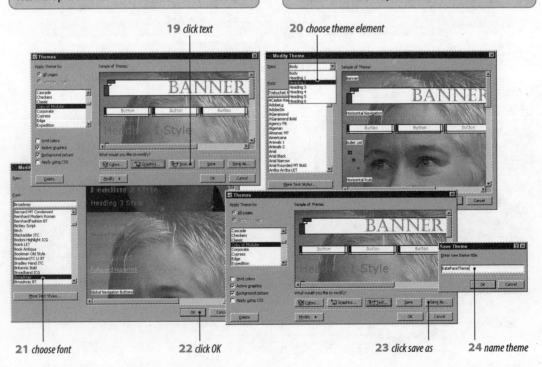

21 *choose font*　　**22** *click OK*　　**23** *click save as*　　**24** *name theme*

Apply Dynamic Effects

Your pages must be dynamic and interactive if you want people to get excited about your site and return to your pages again and again.

Using the Insert Web Component dialog box, you can quickly add a hover button, scrolling marquee, rotating banner ad, hit counter, map, search box, stock quote, and more to your page. And by applying DHTML effects, using the DHTML Effects toolbar, you can animate a page element and apply page transitions, ActiveX controls, Java applets, background sounds, and video to your pages.

Yes, you want your pages to be packed with action, but remember that applying too many dynamic effects can result in a page that looks, at best, chaotic. Compounding the problem, sites laden with effects are slow to download, which could lose your visitors or, worse yet, customers.

179

Configure FrontPage For Dynamic Effects

In order to use all the dynamic effects discussed in this chapter, you must set up FrontPage to handle them. Specifically, you must apply certain *compatibility settings* to your FrontPage workspace using the **Compatibility** tab of the **Page Options** dialog box.

> *tip* Be warned that only those visitors using Microsoft Internet Explorer can enjoy certain DHTML and other dynamic effects on your Web site. Although the content may be wonderful to look at with the correct browser, you may alienate visitors by adding site content that they can't access with different browsers.

1 choose page options

Choose **Tools➭Page Options** to open the **Page Options** dialog box.

2 click compatibility tab

Click the **Compatibility** tab in the **Page Options** dialog box.

3 choose browser

Only Microsoft Internet Explorer supports all the technologies discussed in this chapter. To ensure that you can use them all, open the **Browsers** drop-down list and choose **Microsoft Internet Explorer only.**

4 choose browser version

Only versions 4.0 and later of Microsoft Internet Explorer support all the technologies discussed in this chapter. To ensure that you can use them all, open the **Browser versions** drop-down list and choose **4.0 browsers and later.**

> *tip* When you select **Microsoft Internet Explorer only** and **4.0 browsers and later**, all the checkboxes in the **Available Technologies** area are checked by default. Leave them as they are to ensure that you can use them.

5 click OK

Click **OK** to close the **Page Options** dialog box and apply the compatibility settings.

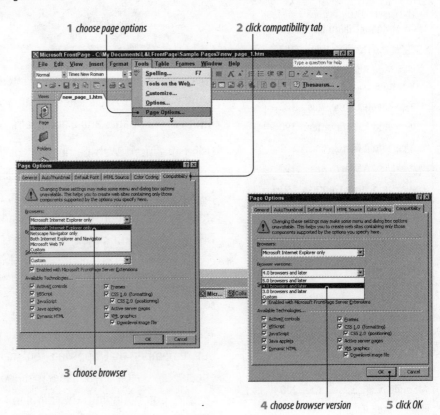

1 *choose page options*

2 *click compatibility tab*

3 *choose browser*

4 *choose browser version*

5 *click OK*

The Insert Web Component Dialog Box

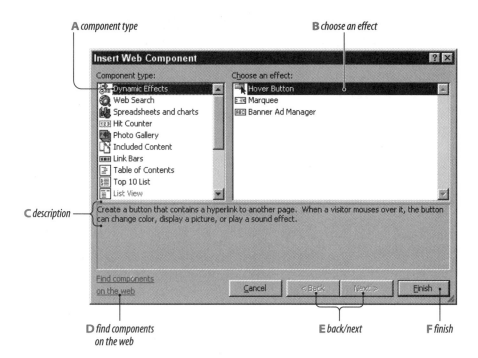

A *component type*

B *choose an effect*

C *description*

D *find components on the web*

E *back/next*

F *finish*

Using the **Insert Web Component** dialog box, you can quickly and easily add a variety of dynamic elements to your page, including a hit counter, a map, a search box, a stock quote, and more. To make this dialog box appear on-screen, choose **Insert▸Web Component.**

A component type

This is your wish-list of component types that you can add to your page, including goodies like dynamic effects, a hit counter, Expedia Components, MSN components, MSNBC components, and advanced controls. (We tell you how to add all of these items, and more, in this chapter.)

B choose an effect

When you select a component type (A), a list of effects pertaining to that component type appears here. Choose the effect you want to apply.

> *tip* The title of this pane changes depending on what's selected in the **Component Type** list.

C description

Read a description of the selected effect in this box.

D find components on the web

Click this link to open Microsoft Office Update and locate additional Web components.

E back/next

The process of inserting some components requires you to step through a wizard-type program. To navigate the program, click the **Back** and **Next** buttons as needed.

> *tip* Don't panic if the Back and Next buttons are grayed out. That just means the effect you've selected doesn't require you to step through a wizard-like program to add it to your page.

F finish

After you select the effect you want to apply, and, if necessary, step through the wizard-like program to apply it, click the **Finish** button. The effect appears on your page, ready to amaze and delight your visitors.

steps Add Hover Buttons

Hover buttons resemble standard buttons in that users click them to navigate your site. Hover buttons differ, however, in that their appearance changes anytime a user clicks or points at (that is, *hovers over*) them with the mouse. For example, the button might glow, display a picture, or play a sound effect when the user's mouse hovers over the button.

1 click web page

Click the spot on your page where you want to insert a hover button.

2 choose web component

Choosing **Insert➤Web Component** opens the **Insert Web Component** dialog box.

3 choose dynamic effects

In the left pane of the Insert Web Component dialog box, choose **Dynamic Effects.**

4 choose hover button

In the right pane of the **Insert Web Component** dialog box, click the **Hover Button** option.

5 click finish

Click **Finish** to open the **Hover Button Properties** dialog box.

6 add button text

In the **Button text** field, type the text that you want to appear on the button.

> *tip* If you plan to add a picture that already contains a text label, leave the **Button text** field blank.

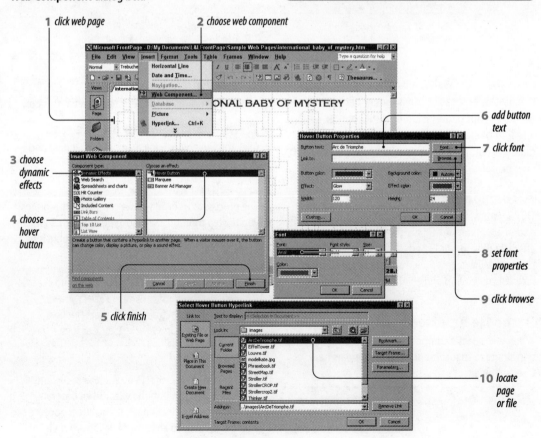

1 *click web page* 2 *choose web component*

3 *choose dynamic effects*

4 *choose hover button*

5 *click finish*

6 *add button text*

7 *click font*

8 *set font properties*

9 *click browse*

10 *locate page or file*

182 ⑩ **Apply Dynamic Effects:** Add Hover Buttons

7 click font (optional)

To format the button text, click the **Font** button.

8 set font properties (optional)

In the **Font** dialog box, choose the button text's font, font style, font size, and font color, and click the **OK** button. (Unfortunately, only a few font choices are available: Arial, Courier New, MS Sans Serif, and Times New Roman.)

9 click browse

Web-page buttons are, in reality, simply links to other pages or files. To specify the page to which you want to link this button, click **Browse.**

> *tip* If you know the path and filename of the page or file to which you want to link, type it in the **Link to** box instead of clicking the **Browse** button.

10 locate page or file

Locate the page or file to which you want the button to link and click **OK.**

11 choose button color

For best visibility, ensure that the color you choose contrasts with the background of the page.

12 choose background color

If you don't want your button's background color to be visible, choose a color that matches the page's background color.

13 choose effect

Choose the effect that appears when a person visiting your site points to the button. (See Hover Effects on page 185 for more information.)

14 choose effect color

In order for the effect you chose to be visible, you must select a color from the **Effect color** drop-down list that contrasts with the button color you selected in step 11.

15 click custom (optional)

To associate a sound or image with your hover button, click the **Custom** button. Otherwise, skip to step 22.

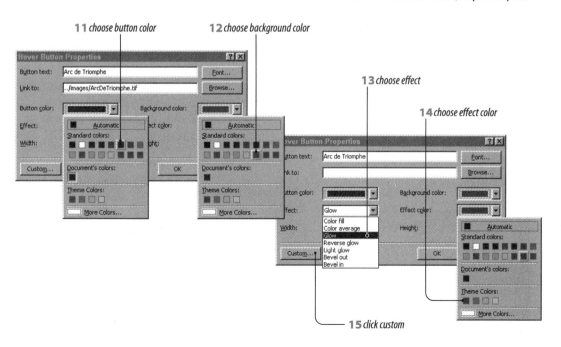

11 *choose button color*   **12** *choose background color*   **13** *choose effect*   **14** *choose effect color*   **15** *click custom*

16 **click browse** (optional)

If you want people visiting your site to hear a sound when they click the button, click the **Browse** button to the right of the **On click** textbox.

> 🛈 If you know the path and filename of the sound files or image files you want to use, simply type the information in the appropriate field rather than clicking the **Browse** button.

17 **locate sound** (optional)

The **Select Sound** dialog box opens. Locate the sound you want to use; when you find it, click it, and then click the **Open** button. (Unfortunately, FrontPage is rather limited on the types of sounds it supports: only .au and .snd files are available.)

18 **specify hover sound** (optional)

If you want site visitors to hear a sound when they point at the button, click the **Browse** button to the right of the **On hover** text field. In the **Select Sound** dialog box, locate and select the sound you want to use.

19 **specify button image** (optional)

To apply an image to the button for times when it's in its normal state (that is, when it's not being hovered over), click the **Browse** button to the right of the **Button** field. In the **Select Image** dialog box, locate and select the image you want to use, and click the **Open** button.

20 **specify hover image** (optional)

To specify an image for instances when a user's mouse pointer hovers over the button, click the **Browse** button to the right of the **On hover** field. In the **Select Image** dialog box, locate and select the image you want to use, and click the **Open** button.

21 **click OK** (optional)

Click **OK** in the **Custom** dialog box.

22 **specify button width**

Type the width of the button in pixels. If you used a picture for your hover button, the number you type here should match the width of the image.

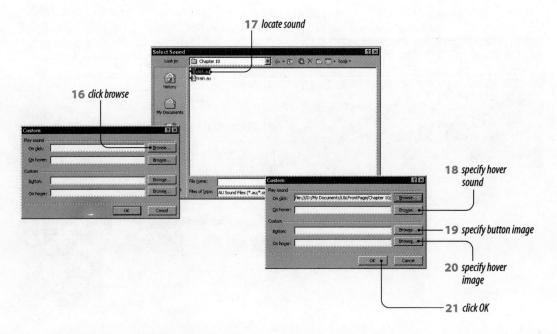

16 *click browse*

17 *locate sound*

18 *specify hover sound*

19 *specify button image*

20 *specify hover image*

21 *click OK*

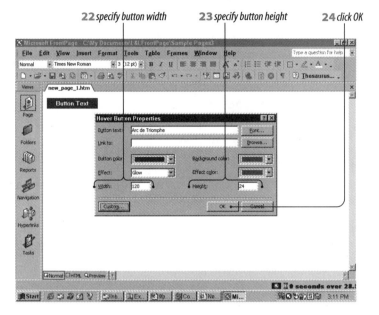

22 *specify button width* **23** *specify button height* **24** *click OK*

23 specify button height

Type the height of the button in pixels. If you used a picture for your hover button, the number you type here should match the height of the image.

tip If you used a picture for your hover button, the size of the button must be the same as the size of the image. If necessary, you can use an image-editing program to change the size of your image.

24 click OK

Click **OK** in the **Hover Button Properties** dialog box.

tip Don't panic if you hover your mouse over the button while viewing the page in FrontPage and nothing happens. In order to view the effect, you must preview the page in your Web browser. For more information about previewing your Web page, refer to Preview A Page on page 72.

Hover Effects

There are several hover effects to choose from. **Color Fill** fills the button with the color selected in the **Effect color** drop-down palette, while **Color Average** averages the effect color and the button color.

Alternatively, you can choose from among three glow settings: **Glow** (the effect color emanates from the middle of the button), **Reverse Glow** (the

effect color emanates from the outer edges of the button), and **Light Glow** (a lighter version of the button color emanates from the button's center).

When someone visiting your site points to a button with the **Bevel Out** effect applied, the button appears to rise from the screen; a button with the **Bevel In** effect applied appears pressed downward.

Unfortunately, there is no preview feature in the **Hover Buttons Properties** dialog box; you just have to choose an effect, click **OK**, and view the button on the page. If you don't like it, you can change it by right-clicking the button and choosing **Hover Button Properties**, and selecting a different effect from the **Hover Button Properties** dialog box.

steps Add A Scrolling Marquee

A *scrolling marquee* is a text message that slides, or *scrolls,* across your screen. A scrolling marquee helps you emphasize information on your page. With FrontPage, you can specify the marquee's message, direction, and behaviors.

1 choose web component

Click on your page where you want the scrolling marquee to appear and choose **Insert➡Web Component**.

2 choose dynamic effects

In the left pane of the **Insert Web Component** dialog box, choose **Dynamic Effects**.

3 choose marquee

In the right pane of the box, click **Marquee.**

4 click finish

The **Marquee Properties** dialog box opens.

5 type text

Type the text for the marquee.

6 choose direction

The text can move across the page right to left (**Left**) or left to right (**Right**).

7 set delay

In the **Delay** box, type the time, in milliseconds, before the marquee begins to move.

8 set speed

In the **Amount** box, type how much, in pixels, the text should "jump" each time it moves onscreen.

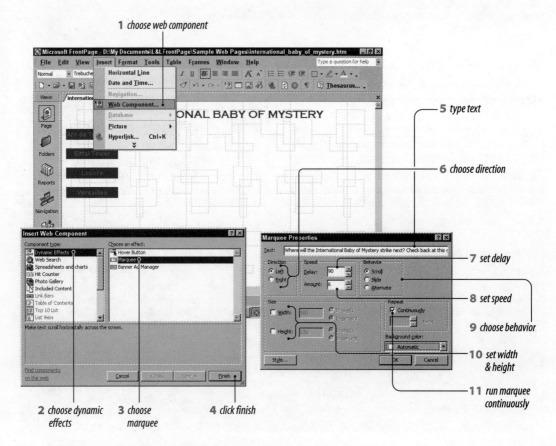

1 *choose web component*

5 *type text*

6 *choose direction*

7 *set delay*

8 *set speed*

9 *choose behavior*

10 *set width & height*

11 *run marquee continuously*

2 *choose dynamic effects*

3 *choose marquee*

4 *click finish*

9 choose behavior

The marquee can scroll across the screen like a stock ticker (**Scroll**), slide into view and remain there once the entire message has been revealed (**Slide**), or alternate between scrolling and sliding (**Alternate**).

10 set width & height

Check the **Width** and **Height** boxes and type the measurements in pixels or as a percentage of the browser window's width or height.

> 💡 Leave the **Width** and **Height** settings unchecked. That way, the marquee is sized to fit the text you typed in the **Text** field.

11 run marquee continuously
(optional)

Check **Continuously** to run the marquee continuously. To run it only a few times, uncheck **Continuously** and type the number of times the marquee should run in the **times** spin box.

12 apply background color (optional)

The **Background** color drop-down palette shows your color choices.

13 click OK

The marquee appears on your page. In order to view the scrolling effect, you must preview the page in your Web browser; refer to Preview A Page on page 72.

14 format text

Click the marquee to select it, choose **Format➡Font** to open the **Font** dialog box, and make changes as needed. (Refer to The Font Dialog Box on page 76 for help.)

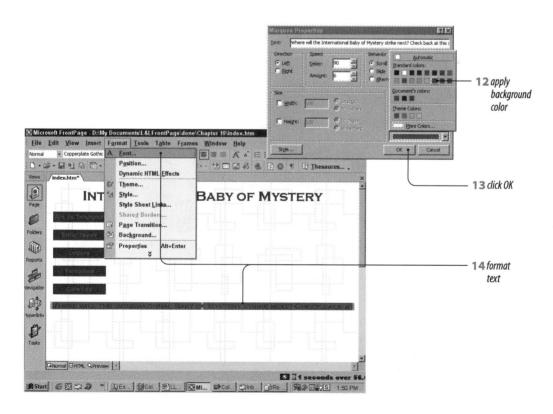

12 *apply background color*

13 *click OK*

14 *format text*

steps Create Banner Ads

A *banner ad* acts like a rotating billboard on your Web page, displaying a sequence of pictures to advertise another site or another area of your site. In addition to acting as an advertisement, the banner ad can act as a link to the site or area it promotes.

> **tip** Before you can add a banner ad to your Web page, you must create the images for the ad using an image-editing program such as PhotoShop. (Check out *Look & Learn Photoshop* by Deke McClelland for help.) For each version of the ad you want to rotate through, you must create a separate image file.

1 choose web component
Click on your page where you want the banner ad to appear and choose **Insert➡Web Component** to open the **Insert Web Component** dialog box.

2 choose dynamic effects
In the left pane of the **Insert Web Component** dialog box, choose **Dynamic Effects.**

3 choose banner ad manager
In the right pane of the **Insert Web Component** dialog box, click **Banner Ad Manager.**

4 click finish
Click **Finish** to open the **Banner Ad Manager Properties** dialog box.

5 type width
Type the width of the banner ad in pixels.

> **tip** The number you type in the **Width** field should correspond to the width of the ad you created.

6 type height
Type the height of the banner ad in pixels.

> **tip** As with the **Width** field, the number you type in the **Height** field should correspond to the height of the ad image you created.

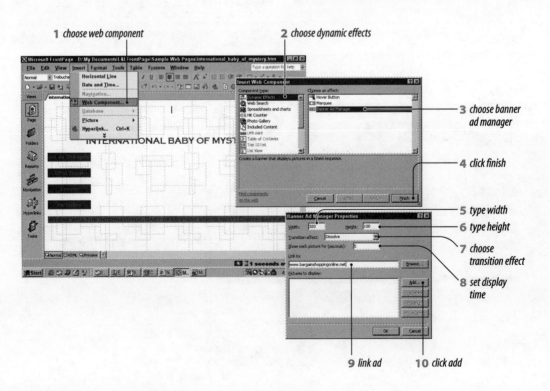

1 *choose web component*

2 *choose dynamic effects*

3 *choose banner ad manager*

4 *click finish*

5 *type width*

6 *type height*

7 *choose transition effect*

8 *set display time*

9 *link ad*   10 *click add*

7 choose transition effect

Choose a transition effect—that is, the effect site visitors see as the banner rotates from one ad to the next.

> 💬 There are several options when it comes to transition effects; experiment to see which one you like best. To simply display the ads in sequential order, with no transition effect in between, choose **None**.

8 set display time

Type the number of seconds you want each ad to be shown before the banner rotates to the next ad.

9 link ad

Banner ads are most effective if they link to the site or page they advertise. To link your banner ad to its corresponding site or page, type the URL in the **Link to** field.

> 💬 If you're not sure of the linking page's URL, click the **Browse** button to locate it.

10 click add

To select the first ad image in the rotation, click the **Add** button.

11 locate ad

Locate and select the first of the files you created using an image-editing program, and then click the **Open** button.

12 repeat

Repeat steps 10 and 11 until you've added all the image files you want the banner ad to rotate through.

> 💬 The banner ad rotates sequentially through the images in the **Pictures to display** list, starting at the top, in an infinite loop. To edit the list, click to select the image you want to remove or move; use the **Remove**, **Move Up**, and **Move Down** buttons as needed.

13 click OK

Click **OK** to close the **Banner Ad Manager Properties** dialog box and apply the banner ad to your page.

Chances are you're building your site on your own computer rather than a server; if so, the banner ad won't function, even when you preview it using your Web browser. Fear not, however; once you publish your site to a server, the ad will function normally. You'll learn more about publishing your site to a server in Chapter 14, Publish A Web.

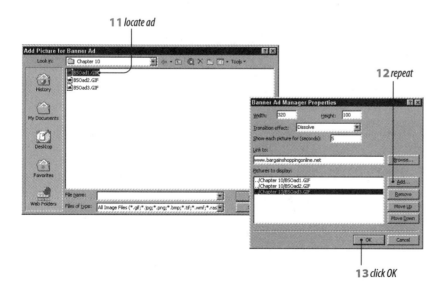

11 *locate ad*

12 *repeat*

13 *click OK*

A *hit counter* displays the number of times a Web page has been visited.

For the hit counter to work, the page containing it must be published to a Web server with Front-Page Server Extensions installed. Read more about publishing your Webs in Chapter 14, Publish A Web.

1 choose web component

Click on your page where you want the hit counter to appear and choose Insert➤Web Component.

2 choose hit counter

In the left pane of the **Insert Web Component** dialog box, choose **Hit Counter.**

3 choose counter style

Select a counter style you like in the right-hand pane.

4 click finish

Click **Finish** to open the **Hit Counter Properties** dialog box.

5 set digits

To configure your hit counter to always display the same number of digits—for example, if you prefer 000010 to 10—check the **Fixed number of digits** checkbox and type 6 (the number of digits in 000010) in the accompanying field.

6 click OK

Click **OK** to close the **Hit Counter Properties** dialog box and add the counter to your page.

If you're building your site on your own computer rather than a server, the hit counter won't work, even when you preview it using your Web browser. Once you publish your site to a server, however, the counter will function normally. For more information about publishing your site to a server, see Chapter 14, Publish A Web.

> *tip* If your counter reflects the times you visited your site for testing purposes, you can easily reset it. Open the page containing the counter, and double-click the hit counter placeholder to open the **Hit Counter Properties** dialog box. Then select the **Reset counter to** checkbox and type the number you want to set the counter at in the accompanying field.

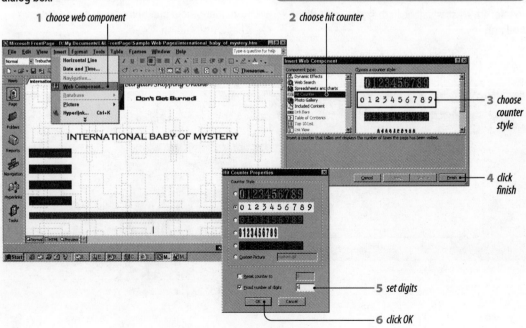

1 *choose web component*

2 *choose hit counter*

3 *choose counter style*

4 *click finish*

5 *set digits*

6 *click OK*

Add A Map

FrontPage lets you add maps from Expedia.com, an Internet travel site, to your pages. Maps can make your site more useful in several ways. For example, if your site details tourist attractions in your city, you can add a map to illustrate the attractions. Or if your site advertises your business, a map showing the location of your physical place of business can help bring customers to your store.

You must be connected to the Internet to complete the steps on this page.

1 choose web component

Click on your page where you want the map to appear and choose **Insert➡Web Component.**

2 choose expedia components

In the left pane of the **Insert Web Component** dialog box, choose **Expedia Components.**

> *tip* When you include a map from Expedia.com, the Expedia.com logo and a link to the site are automatically added next to the map.

3 choose static map

Select the **Static map** option in the right-hand pane.

4 click finish

The **Static Map Properties** dialog box opens.

5 click next

A wizard-like dialog box opens to help you through the process of adding a map. Click **Next** to continue.

6 specify location

Decide whether you're searching for a map of an address or intersection or for a map of a place, and click the appropriate radio button. Then fill out the required information and click **Next.**

> *tip* If Expedia locates multiple matches for your selection, choose the match that best suits your needs and click **Next.**

7 click finish

Click **Finish** to close the **Static Map Properties** dialog box. Notice that a placeholder for the map, rather than the map itself, appears on the page. To view the map, choose **File➡Preview in Browser.**

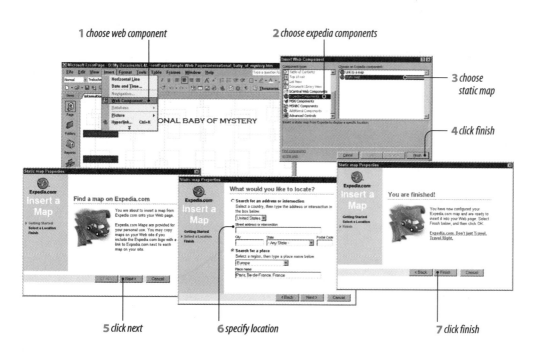

1 choose web component

2 choose expedia components

3 choose static map

4 click finish

5 click next

6 specify location

7 click finish

You can give people who visit your site the ability to search the Web without first having to navigate to a search-engine site. To do so, add a *search box* that allows users to search MSN, a Web portal run by Microsoft, from your site.

You must be connected to the Internet to complete the steps on this page.

1 choose web component
Click on your page where you want the search box to appear and choose Insert➥Web Component.

2 choose msn components
In the left pane of the **Insert Web Component** dialog box, choose **MSN Components**.

3 choose search the web with msn
Select the **Search the Web with MSN** option in the right-hand pane.

4 click finish
Click **Finish** to add the search box to your page.

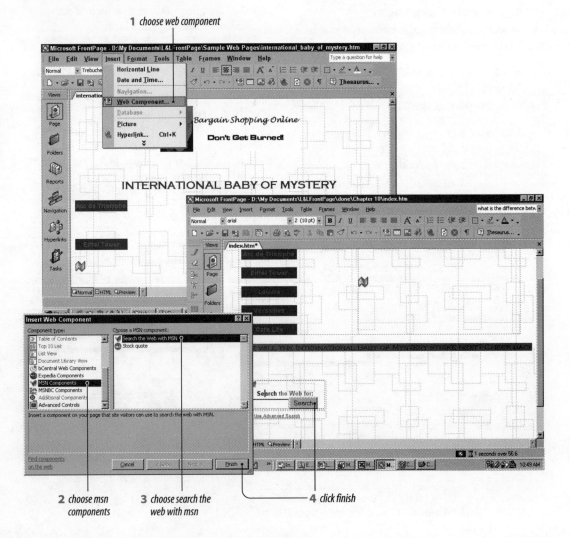

1 *choose web component*

2 *choose msn components*

3 *choose search the web with msn*

4 *click finish*

⬤steps Add Stock Quotes

If you've designed a site geared toward people interested in financial data, offering visitors the ability to quickly obtain a stock quote can be a valuable component of your site. Using FrontPage, you can add a page element that lets people type in the symbol for the stock they want information about. This page element is linked to MoneyCentral, MSN's money-oriented Web site; the stock quotes are updated every half hour.

1 choose web component
Click on your page where you want the stock quote to appear and choose **Insert➡Web Component**.

2 choose msn components
In the left pane of the **Insert Web Component** dialog box, choose **MSN Components**.

3 choose stock quote
Select the **Stock quote** option in the right-hand pane.

4 click finish
Click **Finish** to add the stock quote to your page.

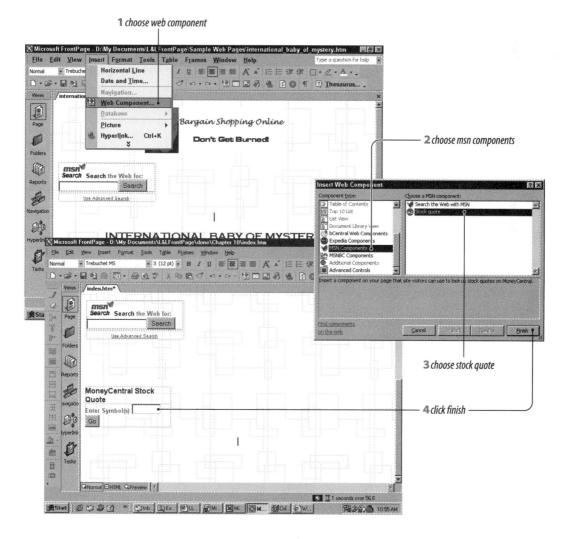

1 *choose web component*

2 *choose msn components*

3 *choose stock quote*

4 *click finish*

🟣steps Add A Java Applet

A *Java applet* is a small application created using the Java programming language. Java applets make it possible to add animations, games, and other active features to your Web site. However, a note of caution: Depending on their browser and settings, some visitors may not be able to use or even view any Java applets on your page. For this reason, it's best to use Java applets sparingly.

Before completing this task, you must first locate an applet you want to use. Good places to find free Java applets include javaboutique.internet.com and www.jars.com. When you find an applet you like, download it to your computer. You may need to use a file-compression utility to extract the applet's files to your hard drive.

1 choose web component
Click on your page where you want the applet to appear and choose **Insert ➥ Web Component**.

2 choose advanced controls
In the left pane of the **Insert Web Component** dialog box, choose **Advanced Controls**.

3 choose java applet
Choose **Java Applet** in the right-hand pane.

4 click finish
Click **Finish** to open the **Java Applet Properties** dialog box.

5 type applet source
Type the name of the file containing the *source code* for the applet you want to add. Typically, applet source files have the filename extension **.class**, as in **Confetti.class**.

6 type applet base url
Type the path and name of the folder containing the applet's *source file* (unless the file is stored in the same directory as the Web page you're creating).

7 type message for non-java users
Type a message to be displayed in lieu of the Java applet for those people visiting your site who use a browser that doesn't support Java.

8 click add
Click the **Add** button to add *parameter names and values* in the **Set Attribute Value** dialog box.

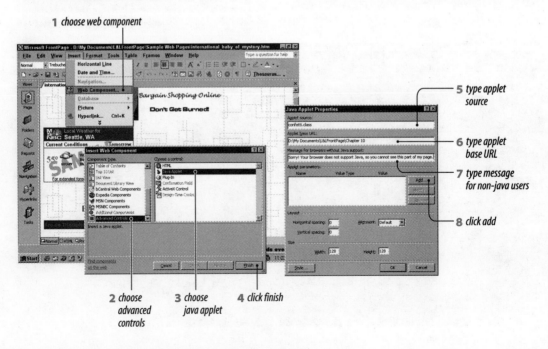

1 choose web component

5 type applet source

6 type applet base URL

7 type message for non-java users

8 click add

2 choose advanced controls

3 choose java applet

4 click finish

> Most Java applets come with documentation containing parameter information, usually in a **.txt** file. If the applet you want to run doesn't have documentation, try contacting the person who made the applet for instructions—contact information is usually provided on the site from which you've downloaded the applet.

9 define parameters

In the **Set Attribute Value** dialog box, type the name of the parameter you want to add. If there is a value associated with the parameter, check the **Specify value** checkbox and choose **Data, Ref,** or **Object**, depending on the instructions provided in your applet's documentation. Then type the value noted in the applet's documentation and click **OK**.

10 set horizontal spacing

Type the amount of space, in pixels, that should separate the applet from the text or other object that is nearest to the sides of the applet.

11 set vertical spacing

Type the amount of space, in pixels, that should separate the applet from the text or other object that is nearest to the top or bottom of the applet.

12 specify alignment

Specify how the Java applet should be aligned on the page. You have several options when it comes to aligning your Java applet. Select **Default** to align the applet using the Web browser's default settings. Choose **Texttop** to align the top of the applet with the top of the tallest text in the line, or select **Middle** to align the middle of the applet with surrounding text. Choosing **Absmiddle, Baseline,** or **Absbottom** aligns the applet with the middle, baseline, or bottom of the current line, respectively.

13 set applet size

Specify how wide and tall you want the applet to be on your page, in pixels, in the **Width** and **Height** textboxes.

14 click OK

Click **OK** to close the **Java Applet Properties** dialog box and add the applet to your page. If you're building your site on your own computer rather than on a server, only a placeholder for the applet appears on your page, even when you preview it using your Web browser. Once you publish your site to a server, however, the applet will function normally. You can learn more about publishing your site to a server in Chapter 14, Publish A Web.

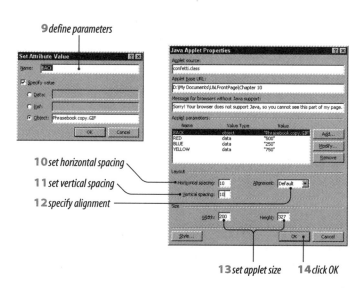

9 define parameters

10 set horizontal spacing

11 set vertical spacing

12 specify alignment

13 set applet size   *14 click OK*

⑩ **Apply Dynamic Effects:** Add A Java Applet   **195**

Add An ActiveX Control

steps

Dynamic page elements, such as streaming stock quotes or interactive games, are probably either *Java applets* or *ActiveX controls*. Some ActiveX controls appear on your computer when you install Windows; you get others when you install certain types of software. In some cases, you acquire ActiveX controls simply by pointing your browser to a Web page containing the controls. Any time you add an ActiveX control to your computer, by downloading it, installing it, or otherwise, that control becomes available for use in your own Web pages. ActiveX controls only work in Windows environments. For all visitors to use your site fully, regardless of their operating system, avoid ActiveX components.

1 choose web component

Click on your page where you want the control to appear and choose **Insert➤Web Component.**

2 choose advanced controls

In the left pane of the **Insert Web Component** dialog box, choose **Advanced Controls.**

3 choose activex control

Choose **ActiveX Control** in the right-hand pane.

4 click next

A wizard-like series of screens begins to help you choose an ActiveX component for your page.

5 choose control

Anytime you add an ActiveX control to your computer, that control becomes available for your own Web pages. Some of these controls are listed in the **Choose a control** list. Click an entry in this list to select it.

6 click finish

A placeholder for the control, rather than the control itself, appears. To view the control, choose **File➤ Preview in Browser.**

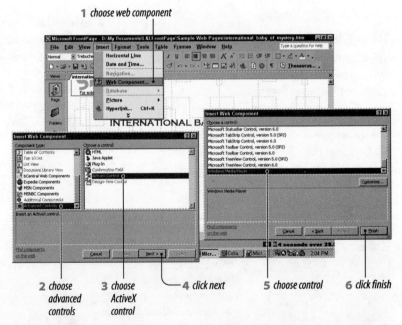

1 *choose web component*

2 *choose advanced controls*

3 *choose ActiveX control*

4 *click next*

5 *choose control*

6 *click finish*

Additional Controls

If the control you want doesn't appear in the **Choose a control** list, but you know it's on your machine, click **Customize.** The **Customize ActiveX Control List** dialog box lists all the ActiveX controls on your machine. To add a con-trol to the list in the **Insert ActiveX Control** dialog box, check the checkbox to the left of the control and click **OK.** To make all the controls in the **Customize ActiveX Control List** dialog box available, click **Select All** and click **OK.**

The DHTML Effects Toolbar

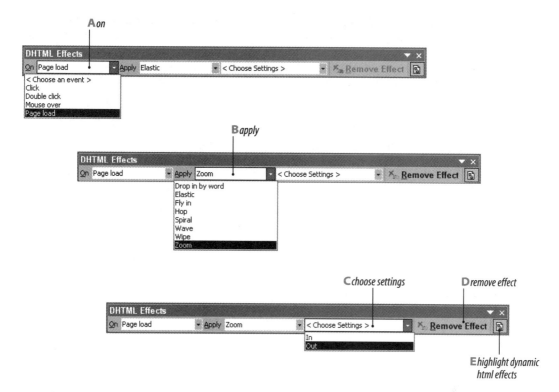

A *on*

B *apply*

C *choose settings*   **D** *remove effect*

E *highlight dynamic html effects*

FrontPage provides a quick, easy way to add dynamic effects to your Web page: by using the DHTML Effects toolbar. (To view the toolbar, choose **View→Toolbar→DHTML Effects.** Alternatively, select the item to which you want to apply a dynamic effect and then choose **Format→ Dynamic HTML Effects.**) Using this toolbar, you can animate page elements when any number of *trigger effects* (clicking, double-clicking, mouse overs, and more) occur.

A on
Open this drop-down list to select the event to trigger the DHTML effect you want to apply. The options in this list may vary depending on what type of page element you've chosen to apply an effect to.

B apply
The **Apply** drop-down list enables you to specify what type of effect you want to apply. The options in this

list vary depending on which item was selected in the **On** list (A).

C choose settings
In the **Choose Settings** drop-down list, you give further instructions regarding the effect you chose in the **Apply** drop-down list (B). For example, if you chose **Zoom** in the **Apply** list, you have the option of choosing **In** or **Out** in the **Choose Settings** list.

Not all effects require you to issue further instructions. In such cases, the **Choose Settings** drop-down list appears grayed out.

D remove effect
Click this button to remove the applied effect from the selected item.

E highlight dynamic html effects
By clicking this button, you toggle between adding a highlight to any items on your page to which DHMTL effects have been applied to removing the highlight.

steps Animate A Page Element

When you animate a page element, you tie it to a *trigger event,* which can be a click, a double-click, a mouse hover, a page transition, or something else, depending on what type of element you want to animate. Any number of page elements can be animated through the use of DHTML: text, paragraphs, pictures, buttons, marquees, and more. There are several options when it comes to animation. For example, if you choose **Page Load** in the **On** drop-down list, you can choose **Drop in by word, Elastic, Fly in, Hop, Spiral, Wave, Wipe,** or **Zoom** to specify how the page element appears to site visitors when the trigger event occurs. To animate page elements, use the **DHTML Effects** toolbar.

1 select page element
Select the page element that you want to animate.

2 choose dynamic html effects
Choosing **Format→Dynamic HTML Effects** brings up the **Dynamic HTML Effects** toolbar.

3 choose event
Choose the event that you want to trigger the effect. Trigger events available in the **On** drop-down list

include **Click** (start the animation when a person visiting your site clicks the selected page element), **Double click** (start the animation when the visitor double-clicks the page element), **Mouse over** (start the animation when the visitor's mouse pointer hovers over the page element), and **Page load** (start the animation when the page is loaded into the visitor's browser). Here, we want the effect to occur when the page containing the selected element opens, so we've chosen **Page load** from the **On** drop-down list.

4 choose effect
The contents of the **Apply** drop-down list vary depending on what trigger event was selected in step 2. Choose the effect that you want to apply when the trigger event occurs.

5 choose settings
If the effect you chose requires further instructions, specify them in the **Choose Settings** drop-down list located to the right of the **Apply** list. Not all effects require you to issue further instructions. In such cases, the **Choose Settings** drop-down list appears grayed out.

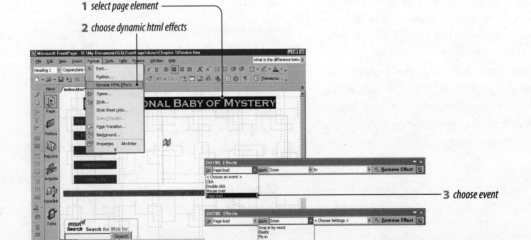

1 *select page element*

2 *choose dynamic html effects*

3 *choose event*

4 *choose effect*

5 *choose settings*

198   ⑩   **Apply Dynamic Effects:** Animate A Page Element

The Page Transitions Dialog Box

A *event*

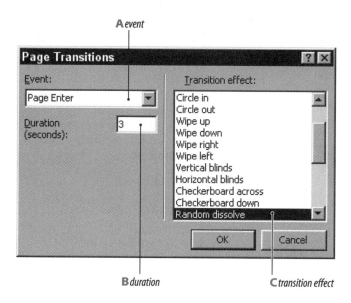

B *duration*　　**C** *transition effect*

If your site contains several pages, consider using page transitions to ease visitors from one page to the next. *Page transitions* are movie-like effects that occur when visitors enter or leave your site, or when they browse to or from specific pages. Using page transitions, you can give your site the look and feel of a slide-show presentation. Note that only visitors using later versions of Microsoft Internet Explorer can view page transitions; they won't be visible to people using other browsers.

A event

Just as you must specify trigger events when animating elements on a single page, you must specify trigger events when employing page transitions. Options are **Page Enter** (the transition effect occurs when the visitor enters the page), **Page Exit** (the effect occurs when the visitor leaves the page), **Site Enter** (the effect occurs when the visitor enters the site), and **Site Exit** (the effect occurs when the visitor leaves the site).

B duration

In the **Duration** box, specify, in seconds, how long you want the transition effect to be displayed. When deciding on a duration, it's probably best to keep it short—site visitors may get annoyed if your page transition takes more than two or three seconds.

C transition effect

Choose the transition effect to be displayed when the trigger event occurs. You have several movie-like options, including *wipes* (where one page appears to be "wiped" off the screen by the page replacing it), *dissolves* (where one page fades out as another page fades in), and more.

> (tip) As with many dynamic features, when it comes to page transitions, moderation is the key. Try not to go overboard, adding transitions to every page on your Web. It's best to use features such as these sparingly to avoid annoying the people who just want to quickly navigate your site.

steps Add Video & Background Sound

Video and sound can go a long way toward making your site more interesting to visitors. For example, if you are making a site to describe your vacation, you might add footage of one of the trip highlights. Alternatively, if your company has an audio jingle or theme, you can play it whenever someone enters your site.

However cool the use of video and sound may be, they are notorious bandwidth hogs. It's best to use these features with considerable restraint. An alternative is to make sound and video optional, selectable features for those users who have the bandwidth to access them easily.

You have several options when it comes to sound and video formats that are acceptable for use over the Web—MP3, WAV, Real, Windows Media, Quick-Time, MPG, AV… the list goes on and on.

1 choose video
After you click the spot on your site where you want the video to appear, choose **Insert➠Picture➠Video** to open the **Video** dialog box.

2 select video
Locate the video you want to add to your Web site, click it to select it, and then click the **Open** button.

3 open picture properties dialog box
A placeholder for the video appears on your page. To set properties for the video, right-click the placeholder and choose **Picture Properties** from the menu that appears. The **Picture Properties** dialog box opens with the **Video** tab displayed.

4 set loop parameters
Specify the number of times the video should be looped in the **Loop** spin box, or check the **Forever** checkbox. Type the number of milliseconds you want to pass between each playing of the video in the **Loop delay** spin box.

5 set start parameters
If you want the video to start when the page opens, choose the **On file open** radio button. To start the video when the site visitor's mouse hovers over it, choose **On mouse over**.

6 click OK
Click **OK** to close the **Picture Properties** dialog box.

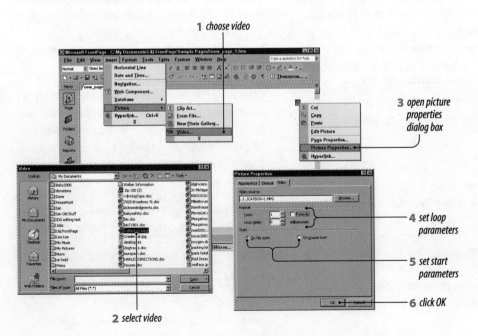

1 choose video

3 open picture properties dialog box

4 set loop parameters

5 set start parameters

6 click OK

2 select video

To view the video, choose **File→Preview in Browser.** For more information about previewing your Web page, see Preview A Page on page 72.

If you know the path and filename of the sound file, type it in the **Location** box instead of clicking the **Browse** button.

7 open page properties dialog box

To add a background sound to your page, right-click the page and choose **Page Properties** from the short-cut menu that appears. The **Page Properties** dialog box opens, with the **General** tab displayed.

8 click browse

Click the **Browse** button in the **Background sound** area of the **General** tab to locate the file containing the sound you want to play when someone visits your page.

9 select file

Locate the sound file you want to use, click it to select it, and click the **Open** button.

10 set loop parameters

Specify the number of times the sound should be looped in the **Loop** spin box, or check the **Forever** checkbox.

11 click OK

Click **OK** to close the **Page Properties** dialog box.

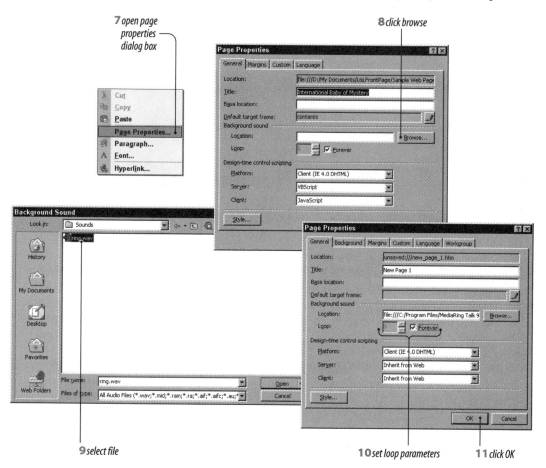

7 open page properties dialog box

8 click browse

9 select file

10 set loop parameters

11 click OK

⑩ **Apply Dynamic Effects:** Add Video & Background Sound   201

Add Page Transitions

Page transitions make your site more polished by easing visitors into and out of your site, and from one page in your site to the next.

1 choose page transitions
After you've opened the page to which you want to apply the page-transition effect, choose **Format→ Page Transition** to open the **Page Transitions** dialog box.

2 choose event
Select **Page Enter, Page Exit, Site Enter, or Site Exit** from the **Event** drop-down list in the **Page Transitions** dialog box. For more information about each of the options in the Event drop-down list, see The Page Transitions Dialog Box on page 199.

3 enter duration
In the **Duration** box, type the number of seconds that you want the effect to be displayed.

4 choose effect
In the **Transition effect** list, click the transition you want to apply. (Use the scrollbar to the right of the list to view all the options.)

click OK
Click the **OK** button to close the **Page Transitions** dialog box and apply the page-transition effect to your page.

If you're creating your page on your own computer rather than a server, the you won't be able to preview the page-transition effect until you publish your site to a server. You'll learn more about publishing your site to a server in Chapter 14, Publish A Web.

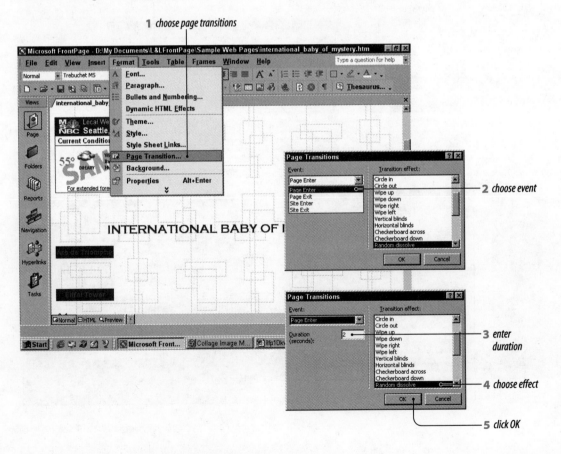

1 *choose page transitions*

2 *choose event*

3 *enter duration*

4 *choose effect*

5 *click OK*

Divide A Page Into Frames

Suppose you want to create a Web page that simultaneously displays multiple pages at one time. For example, if you were building an online catalog, you might want your page to have a banner ad touting the name of the catalog, a page containing a list of links to the goods you plan to sell, and a page with information about whatever product the user has requested. Creating such a page in Front-Page 2002 is a snap; you simply use a *frames page*. A frames page contains no visible content of its own. Instead, it acts as a vessel for the content you want to display.

To create a frames page, you use one of FrontPage 2002's myriad frames-page templates. FrontPage also lets you change frame properties and provides ways for you to present no-frames content for browsers that don't support frames.

203

The Frames-Page Templates

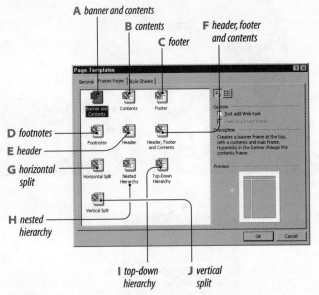

A *banner and contents*

B *contents*

C *footer*

F *header, footer and contents*

D *footnotes*

E *header*

G *horizontal split*

H *nested hierarchy*

I *top-down hierarchy*

J *vertical split*

FrontPage 2002 offers several frames-page templates that you can use to build a frames-based Web.

A banner and contents

Select **Banner and Contents** to create a page with a banner frame at the top, a contents frame along the left side, and a main frame. The banner frame might contain an image of the Web site's logo along with the site name. The contents frame contains links that you create; users click the links to specify what content appears in the main frame.

B contents

Select **Contents** to create a page with a contents frame along the left side and a main frame along the

right side. Links you create in the contents frame let the user specify what content appears in the main frame.

C footer

Select **Footer** to create a page that features a main frame with a footer underneath it. Hyperlinks you place in the footer let users determine what content appears in the main frame.

D footnotes

Select **Footnotes** to create a page with a main frame, with a footnote frame underneath it. Hyperlinks you place in the main frame allow users to specify what content is displayed in the footnote frame.

E header

Select **Header** to create a page that offers a navigation header with a main frame underneath it. Hyperlinks you place in the header enable users to change the content in the main frame.

F header, footer and contents

Select **Header, Footer and Contents** to create a page with a header frame, a footer frame, a contents frame, and a main frame. The header and footer frames are designed to contain hyperlinks that change the available links in the contents frame; users can click a link in the contents frame to specify what appears in the main frame.

G horizontal split

Select **Horizontal Split** to create a page with independent top and bottom frames.

H nested hierarchy

Select **Nested Hierarchy** to create a page with a *nested information hierarchy*. Users can choose from the general hyperlinks you provide on the left frame to view more specific links in the top frame, and then select a link in the top frame to view content in the main frame.

I top-down hierarchy

Select **Top-Down Hierarchy** to create a page with a *top-down information hierarchy*. Users can choose from the general hyperlinks you provide in the top frame to view more specific links in the middle frame; users then select a link in the middle frame to view content in the bottom (main) frame.

J vertical split

Select **Vertical Split** to create a page with independent left and right frames.

Design Tips

If you want to add frames to an existing no-frames page, you might want to think again. This is especially true if you have applied shared borders (refer to The Borders Tab on page 92 and The Shading Tab on page 93) or navigation bars (you learn about those in Chapter 12, Add Navigation Elements, starting on page 216), or if you have spent a great deal of time setting up a navigation structure (again, discussed in the next chapter). In such cases, a frames page may interrupt the flow of links from page to page. Consider setting up a new

frames site, or creating a site that combines frames and no frames so that visitors can make a choice (find out how in Insert No-Frames Content on page 209).

If, after thinking it over, you've decided that frames are appropriate for your site, you'll need to decide which frames-page template to use. Although deciding which frames-page template to use for your Web is often a matter of personal preference, some frames-page templates are best suited for certain types of Webs. For

example, if you want your page to contain one frame with a list of links and another frame showing the result of clicking one of those links, you probably want to use the Contents template, the Footer template, or the Header template. If, however, you also want to display a banner touting your company or site's name, try the Banner and Contents template. If your site is more complicated, containing categories of links, try the Header, Footer and Contents template, the Nested Hierarchy template, or the Top-Down Hierarchy template.

FrontPage provides several frames-page templates that you can choose from to create a frames page.

Before you create a frames page, you should make sure your browser supports frames. To do so, choose **Tools→Page Options**. Click the **Compatibility** tab and select your browser from the Browsers drop-down list. Locate the **Frames** checkbox in the Available Technologies area; if it's checked, then your browser supports frames.

1 choose page or web

Make sure Page view is selected. Then choose **File→New→Page or Web.**

2 select page templates

Find the **New from template** section of the New Page or Web task pane and click **Page Templates.** The **Page Templates** dialog box opens.

3 click frames pages tab

Click the **Frames Pages** tab to view the available frames-page templates.

4 select template

There are several frames-page templates to choose from; select the one that best suits your needs. (Refer to Design Tips on page 205 and The Frames-Page Templates on page 204 if you need help choosing.)

5 click OK

The empty frames page appears on your screen.

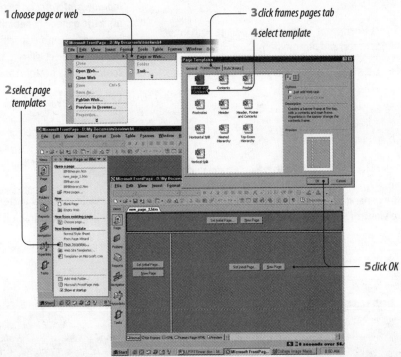

1 choose page or web

2 select page templates

3 click frames pages tab

4 select template

5 click OK

Inline Frames

Inline frames are similar to regular frames, except that they are embedded within a regular Web page rather than being part of a frames page.

To add an inline frame to your page, open the page in Page view. Then choose **Insert→Inline Frame.** Set the initial page as described in the sections Insert An Existing Page In A Frame and Insert A New Page In A Frame, starting on page 208. To change the properties of the frame, click anywhere within the frame (except on a button) to select it, choose **Format→Properties,** and

make changes in the Inline Frame Properties dialog box as needed. (Many of the options in this dialog box are similar to the options in the Frame Properties dialog box discussed later in this chapter; read The Frame Properties Dialog Box on page 212 for more information.)

The Frames Page Window

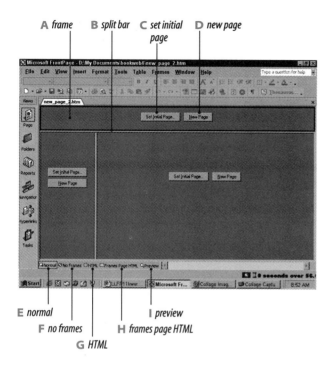

A *frame* B *split bar* C *set initial page* D *new page*

E *normal*
F *no frames*
G *HTML*
H *frames page HTML*
I *preview*

When you create a frames page, you select a frames-page template (see Create A Frames Page on page 206 for more information).

Depending on the template you selected, the frames-page window shows two, three, or four frames, which you can fill with content and adjust for size.

A frame
A frame will eventually contain an individual Web page. Some frames show *static* (non-changing) content; other frames' contents change whenever a visitor clicks a link.

B split bar
A *split bar* represents the border between one frame and another. You can resize a frame by dragging the split bar. Resizing one frame affects the size of at least one adjacent frame.

C set initial page
Click to specify an existing page that will appear in the current frame when a user first views the frames page.

To learn how to add an existing Web page to the frame, read Insert An Existing Page In A Frame on page 208.

D new page
Click to create a new page that will appear in the current frame when a user first views the frames page. To learn how to add a new Web page to the frame, read Insert A New Page In A Frame on page 209.

E normal
Click **Normal** to show the frames page and its frames as you create them, with text, graphics, and links. Normal view is the default view.

F no frames
Click **No Frames** to view the page that will contain no-frames content. For more information, read the sidebar Insert No-Frames Content on page 209.

> *tip* You should add a no-frames page for users whose browsers don't support frames. When a non-frames browser encounters a frames page, the browser ignores the frames code, locates the no-frames page, and displays its contents. That way, these visitors aren't left hanging.

G HTML
Click **HTML** to view the current page as FrontPage has coded it: a combination of the text you have entered and the HTML that formats the text.

H frames page HTML
Click **Frames Page HTML** to view the HTML code for the structure of the frames page.

I preview
Click **Preview** to show the frames page as it will look in a browser window.

After you set up your frames page, you can start filling the frames with content. (See Create A Frames Page on page 206 for more information.) You are apt to insert an existing page in a frame if you're gradually evolving from a no-frames site to a frames site, or if you're adding frames pages to a current site to offer your users a choice between frames or no frames.

1 choose frame

Decide which frame you want to add an existing page to.

2 click set initial page

Click the frame's **Set Initial Page** button. The **Insert Hyperlink** dialog box appears.

In the **Insert Hyperlink** dialog box, you can select the page you want to insert from among the pages you have already created in the current working folder, or use the **Look in** box to locate the page you want to open. Alternatively, type the URL of the page in the **Address** box.

3 choose file

Select the file you want to insert in the frame.

> When you create a frames page in a no-frames site, FrontPage opens both the **Insert Hyperlink** and **Select File** dialog boxes. The **Select File** dialog box suddenly appears to help you select a page from any folder on your computer. Once you click **OK**, the **Insert Hyperlink** dialog box remains on-screen so that you can make a link between the frames page and the newly inserted Web page.

4 click OK

Or press **enter** to close the dialog box and display the page in the frame.

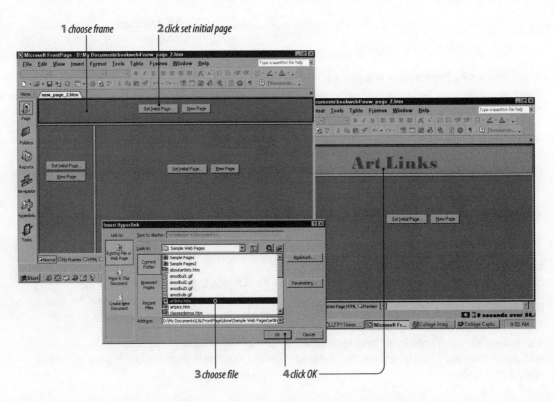

1 *choose frame*   **2** *click set initial page*

3 *choose file*   **4** *click OK*

Insert A New Page In A Frame

1 *choose frame*   **2** *click new page*

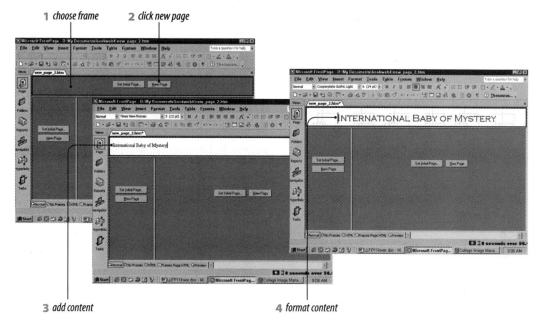

3 *add content*   **4** *format content*

You aren't limited to inserting pages you've already created into frames. FrontPage lets you create a new page in a frame; you can then insert content directly into the frame. For example, if the template you have chosen provides a frame for your company's name or the site's name, you can type the name directly into the frame.

1 choose frame
Decide which frame you want to add a new page to.

2 click new page
FrontPage places an empty Web page in the frame.

3 add content
Type text and insert other content in the page as you would any other Web page.

4 format content
Use the buttons in the **Formatting** toolbar and other formatting resources to change the look of the content. To learn formatting basics, read Chapter 5, Enhance Page Design, which starts on page 73.

> *tip* To edit in a larger window, right-click the frame and choose **Open Page in New Window** from the menu. The page you're editing opens in Page view alongside the frames page; changes you make in the larger window are automatically reflected in the frame.

Insert No-Frames Content

When you use a template to create a frames page, FrontPage automatically adds a page for those visitors whose browsers don't support the use of frames. By default, the no-frames page created by FrontPage features a short message that tells visitors if their browser doesn't support frames.

To make your site more user-friendly, consider creating two sets of pages for your site—one a frames version and the other for those whose browsers don't support frames. Then you can construct a no-frames home page with links to both sets of pages.

steps Build A Table Of Links

A *table of links* lets visitors look through selected pages at a site. To learn more about the variety of links that FrontPage provides, read Chapter 7, Create Hyperlinks, which starts on page 131.

1 click new page
Click the **New Page** button in the frame that you want to devote to the table of links.

2 type heading (optional)
If you wish, type a heading and introductory text.

3 place insertion point
Move the insertion point to the spot on the page where you want the first link to appear.

4 click hyperlink button
Click the **Insert Hyperlink** button on the **Standard** toolbar. FrontPage opens the **Insert Hyperlink** dialog box.

5 select file
Select the file you want the hyperlink to open.

6 name link
Type the text you want the link to display in the **Text to display** textbox.

7 click OK
Or press **enter** to close the dialog box and insert the link at the insertion point.

8 repeat
Repeat steps 3 through 7 until you've added all the links you want displayed on this page.

> 💡 You can use the **Formatting** toolbar to change the look of the hyperlinks, just as you would format any other text on your page. For more information on formatting text, refer to Chapter 5, Enhance Page Design, starting on page 73.

9 preview links
Check your links by clicking **Preview** and then clicking each link.

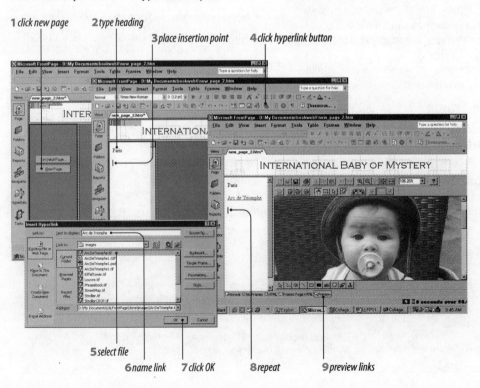

1 *click new page* 2 *type heading* 3 *place insertion point* 4 *click hyperlink button*

5 *select file* 6 *name link* 7 *click OK* 8 *repeat* 9 *preview links*

𝘴𝘵𝘦𝘱𝘴 Split A Frame

When you select a frames-page template, it has a set number of frames—two, three, or four. So what do you do if you want to add another frame to contain navigation buttons, copyright information, or another frame's worth of content? Simply *split* an existing frame.

1 choose split frame

Click the frame that you want to split. Then, choose **Frames→Split Frame**. FrontPage reveals the **Split Frame** dialog box.

tip When you work with frames pages and frames, the more frames in a frames page, the more cluttered the browser window becomes. So, when adding new frames, plan carefully.

2 specify columns or rows

Click the **Split into columns** radio button (our choice for these steps) to split the frame into two columns, or click **Split into rows** to split the frame into two rows.

3 click OK

Or press **enter** to close the **Split Frame** dialog box and split the frame.

4 add content

Click the **Set Initial Page** button in the new frame to place an existing page in the new frame; alternatively, click the **New** button to create a new page. Add content and format the page as desired. (**Review** Insert An Existing Page In A Frame on page 208 and Insert A New Page In A Frame on page 209 for more information about setting a frame's initial page. For information about resizing a frame, read Resize A Frame on page 213.)

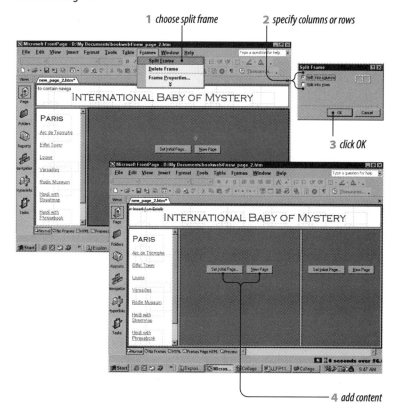

1 choose split frame

2 specify columns or rows

3 click OK

4 add content

Delete A Frame

To delete a frame immediately after adding it, click the **Undo** button on the Standard toolbar or press **ctrl+Z**. Otherwise, delete a frame by selecting it and choosing **Frames→Delete Frame**. The content within the frame is actually a separate file, so you won't lose the content when you delete the frame.

The Frame Properties Dialog Box

The **Frame Properties** dialog box allows you to change several characteristics of a selected frame.

A name

Initially, the **Name** textbox contains the frame name assigned by FrontPage. You can replace the name with your own unique frame name.

> **tip** Don't give frames any of the following frame names: _blank, _parent, _self, and _top. These are all HTML reserved keywords.

B initial page

This textbox displays the URL of the Web page that appears when a visitor first sees the frame. You can switch to a different initial page by typing a new URL in the **Initial page** textbox.

C browse

If you don't know the URL for the replacement initial page, click the **Browse** button. This opens the **Edit Hyperlink** dialog box from which you can select the appropriate page.

D frame width

You can set a *relative width* (one that changes to reflect the size of the visitor's browser window) or *absolute width* (one that never changes no matter how large or small the visitor's browser window is) for the selected frame. Type or select a number in

the option box. Then, from the pop-up menu, select **Relative, Percent,** or **Pixels.** (See Relative, Percent, or Pixels? on page 213 for more information.)

E frame row height

You can set a relative or absolute height for the selected frame. Type or select a number in the option box. Then, from the pop-up menu, select **Relative, Percent,** or **Pixels.**

F margins width

From the **Width** option box, select the width, in pixels, between the left and right edges of the frame and the frame's contents.

G margins height

From the **Height** option box, select the height, in pixels, between the top and bottom edges of the frame and the frame's contents.

H resizable in browser

The **Resizable in Browser** checkbox, checked by default, enables users to resize the frame to fit the size of their browser windows.

I frames page

Click the **Frames Page** button to open the **Frames** section of the **Page Properties** dialog box, in which you can control spacing between all the frames in the frames page and either display or hide frame borders.

J show scrollbars

With the **Show scrollbars** pop-up menu, you can choose if or when to show scrollbars on the selected frame. Select **If Needed, Always,** or **Never.**

K style

Click this button to modify the frame's style. To learn more about styles, see Chapter 9, Work With Styles, which starts on page 163.

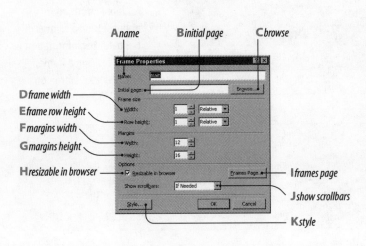

A *name* B *initial page* C *browse*

D *frame width*
E *frame row height*
F *margins width*
G *margins height*
H *resizable in browser*

I *frames page*
J *show scrollbars*
K *style*

 **Resize A Frame**

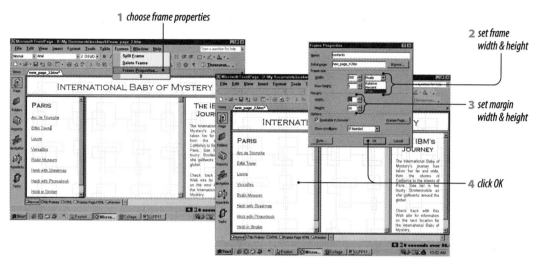

1 *choose frame properties*

2 *set frame width & height*

3 *set margin width & height*

4 *click OK*

One of your frames may need to be resized to fit all its contents, or for aesthetic reasons. When you resize a frame, adjacent frames adjust accordingly to fill the space. Although you can resize a frame by dragging the split bar bordering the frame, using the **Frame Properties** dialog box, discussed here, affords you more resizing options.

1 choose frame properties

Click the frame that you want to resize. Then, choose **Frames→Frame Properties** to make the **Frame Properties** dialog box pop up.

2 set frame width & height

Type or select a number in the **Frame size** area's **Width** and **Height** spin boxes, and, from the drop-down menus, select **Relative**, **Percent**, or **Pixels**.

The **Height** box changes to **Row Height** if the frame you want to resize is part of a row of frames. Changes

made to the row height affect the entire row. Likewise, if the frame is part of a column, the **Width** box changes to **Column Width**.

3 set margin width & height

In the **Margin** area's **Width** and **Height** spin boxes, select the number of pixels between the edges of the frame and the frame's contents. Increasing the margin width and height adds space between the edges of the frame and its contents, making the contents easier to read.

> *tip* Check the **Resizable in Browser** checkbox. That way, users can resize the frame to fit their browser windows.

4 click OK

Or press **enter** to close the **Frame Properties** dialog box and see your resized frames.

Relative, Percent, Or Pixels?

If you choose **Pixels** in the **Width** or **Height** drop-down boxes in the Frame Properties dialog box, the frame remains the same size no matter how big the viewer's browser dialog box is. If you select **Percent**, the frame

size is a percentage of the entire browser window. If you select **Relative**, the size of the frame depends on how much room is available in the browser window.

Hide Frame Borders

If you hide the frame borders on a frames page, the entire browser window appears to be a single entity rather than a set of separate windows.

1 choose frame properties

Click the frame whose borders you want to hide. Then choose **Frames➡Frame Properties** to make the **Frame Properties** dialog box appear.

2 hide scrollbars (optional)

If the frame whose borders you've hidden features scrollbars, you can hide them to promote a more seamless-looking page. Open the **Show scrollbars** drop-down list in the **Frame Properties** dialog box and choose **Never**. Note that you should hide the scrollbars in a frame only if the frame contains very little content.

3 click frames page

Click the **Frames Page** button. FrontPage displays the **Page Properties** dialog box.

4 click frames tab

This is where you're going to make those borders disappear.

5 hide borders

Uncheck the **Show Borders** checkbox.

6 click OK

Or press **enter**. FrontPage removes all the borders from the frames page and redisplays the **Frame Properties** dialog box.

7 click OK

Or press **enter** to close the **Frame Properties** dialog box and return to the frames page.

8 edit page (optional)

When the frames page reappears on-screen, you may have to edit the contents to create a more seamless-looking site.

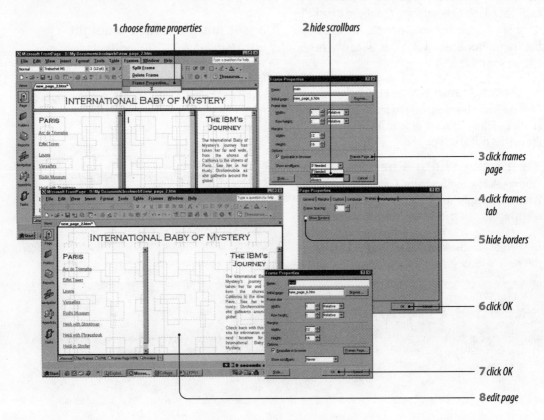

1 choose frame properties

2 hide scrollbars

3 click frames page

4 click frames tab

5 hide borders

6 click OK

7 click OK

8 edit page

Add Navigation Elements

An important component of any Web is its *navigation structure*—how the user moves from one page to the next within your site. Of course, you can manually link the pages in your site to create the navigation structure, but FrontPage 2002's **Navigation view** offers easier and smoother solutions.

After you create your Web's navigation structure, you can implement any of the several navigation tools that FrontPage puts at your disposal. For instance, you can create *link bars* and *shared borders* so that site visitors can always access links to other pages on your site, no matter what page they're on. You can also create a table of contents for your site, and a site map, helping visitors quickly and easily locate the page they need.

Navigation View

A Web starts with a *parent page* and branches out to include *child pages*. As with a family tree, a Web's navigation structure can contain generations; that is, the first parent page branches out to include the first generation of child pages; those pages might branch out to include a second generation of child pages; and so on.

You establish your Web's navigation structure by using **Navigation** view. In this view, you can specify which pages in your Web are parent pages, which are child pages, and how they are linked.

A navigation button
Click this button to switch to **Navigation** view.

B folder list
This pane lists the folders and files comprising the Web that is currently open.

> (tip) If you don't see the folder list, click the **Toggle Pane** toolbar button and choose **Folder List**. (See step 1 on page 218 if you're not sure which button is the **Toggle Pane** button.)

C navigation structure
This pane shows the navigation structure of the open Web. Here you can add, move, or delete pages in the Web.

D home
The *home page* serves as the top level of the navigation structure.

E parent pages
Parent pages contain links to child pages.

F child pages
Child pages branch out from parent pages.

G navigation toolbar
You can use the **Navigation** toolbar to perform certain simple tasks while you build your Web's navigation structure.

> (tip) The **Navigation** toolbar isn't displayed by default. To view it, choose **View➡Toolbars➡ Navigation**.

H zoom
Zoom in and out of your navigation structure using this drop-down list. This feature comes in handy if

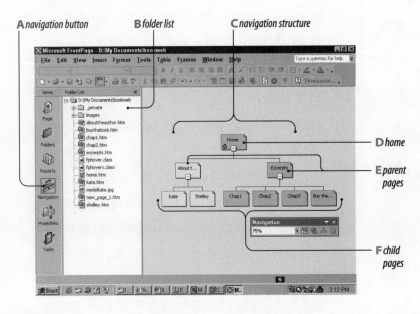

A *navigation button*   B *folder list*   C *navigation structure*

D *home*

E *parent pages*

F *child pages*

your navigation structure is large and won't fit on your screen when viewed at 100%.

> **tip** You can also zoom in and out of your navigation structure by right-clicking the background and choosing Zoom. You are given several options: 150%, 100%, 75%, 50%, 25%, and Size To Fit. Choose Size To Fit to automatically size a large navigation structure to fit in the Navigation window.

I portrait/landscape

Toggle between a *portrait* (vertical) layout and a *landscape* (horizontal) layout by clicking this button. Choose Portrait if your navigation structure is complex, containing many generations of child pages; that way, you can see more of the structure.

J add existing page

Add a hyperlink to your navigation structure to a page that isn't in this Web.

K included in navigation bars

Click this button to include the selected page in a link bar or, if the page already appears on a link bar, to

exclude it from the bar. (See The Link Bar Properties Dialog Boxes on page 220.)

> **tip** To determine whether the selected page is included in a link bar, right-click the page. If the **Included in Navigation Bars** option is selected, then the page is included in a link bar.

L view subtree only

Click the **View Subtree Only** button to display only a portion of the navigation structure, starting at the selected page. Alternatively, if only the subtree is displayed, click this button to toggle back to the full-structure view.

> **tip** Alternatively, you can view the subtree of a selected page by right-clicking the page and choosing **View Subtree Only**. To view the navigation structure in its entirety, right-click the background of the **Navigation** window and choose **Expand All** from the menu that appears.

G *navigation toolbar*

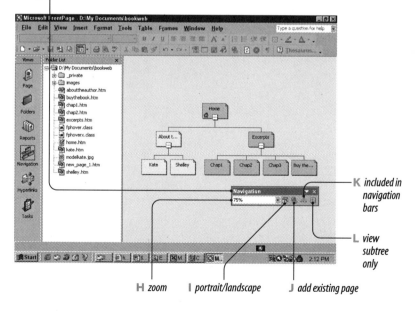

K *included in navigation bars*

L *view subtree only*

H *zoom*   I *portrait/landscape*   J *add existing page*

ⓢ𝑡𝑒𝑝𝑠 Set Up A Navigation Structure

Using Navigation view, you can easily add, move, and delete pages to and from your Web's navigation structure. Open Navigation view by clicking the Navigation button in the **Views** bar on the left side of the screen (if you don't see the **Views** bar on-screen, choose **Views➧Views Bar** to open it).

1 display folder list

After you open the Web you want to work on in **Navigation** view, click the **Toggle Pane** button and choose **Folder List**.

2 add home page

In the folder list, locate a page that you want to use as the home page of your Web's navigation structure. Click the file and drag it to the **Navigation** pane.

3 choose rename

The home page appears in the navigation structure, named simply New Page 1. To assign a more descriptive

name, right-click the newly added page and choose **Rename** from the menu that appears.

> 𝑡𝑖𝑝 If you haven't yet created the page you want to use as your Web's home page, click the New Page button on the toolbar instead of dragging a page from the Folder list. Name the page as described in steps 3 and 4, and then switch to Page view to add content to and format the page as normal.

4 type name

Type a descriptive name for the newly added page and press **enter**.

5 add first generation

Add a first-generation page to your Web by dragging a file from your folder list and "attaching" it to your home page (you'll see a line attaching the home page to the

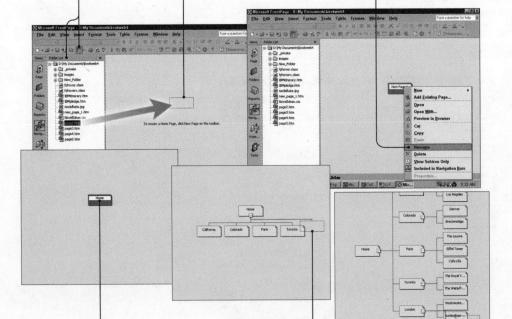

1 *display folder list* 2 *add home page* 3 *choose rename*

4 *type name* 5 *add first generation* 6 *add second generation*

new page). Name the new page using the instructions outlined in steps 3 and 4. Continue adding pages in this manner until the navigation structure contains all the first-generation pages you want.

> *tip* To add a page that you haven't yet created, right-click the page you want to serve as the new page's parent and choose **New➧Page.** FrontPage adds the new page to the Web and navigation structure under the page you selected. To name the new page, right-click it and choose **Rename** from the menu that appears; then type a descriptive name for the page and press **enter.** To add content to the page you just added, simply double-click the page's icon in the navigation structure. FrontPage opens the page in Page view; add content and format the page as you would any other.

6 add second generation
Following the instructions outlined in step 5, add second-generation pages to your navigation structure—but instead of attaching these pages to your home page, attach them to pages in the first generation. (It may be helpful to switch to Portrait view so you can see more of your navigation structure.) If the Navigation toolbar is open on your desktop, click the

Portrait/Landscape button to toggle to Portrait view; otherwise, right-click the Navigation window's background and choose Portrait/Landscape from the menu that appears.

7 move page (optional)
To move a page from one parent to another, drag it to the desired location in the navigation structure.

8 delete page (optional)
To delete a page from your navigation structure, right-click it and choose **Delete** from the menu that appears.

9 choose delete option (optional)
You can choose to remove the page from the navigation structure or from the entire Web; choose the option that best suits your needs and click **OK.**

> *tip* Unless you're absolutely positive that you won't ever use the page you're deleting again, simply remove it from the navigation structure as opposed to deleting it from the Web. That way, if you need to, you can always re-add it to the structure. Who knows when you may want to re-use that page of your Aunt Mabel's vacation photos?

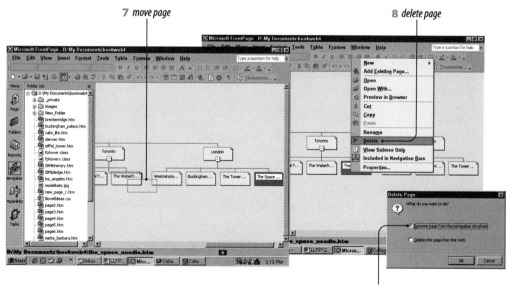

7 *move page*

8 *delete page*

9 *choose delete option*

The Link Bar Properties Dialog Boxes

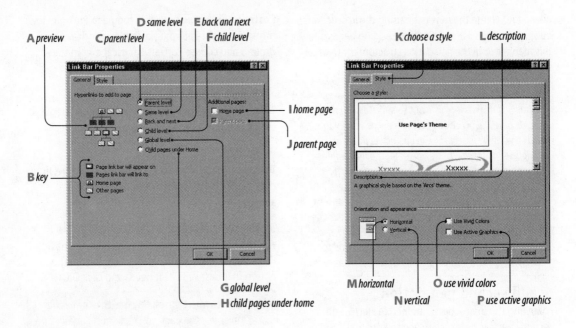

A preview **C** parent level **D** same level **E** back and next **F** child level **K** choose a style **L** description

B key

I home page
J parent page

G global level
H child pages under home

M horizontal **N** vertical **O** use vivid colors **P** use active graphics

On many Web sites you see a *link bar*, also called a *navigation bar*, which is a set of hyperlinks placed on pages in a Web to help visitors navigate the site. The link bar provides a central, convenient location for the Web's links; on sites with pages containing link bars, a visitor knows where to go to quickly access another page. For example, you might decide to add a link bar with links to your Web's home page and other main pages to make it easier for people to get to those pages.

You can form a link bar by creating a set of links by hand, adding a series of buttons, and linking them to relevant pages on each page where you want them to appear. Alternatively, you can set up your Web's navigation structure and let Microsoft FrontPage create a link bar for you. If you decide to let Microsoft create the link bar for you, you use the **Link Bar Properties** dialog box to establish how you want the link bar to behave. (For help opening this dialog box, see Insert A Link Bar on page 222.)

If you allow FrontPage to create your link bar for you, the program maintains the link bars it creates. That means if you move a page, FrontPage updates the hyperlinks in the link bar to reflect the change. A major plus for this method, we think, because having FrontPage take care of this for you ensures that the links are always functional—and you don't have to spend any extra time maintaining the links.

A preview

View the **preview** area to see what types of pages on your Web are included on the link bar.

B key

The **key** is your Rosetta Stone, indicating which symbols in the preview area represent which types of pages.

C parent level

Choose **Parent level** to create a link bar that includes hyperlinks to all pages on the same level as the parent page.

D same level

Choose **Same level** to create a link bar that includes hyperlinks to other pages on the same level as the active page. (Note that only pages with the same parent page as the active page are included.)

E back and next

Choose **Back and next** to create a link bar that includes hyperlinks to adjacent pages on the same level as the active page.

F child level

Choose **Child level** to create a link bar that includes hyperlinks to pages on the level below the active page.

G global level

Choose **Global level** to create a link bar that includes hyperlinks to pages back up the tree on all levels.

H child pages under home

Choose **Child pages under home** to create a link bar that includes hyperlinks to pages under the home page.

I home page

Check the **Home page** checkbox to include a link to the Web's home page in the link bar.

J parent page

Check the **Parent page** checkbox to include a link to the active page's parent page in the link bar.

K choose a style

Choose a link bar style from the list (scroll down to see a preview of each style). If you've applied a theme to your page, select **Use Page's Theme.**

L description

The **Description** box describes the style selected in the Choose a style (K) list.

M horizontal

Select the **Horizontal** radio button to create a horizontal link bar along the top of the page.

N vertical

Select the **Vertical** radio button to create a vertical link bar along the left side of the page.

O use vivid colors

Some themes allow you to choose one of two color sets: *vivid* and *normal*. If the theme you selected in the Choose a style list (K) supports the use of vivid colors, you can check this checkbox to apply them to your link bar.

P use active graphics

Some themes let you apply animated page elements, such as hover buttons. If the theme you selected in the Choose a style list (K) supports the use of these animated elements, you can check this checkbox to apply them to your link bar.

Types Of Link Bars

FrontPage 2002 supports the use of three types of link bars: *Custom link bars* (these can include links to pages within your Web as well as to external pages), link bars with *Back and Next links* (FrontPage examines your Web's navigation structure to determine which page appears when site visitors click **Back** or **Next**), and link

bars based on the navigation structure of your Web (discussed in Insert A Link Bar on page 222).

If you publish your Web to a disk-based Web site, you can use any type of link bar you like. If, however, you plan to publish your site to a Web server, you can only use link

bars based on the navigation structure of your Web unless Microsoft FrontPage 2002 Server Extensions or SharePoint Team Services from Microsoft are installed on the server. For this reason, this section, as well as the ones that follow, focus on the implementation of a link bar based on a Web's navigation structure.

Insert A Link Bar

You insert a link bar in much the same way you insert Web components such as hit counters and hover buttons: You use the **Insert Web Component** dialog box (refer to Chapter 10, Apply Dynamic Effects, for more information about this dialog box).

This section describes how to insert a link bar based on your Web's navigation structure, which means you should establish your site's navigation structure before completing the steps on this page. For help building a navigation structure, see Set Up A Navigation Structure on page 218.

1 choose navigation

After you open a page to which you want to add a link bar and click in the spot where you want the bar to be added, choose **Insert➧Navigation**. The **Insert Web Component** dialog box opens, with **Link Bars** selected in the **Component type** column.

tip If you wish, you can add multiple link bars to pages—for example, if you want users to navigate to different page levels.

2 choose bar type

In the **Choose a bar type** column, click **Bar based on navigation structure** and then click the **Next** button.

3 choose bar style

Choose a bar style from the list that appears in the **Insert Web Component** dialog box and click the **Next** button.

tip If you've applied a theme to your page, select **Use Page's Theme** at the top of the **Choose a bar style** list. The link bars then use the fonts, colors, and other style elements of the theme. If your page doesn't use a theme, choose **Use Page's Theme** to create a link bar that uses the default text style of your page.

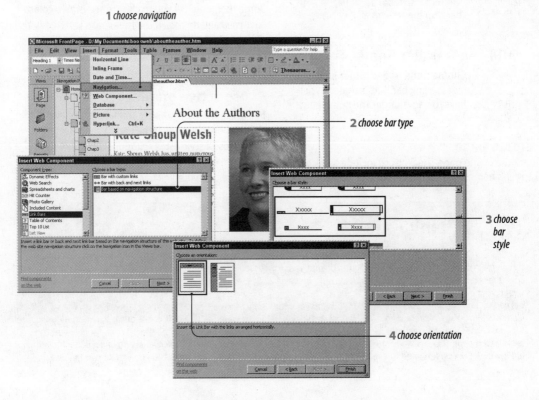

1 choose navigation

2 choose bar type

3 choose bar style

4 choose orientation

7 *click OK*

4 choose orientation

Specify whether you want the link bar to appear along the top or the left side of the page and click **Finish**. The **Link Bar Properties** dialog box opens.

5 set link bar level

Specify the pages you want the link bar to link by choosing a radio button in the **Hyperlinks to add to page** area. To include links to the Web's home page or the active page's parent page, check the **Home page** and/or **Parent page** checkbox.

6 set link style (optional)

Click the **Style** tab to change the settings you chose in steps 3 and 4, including the theme of the link bar and the link bar's orientation. This tab also lets you specify whether vivid colors or active graphics are used in the event you've chosen a theme.

7 click OK

Click the **OK** button to close the **Link Bar Properties** dialog box and add the link bar to your page.

Edit A Link Bar

The links in the link bar are named and ordered to reflect your Web's navigation structure. To change the name of a link or the order in which links appear on a link bar, you must rename the link page or change the navigation structure of the Web (refer to Set Up A Navigation Structure on page 218). After you do so, right-click the blue background in **Navigation** view and choose **Apply Changes** to update the link bar.

To change which pages appear on the link bar, you use the **Link Bar Properties** dialog box (double-click the link bar to open this dialog box). If none of the options in the **Hyperlinks to add to page** area quite suits your needs, select one that includes all the pages you want to link to, even if it also includes pages you don't want in the bar. Then, exclude pages you don't want by switching to **Navigation** view and right-clicking a page you want to exclude. In the shortcut menu that

appears, click **Included in Navigation Bars** so that it's no longer selected.

To change the style of a link bar made of buttons, including its orientation, use the **Style** tab of the **Link Bar Properties** dialog box, as described in step 6. Alternatively, if the link bar features text links instead of buttons, format the bar just as you would any other type of text: Click the link bar and then choose **Format ➡ Font**. Change the font as desired and click **OK**.

The Shared Borders Dialog Box

A *shared border* is a page border design that is shared among one or more pages within a Web. You might use shared borders to display your company's logo, a copyright notice, or some other important item on each page in your Web. You can also add link bars to a shared border. Shared borders ultimately add continuity to your site.

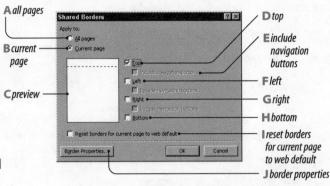

A *all pages*

B *current page*

C *preview*

D *top*

E *include navigation buttons*

F *left*

G *right*

H *bottom*

I *reset borders for current page to web default*

J *border properties*

A all pages
Apply shared borders to all the pages on your Web.

B current page
Apply a shared border to only the current or selected pages.

C preview
Preview your border selections in this area.

D top

Apply a shared border to the top of the page or pages in your Web.

E include navigation buttons
Check this box to create a shared border that contains the title of the page and a link bar generated according to the Web's navigation structure. (Note that this option is available only if you've selected the **All pages** option in the **Apply to** area.)

> You specify page titles and the navigation structure in **Navigation** view, as discussed in Navigation View and Set Up A Navigation Structure on pages 216- 219.

F left

Apply a shared border to the left side of the page or pages in your Web.

G right

Apply a shared border to the right side of the page or pages in your Web.

H bottom

Apply a shared border to the bottom of the page or pages in your Web.

I reset borders for current page to web default
Return the shared-border settings on the active page to the default for the page's Web.

> This option is available only if you select **Current page** in the **Apply to** area.

J border properties
Open the **Border Properties** dialog box, where you can apply a background color or picture to the selected shared border.

⚙steps Add Shared Borders

You can give a consistent look to multiple pages by applying a shared border. Similarly, if you need to change the contents within a shared border, you modify the contents in one place rather than modifying each affected page one at a time.

1 open web

In **Navigation** view, open the Web containing pages to which you want to apply shared borders.

> 💡 If you prefer to work in Page view, you can open a page within the Web to which you want to apply shared borders instead of opening the Web in Navigation view. Then, you have the option of applying the shared borders to the entire Web or to the page you have open in Page view.

2 select pages (optional)

Move your mouse pointer to the **folder list**. Press and hold down the **ctrl** button on your keyboard, and click all pages in the folder list to which you want to apply shared borders. (If you want to apply the shared borders to your entire Web, skip this step.)

> 💡 To display the folder list, click the **Toggle Pane** button in the toolbar. (Refer to Set Up A Navigation Structure on page 218 if you're not sure which button is the Toggle Pane button.)

3 choose shared borders

Choose **Format➡Shared Borders** to open the **Shared Borders** dialog box.

4 choose application setting

Choose **All pages** to apply the shared border to all pages in the open Web, or choose **Current page** to apply the border to pages you selected in step 2. (Notice that the Current page option is grayed out unless you selected pages from the folder list or opened a page in Page view.)

5 choose border location

Choose **Top, Left, Right,** or **Bottom** to specify where the shared border should appear on the page.

> 💡 You aren't limited to applying a single shared border; in fact, you can apply shared borders to all four edges of your page if you wish.

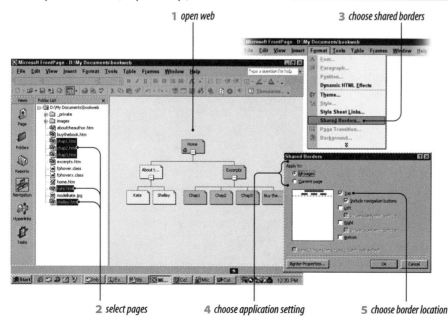

1 *open web*

3 *choose shared borders*

2 *select pages*   4 *choose application setting*   5 *choose border location*

6 add link bar (optional)

If you want to add a link bar to one of the shared borders, check the **Include navigation buttons** checkbox under the border location checkbox. (If you don't wish to add a link bar, skip this step.)

> 🄫 Adding a link bar to a shared border can be problematic. Unlike link bars you insert by hand, which may change depending on which page you view, the available links in a link bar that resides in a shared border never change.

7 click border properties

Click the **Border Properties** button to set the properties of the shared border.

> 🄫 If you've elected to place multiple shared borders on your page, you need to select the border whose properties you want to set from the **Border** drop-down list in the **Border Properties** dialog box.

8 choose background color

Check the **Color** checkbox and open the accompanying drop-down list to choose a background color.

9 choose background picture (optional)

If you wish to place a picture in the background of the shared border, check the **Picture** checkbox and type the path and filename of the image you want to add in the accompanying textbox. If the image you want to use resides outside the current Web, you need to copy or move it to your Web's folder.

> 🄫 Unless the image you choose is the exact same size as the shared border, it appears tiled on the border. You may need to resize your image in an image-editing program before placing it in the shared border if you want it to fit exactly.

10 click OK

Click **OK** twice to close the dialog boxes and apply the shared borders.

6 *add link bar*

7 *click border properties*

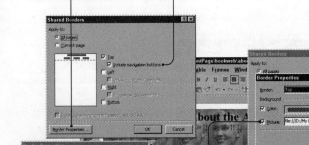

8 *choose background color* **9** *choose background picture* **10** *click OK*

Table Of Contents Properties Dialog Box

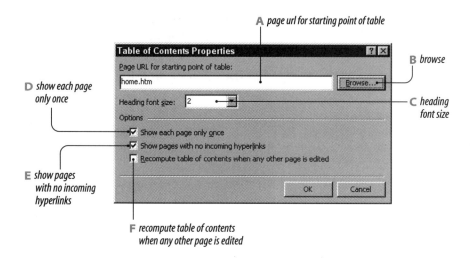

A *page url for starting point of table*

B *browse*

C *heading font size*

D *show each page only once*

E *show pages with no incoming hyperlinks*

F *recompute table of contents when any other page is edited*

A great addition to any site is a *table of contents* (TOC), or *site map,* helping visitors to quickly link to any page on the Web with the click of a mouse. If your Web is large, it's best to place the table of contents on a page of its own (be sure to add it to your navigation structure using Navigation view); otherwise, you can add it to a page that contains other content. Either way, you use the **Table of Contents Properties** dialog box to create a table of contents for your site; for help opening this dialog box, see Create A Table of Contents on page 228.

A page url for starting point of table

Type the URL of the top-most page in the TOC—the parent page under which all child pages appear. If you want your table of contents to cover your entire Web, enter the URL of the Web's home page here.

B browse

If you're not sure of the exact URL of the page you want to use as the starting point for the TOC, click the **Browse** button to select a page in the current Web.

C heading font size

Choose a heading size for the first entry in the TOC from this drop-down list. If you prefer to create a table of contents with no heading, choose **None.**

D show each page only once

Many pages in your Web may be accessible via multiple hyperlinks. If you want those pages to appear only once in your table of contents, check this checkbox.

E show pages with no incoming hyperlinks

There may well be pages in your Web that can't be reached by following hyperlinks from your home page. If you want to include these pages, called *orphan pages,* in your TOC, check this checkbox.

F recompute table of contents when any other page is edited

If you want your TOC page to be updated each time you alter your Web, check this checkbox.

> *tip* Checking this checkbox sounds like a good idea in theory, but this feature can be problematic in practice. If your Web is large, it can take some time to update the table of contents each time you make a change. It may be better to manually update the table of contents by opening and saving the page that contains the table.

Follow these steps to create a table of contents based on the navigation structure of your Web.

1 choose web component

After you click on the spot on the page where you want to insert the TOC, choose **Insert➡Web Component.**

2 choose table of contents

In the **Component type** list of the **Insert Web Component** dialog box, click **Table of Contents.**

3 choose for this web site

In the **Choose a table of contents** list, click **For This Web Site.**

4 click finish

Click the **Finish** button to open the **Table of Contents Properties** dialog box.

5 enter url

Type the URL of the page you want to act as the starting point for the TOC (choose your Web's home page to make the TOC cover your entire site). If you don't know the page's URL, click **Browse** to locate it.

6 set heading size

Open the **Heading font size** drop-down list to select the style for the top-level entry in the TOC.

7 show each page only once (optional)

If your Web has pages accessible via multiple hyperlinks, check this box to ensure that they appear only once in your TOC.

8 show pages with no incoming hyperlinks (optional)

If your Web contains pages that visitors can't access by following hyperlinks from your home page, check this box to include those pages in your TOC.

9 recompute table of contents (optional)

If you want your TOC page to be updated each time you alter your Web, check this checkbox.

10 click OK

Click **OK** to close the **Table of Contents Properties** dialog box and insert the table of contents on your page.

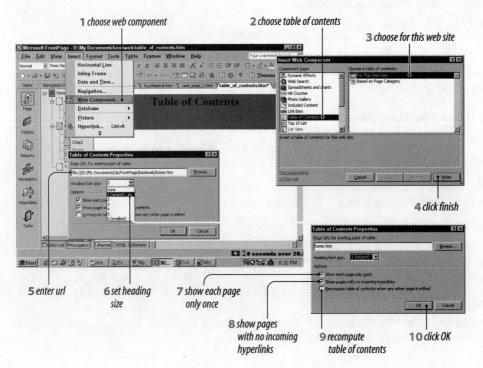

1 *choose web component*

2 *choose table of contents*

3 *choose for this web site*

4 *click finish*

5 *enter url*

6 *set heading size*

7 *show each page only once*

8 *show pages with no incoming hyperlinks*

9 *recompute table of contents*

10 *click OK*

steps Create A Category-Based Site Map

You can create a site map or TOC based on categories that you assign to each page on your Web. This type of TOC is appropriate especially for large, complex Webs. To do this, you must first assign a category to each page in your Web, and then you can generate the site map. Anytime you add files to or remove files from a category, FrontPage 2002 updates your site map automatically.

1 open page properties window
In any view but **Tasks** view, right-click a page you want to appear on your site map and choose **Properties** from the shortcut menu that appears.

2 click workgroup tab
The page's **Properties** dialog box opens. Click the **Workgroup** tab.

3 click categories
FrontPage offers several pre-defined categories that you can apply to your page. If one suits your needs, skip to step 7. Otherwise, you can create your own category. Click the **Categories** button; the **Master Category List** dialog box opens.

4 name category
Type a name for the new category in the **New category** textbox.

5 click add
Click **Add** to add the new category to the list.

6 click OK
Click **OK** to add the new category to the **Properties** dialog box's list of available categories.

7 select category
Check the checkbox for the category you want to apply to the page.

8 click OK
Click **OK** to close the page's **Properties** dialog box and to apply the selected category to the page. Repeat

steps 1-8 for each page you want to appear on your TOC, categorizing them as needed.

9 type heading
After you categorize all the pages you want to appear on your site map, open the page on which the site map will be placed, and type a heading for the first category you want to appear on the map. (Format the heading in the font, color, and style you prefer.)

> *tip* This heading doesn't need to mirror the category name you assigned in step 4; it should be what you want visitors to see when they view the TOC.

10 choose web components
Click where you want the site map to be inserted, and choose **Insert➤Web Component**.

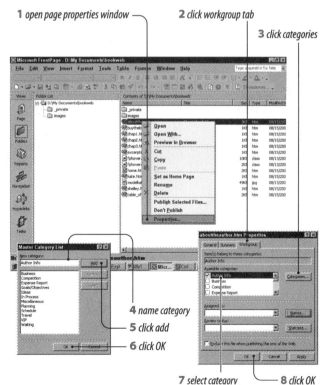

1 *open page properties window* — **2** *click workgroup tab*

3 *click categories*

4 *name category*
5 *click add*
6 *click OK*

7 *select category* — **8** *click OK*

11 choose table of contents

In the **Component type** list, click **Table of Contents**.

12 choose based on page category

In the **Choose a table of contents** list, click **Based on Page Category**.

13 click finish

Click **Finish** to open the **Categories Properties** dialog box.

14 choose category

Check the checkbox for the category whose pages you want to appear under the heading you added in step 9.

15 set sort options

Open the **Sort files by** drop-down list and select **Document Title** to sort pages alphabetically by document title within the category on the site map, or **Date Last Modified** to sort pages according to the date the page was last modified.

16 include additional information

Check the appropriate checkboxes in the **Include the following information** area to include the date each page was last modified or comments about pages in your site map.

17 click OK

Click **OK** to close the **Categories Properties** dialog box and add links to the site map. Repeat steps 9-17 to add all your categories to your site map.

tip You can add comments about a page to provide a description or a note about the file. Comments are not visible on the page that readers see, but you can access them in the Site Summary report in Reports view (see The Site Summary Report on page 270). To add a comment, open any view but **Tasks** view, right-click the page to which you want to add a comment, and choose **Properties** from the menu that appears. Click the **Summary** tab, type a comment in the **Comments** field, and click **OK**.

tip You have to preview your site map page in your browser to see all the links. For more information about previewing your Web page, see Preview A Page on page 72.

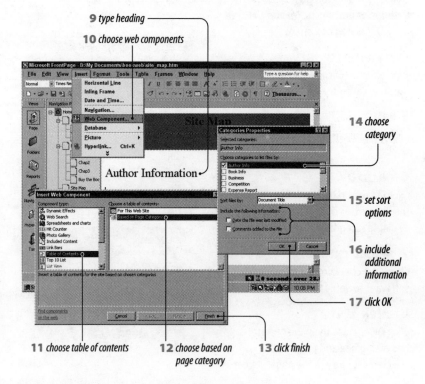

9 *type heading*

10 *choose web components*

14 *choose category*

15 *set sort options*

16 *include additional information*

17 *click OK*

11 *choose table of contents*

12 *choose based on page category*

13 *click finish*

Title ☐ ▼

◉ Region

A *form* is an area in a Web page that contains text-boxes, checkboxes, option buttons, and drop-down lists. Using forms, you can gather information from people who visit your site, such as their names, street addresses, e-mail addresses, and any feedback they have regarding your site, product, or service.

In Microsoft FrontPage 2002, you can create forms from scratch or by using a wizard. You can also set the properties of any form elements you add. For example, you can create a confirmation page to notify site visitors when the information-gathering process is done, and specify how you want to save the data that your visitors provide. We tell you how to do all this and more in this chapter.

Before you add a form page to your Web, make sure the server that hosts your site has **FrontPage Server Extensions** or **SharePoint Team Services** installed. Otherwise, the forms on your site won't work.

The Form Page Wizard

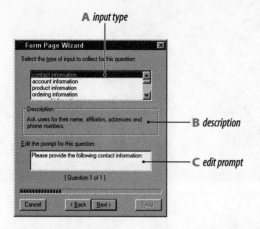

A *input type*

B *description*

C *edit prompt*

The easiest way to collect data on your site is to use the **Form Page Wizard** to create a form page. Using the wizard, you simply specify the questions you want to ask site visitors; the wizard then creates a form page based on your input, including Submit and Reset buttons that enable visitors to submit their form to you or to reset the fields in the form to their default values.

A input type

The **Select the type of input to collect for this question** list contains the types of input you can receive from site visitors.

You can opt to receive one of several types of user input, including contact, account, product, ordering, or personal information. In case none of these options suits your needs, the wizard offers alternative choices to help you create more specialized forms. Choose **one of several options** to ask visitors to choose only one item from a list of options, or **any of several options** to choose as many or as few items as they wish. To ask visitors for a yes/no or true/false response, choose **boolean.** Select **date** or **time** to prompt users for date or time information. The **range** option lets you receive rating information from visitors; **number** allows visitors to cite numeric values, such as quantities. Select **string** if you want visitors to type a short *character string* (useful if you use promotional codes); choose **paragraph** to allow users to

type one or more paragraphs in a textbox (useful for feedback).

B description

Read a brief description of the selected input type in the **Description** area.

C edit prompt

Depending on the type of input you want, the Form Page Wizard provides a default question to ask site visitors. To change the default question, type a new question in the **Edit the prompt for this question** box.

D choose items to collect

Use the **Choose the items to collect from the user** area to specify the exact data items you want to collect from site visitors. The options in the **Choose the items to collect from the user** area differ depending on what type of input you elect to gather.

E enter base name

Specify a name for the group of variables you've just configured in the **Choose items to collect** area (**D**). FrontPage needs this name in case you decide to generate a table of contents for your form page.

F presentation options

Choose whether your list of questions should be presented as normal paragraphs, a numbered list, a bulleted list, or a definition list in the **How should the list of questions be presented?** list.

> ***tip*** You use a *definition list* when you want to define any of the terms in your list; a definition list displays the term flush left, and indents the definition. When used in a form, a definition indents an explanation of the request (such as "Please provide the following contact information"), but not the form fields.

G table of contents

Choose **yes** or **no** in the **Would you like a Table of Contents for this page?** area to specify whether you

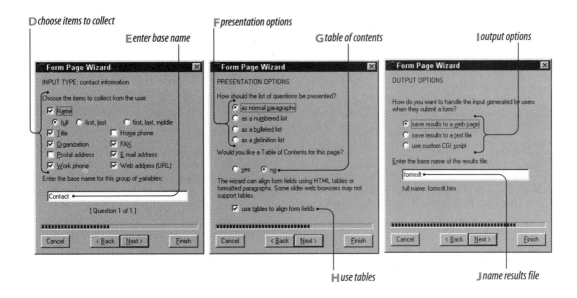

D *choose items to collect*

E *enter base name*

F *presentation options*

G *table of contents*

I *output options*

H *use tables*

J *name results file*

want a table of contents for your form page. If you choose **yes**, FrontPage generates a table of contents for your form page with links to the different sections of the page.

H use tables

Tables help you artfully align your form fields. The downside, as noted in the **Form Page Wizard** dialog box, is that some Web browsers don't support tables. If you're confident that the majority of your site visitors use relatively new browsers, feel free to check the **use tables to align form fields** checkbox.

I output options

You need a place to store the data that visitors input on your form page; choose **save results to a web page, save results to a text file,** or **use custom CGI script** here. Unless you're an experienced programmer, or at the very least know how to create or use custom *CGI scripts* (that is, programs designed to accept and return data), choose one of the first two options.

J name results file

If you choose to save data input to a Web page or text file, you need to name the file; type a *base name* (that is, the name minus the file extension) here.

Other Form Options

FrontPage 2002 features the **Database Interface Wizard,** which helps you create a form based on a database you already have and saves user input to that database; the Discussion Web Wizard creates a discussion forum for visitors. Alternatively, FrontPage page templates can help you quickly and easily create guest-book pages (the **Guest Book template**), feedback forms (the **Feedback Form template**), user registration pages (the **User Registration template**), and more. You access these templates and wizards via the **Web Page Templates** dialog box.

Create A Form With The Wizard

The Form Page Wizard helps you specify what questions to ask visitors in order to collect data from them. Using this wizard, FrontPage creates a form page based on your input.

1 choose page templates

After you've opened the Web for which you want to create a form page, click **Page Templates** in the New Page or Web task pane. (If you don't see the task pane, choose **View→Task Pane.**)

2 choose form page wizard

On the **General** tab of the **Page Templates** dialog box, click **Form Page Wizard** and then click **OK.**

3 click next

The **Form Page Wizard** dialog box opens, outlining the process of creating form pages. Click **Next.**

4 click add

Click **Add** to add a question for your site visitors to the form.

5 select input type

Select an input type. (Refer to The Form Page Wizard on page 232 for information about the options in this list.)

6 edit prompt

Depending on your choice in step 5, the wizard provides a default question or command to which site visitors must respond. To change the default, type a new question or command in the **Edit the prompt for this question** box. Then click **Next.**

7 enter input information

Select the data items you want to collect from the visitor. (The contents of this screen vary depending on the option you chose in step 5.)

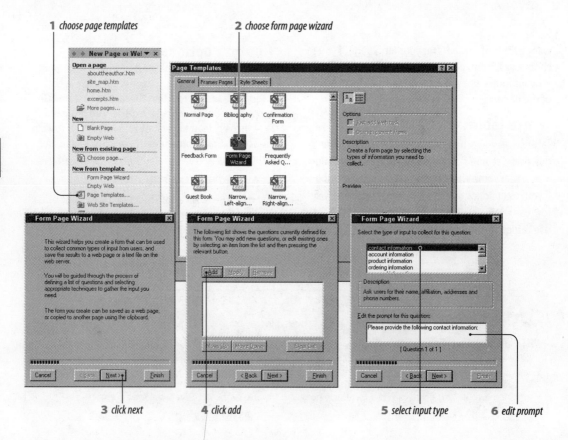

1 *choose page templates*   2 *choose form page wizard*

3 *click next*   4 *click add*   5 *select input type*   6 *edit prompt*

8 type base name (optional)

Type a name for the group of variables you selected; FrontPage needs this name if you decide to generate a table of contents for your form page. Then click **Next**.

9 repeat (optional)

Repeat steps 4-8 until you add all the questions you want to define for your form. Then click **Next**.

10 specify presentation options

Choose **as normal paragraphs**, **as a numbered list**, **as a bulleted list**, or **as a definition list** to specify the presentation of questions.

11 add table of contents (optional)

To add a table of contents to your form, choose **yes** under **Would you like a Table of Contents for this page?**

12 check use tables (optional)

To use tables in your form, check **use tables to align form fields**. Then click **Next**.

13 select output option

Choose **save results to a web page**, **save results to a text file**, or **use custom CGI script**.

14 name results file

If you save data to a Web page or text file, you must name the file; type a *base name* (the file name minus the file extension). Then click **Next**.

15 click finish

Click **Finish** to generate the form page, which is saved in your Web's main folder by default. You can now format your form page just as you would any other page. Link the form to your Web's home page so that visitors can access it; refer to Set Up A Navigation Structure on page 218.

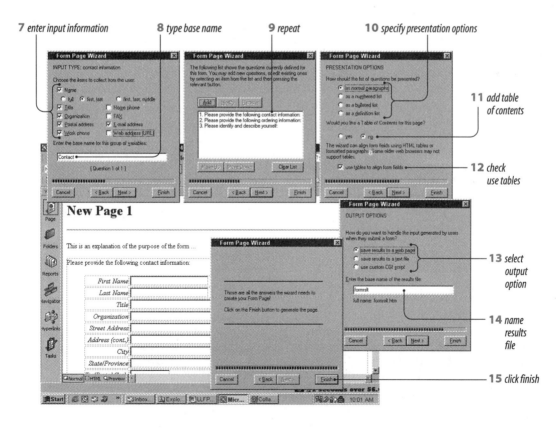

7 *enter input information* **8** *type base name* **9** *repeat* **10** *specify presentation options*

11 *add table of contents*

12 *check use tables*

13 *select output option*

14 *name results file*

15 *click finish*

The Insert Form Menu

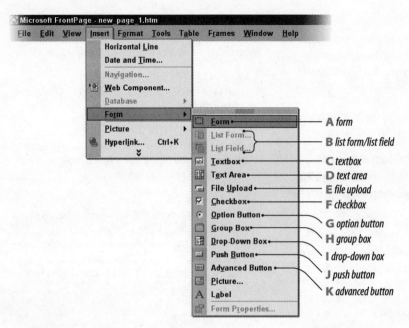

- **A** form
- **B** list form/list field
- **C** textbox
- **D** text area
- **E** file upload
- **F** checkbox
- **G** option button
- **H** group box
- **I** drop-down box
- **J** push button
- **K** advanced button

In addition to using the Form Page Wizard, you can create your form pages from scratch; this method offers greater flexibility and more options. To do so, you use the selections in the **Insert→Form** menu.

A form

Choose **Insert→Form→Form** to insert the form on your Web page. (You should insert the form before adding any form fields.) When you choose this command, a rectangular area containing **Submit** and **Reset** buttons (used to submit the form or clear its fields, respectively) appears on your page. In it, you can add any text and form fields you wish.

B list form/list field

A *list form* on a Web page lets visitors add or edit items in a *document library* (a folder containing a collection of shared files) or an *interactive list* (such as a survey). *List fields* are the fields comprising a list form.

> **tip** In order to use list forms and list fields on your Web site, your Web must be published to a server running **Microsoft SharePoint Team Services.**

C textbox

Insert a *textbox* into your form if you wish to collect a single short line of text from site visitors, such as a name.

D text area

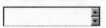

Insert a *text area* if you want to collect multiple lines of text from site visitors, such as a comment or other type of feedback. Scrollbars help visitors scroll through long missives.

E file upload

If you want to allow site visitors to upload a file to your Web site—for example, if you hold a photography contest, and you want contestants to upload their digital images—insert a *file upload field*. Visitors can then type the path and filename of the file they want to upload, or click the **Browse** button to locate the file on their system.

F checkbox

Checkboxes are used for optional items of which users can select as many or as few as they like.

G option button

⊙

Option buttons, which always occur in groups of two or more, let visitors select only one option from a group of choices.

H group box

┌─ Group box ──────────────────┐
│   │
└──────────────────────────────┘

Group boxes let you group related controls or text in their own separate area. Simply insert the group box onto your page, and then insert desired controls into the group box.

I drop-down box

Drop-down boxes are similar to option buttons (G) in that they contain a list of items from which the site visitor can select only one. Drop-down boxes, however, require less space than a large group of option buttons.

> **tip** Although drop-down boxes allow visitors to select only one option by default, you can configure them to allow multiple selections. See Set Form Element Properties on page 243 for more details.

J push button

Button

Two *push buttons* are added to forms by default: **Submit** and **Reset.** If you want to add additional push buttons, which can be configured to perform any number of operations, choose this option.

K advanced button

Type Here

Choose **Advanced Button** to insert a button that offers the same options as a push button, but enables you to specify its size. (When you insert an advanced button, FrontPage lets you immediately type a name for it.)

> **tip** After you build your form, you can format it just as you would any other page. Add a background, picture, or any other elements you like; change the font of your fields' labels; drag the fields on the page to position them; apply a theme; and more.

> **tip** You should always preview and test your form before making it available to your visitors. To preview your form page in your browser, refer to Preview A Page on page 72. To test your form, access it via the Internet. Fill out the form just as a visitor would, submit the form, and retrieve the results. Note that certain page elements won't display properly unless the form is published to a Web server supporting **Microsoft FrontPage Server Extensions** or **SharePoint Team Services.** Likewise, you must publish the site before you can test your form to make sure it works properly. (See Chapter 14, Publish A Web, for more information.)

Retrieve Data From Forms

To retrieve the data site visitors enter into your form, whether the form is created from scratch or via the Form Page Wizard, first open the Web in FrontPage. In Folder view, navigate to the _private folder and double-click the results file to open it. You can now view all of the information gathered by your forms page.

steps Create A Form From Scratch

Creating a form page from scratch affords you greater flexibility and more options in terms of the types of elements that appear on your form. Here we create a form to gather customer information and feedback. We show your how to set the properties of the form's fields, such as their size, contents, and so on, in Set Form Element Properties starting on page 243.

> **tip** Before you create your form, think about what you want the form to contain. Sketch out the layout of your form so that you have a clear picture of what you're shooting for.

1 choose form
In Page view, click the page where you want the form to appear and choose **Insert➜Form➜Form**. FrontPage inserts the form on the page.

2 press enter
Press **enter** several times to enlarge the form area. This gives you some working room.

3 choose group box
Before you start adding form fields, add a group box so that you can group related fields by choosing **Insert➜Form➜Group Box**.

1 *choose form* **2** *press enter* **3** *choose group box*

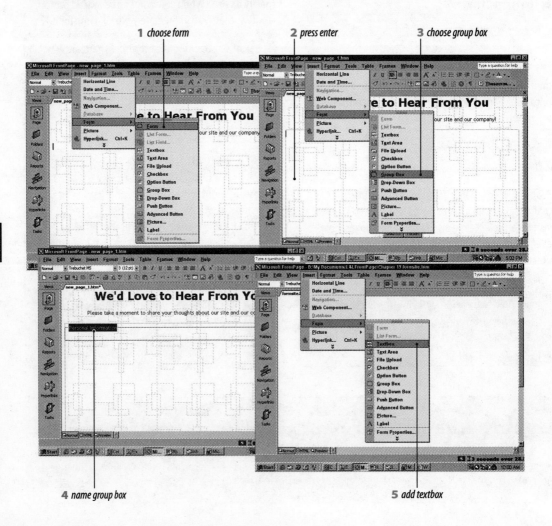

4 *name group box* **5** *add textbox*

⑬ Title ☐▽
⊙Region

4 name group box

Select the **Group box** text and type a descriptive name for the group box.

5 add textbox

Click in the group box where you want to add a textbox and type a label for it. Then, choose **Insert➠Form➠Textbox** to insert the textbox to the right of your label (you can change the placement of your textbox by clicking it and dragging it to a location you prefer).

6 repeat

Continue adding textboxes to the group box until it contains all the textboxes you require.

7 add form elements

Add any other form elements you need to gather the information you want by clicking the spot where you want to add the form element, typing a label for it, choosing **Insert➠Form,** and selecting the form element you want to add from the submenu that appears. The form element is placed to the right of the label by default; move it by clicking it and dragging it to the spot you prefer.

8 add text area

Click the form somewhere outside the group box, type a label for the text area you're about to add, and then choose **Insert➠Form➠Text Area.** After you've added all the form elements you want on your form page, be sure to save it (choose **File➠Save As,** locate the folder where you want to save the page, and give it a distinctive name), and link it to your Web's home page so that visitors can access it (refer to Set Up A Navigation Structure on page 218).

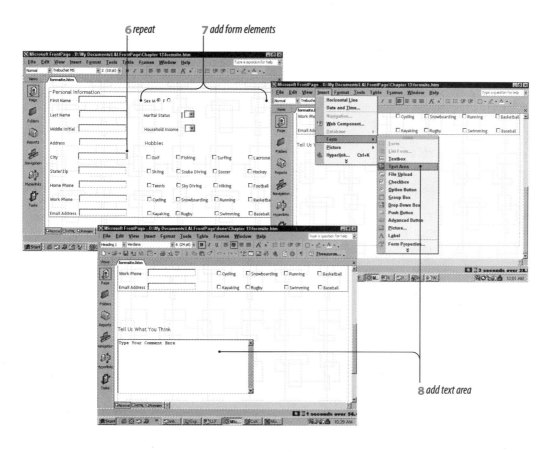

6 repeat   **7** add form elements

8 add text area

The Form Field Properties Dialog Boxes

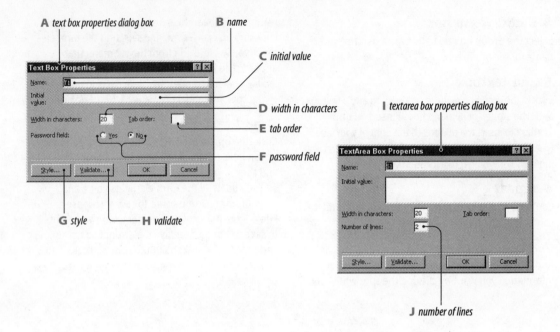

A *text box properties dialog box*

B *name*

C *initial value*

D *width in characters*

E *tab order*

F *password field*

G *style*

H *validate*

I *textarea box properties dialog box*

J *number of lines*

Each type of *form field,* be it a textbox, a checkbox, or text area, has its own **Properties** dialog box that enables you to apply various settings to the form field.

A text box properties
Set the properties for a *textbox field.*

B name
Holds the name used to internally identify the form field when the visitor submits the form, not the name displayed on the form. You can enter any name you like here.

> *tip* Spaces and certain characters, including slashes and commas, can't be used in the various **Properties** boxes' **Name** fields. If you try to use a character that's not allowed, FrontPage prompts you to rename the field.

C initial value
Contains the text that appears in the form field by default when the form first opens.

D width in characters
Specify the form field's width, in characters.

E tab order
When a visitor tabs through your form, the tab goes from the top of the form to the bottom by default. To change this tab order, type a numeric value to indicate the selected form field's new position in the order. For example, if you want the form field to be first in the tab order even if it isn't at the top of the page, type 1. If you don't want the selected field to appear in your form's tab order, type -1.

> *tip* Leave the **Tab order** field blank if you want visitors to use the default tab order.

F password field
Select this option if the textbox you've created is a *password field,* a field where site visitors enter a password. Then, when the visitor types his password, it appears in his browser as asterisks.

G style
Click to open the **Modify Style** dialog box and apply style-sheet formatting to the field.

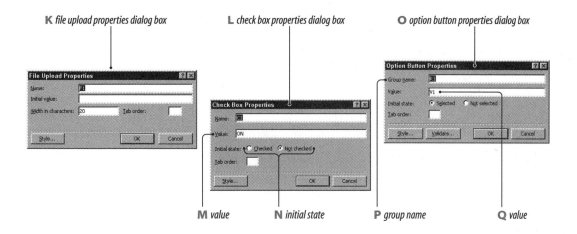

K *file upload properties dialog box* **L** *check box properties dialog box* **O** *option button properties dialog box*

M *value*   **N** *initial state*   **P** *group name*   **Q** *value*

H validate

Click to open the **Validation** dialog box, in which you can set rules for data entry. (See Set Rules For Data Entry on page 248 for details.)

I textarea box properties

Set the properties for a *textarea field*. The **Name, Initial value, Width in characters, Tab order, Style,** and **Validate** options work just like the ones in the **Text Box Properties** dialog box (A).

J number of lines

Enter the number of lines of text that the textarea field can contain.

K file upload properties

Set the properties for a *file upload field*. The **Name, Initial value, Width in characters, Tab order,** and **Style** options work just like the ones in the **Text Box Properties** dialog box (A).

L check box properties

Set the properties for a *checkbox field*. The **Name, Tab order,** and **Style** options function just like the ones in the **Text Box Properties** dialog box (A).

M value

Type a value, such as CHECKED, to associate with the checkbox; if the visitor selects the checkbox, this value appears in the file you use to gather form results.

N initial state

Specify whether the field should be selected by default when the form appears in the browser.

O option button properties

Set the properties for an *option button field*. The **Initial State** option acts like the one in the **Check Box Properties** dialog box (L); the **Tab order, Style,** and **Validate** options work like the ones in the **Text Box Properties** (A).

P group name

The **Group name** box acts like the **Name** box in the **Text Box Properties** dialog box (A).

Q value

You assign each option button a *unique value;* if the visitor selects the option button, this value appears in the file you use to gather form results.

R group box properties

Set the properties for a *group box*. This option works just like the Style option in the **Text Box Properties** dialog box (G).

S label

Specity the label on the group box.

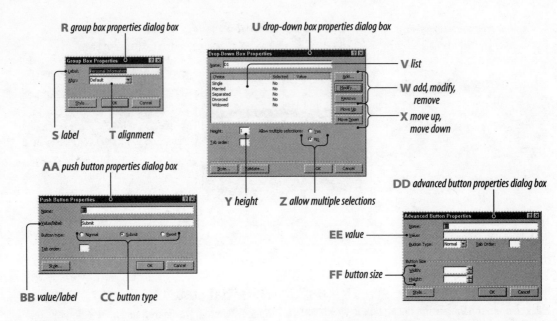

R *group box properties dialog box*

U *drop-down box properties dialog box*

S *label* **T** *alignment*

V *list*

W *add, modify, remove*

X *move up, move down*

AA *push button properties dialog box*

Y *height* **Z** *allow multiple selections*

DD *advanced button properties dialog box*

EE *value*

FF *button size*

BB *value/label* **CC** *button type*

T align

Set the alignment of the group box's label (the default is Left).

U drop-down box properties

Set the properties for a *drop-down box*. The **Name, Tab Order, Style,** and **Validate** options work like the same-named options in the **Text Box Properties** dialog box (A).

V list

Displays options defined for the drop-down box.

W add, modify, remove

Add, modify, or remove a choice in the box list.

X move up, move down

Move the selected choice up or down in the list.

Y height

Set the number of lines of text the drop-down menu displays by default.

Z allow multiple selections

Click **Yes** to allow multiple menu choices or **No** to allow only one choice.

AA push button properties

Set the properties for a *push button*. The **Name, Tab Order,** and **Style** options operate just as the same-named options in the **Text Box Properties** dialog box (A).

BB value/label

Type a label for the button.

CC button type

Specify whether the button is a **Submit** button, **Reset** button, or **Generic** button (normal), to which you can assign a script.

DD advanced button properties

Set the properties for an *advanced button*. The **Name, Tab Order,** and **Style** options work like the same-named options in the **Text Box Properties** dialog box (A); the **Button Type** drop-down list offers the same options as the **Button Type** section in the **Push Button Properties** dialog box (AA).

EE value

Type a label for the button in the **Value** box.

FF button size

Set the width and height of the button, in pixels.

Set Form Element Properties

This section illustrates how to set the properties of a text area, a checkbox, an advanced button, and a drop-down list.

1 choose form field properties

Right-click the text area whose properties you want to set and choose **Form Field Properties.** The **TextArea Box Properties** dialog box opens.

2 type name

Type a name in the **Name** box; this name appears in the form results, not on the actual form.

3 set initial value (optional)

Enter text, such as **Type your comment here**, to appear in the form by default.

4 set width

Specify the width of the text area, in characters.

5 set height

Specify the height of the text area, in lines.

> **tip** Alternatively, you can drag the text area's *size handles* to change its size.

6 set tab order (optional)

Let visitors tab through your form's fields in a specific order (instead of the default, top to bottom) by specifying the text area's position in that order.

7 click OK

Click **OK** to apply your settings.

8 choose form field properties

Right-click the checkbox whose properties you want to set and choose **Form Field Properties.** The **Check Box Properties** dialog box opens.

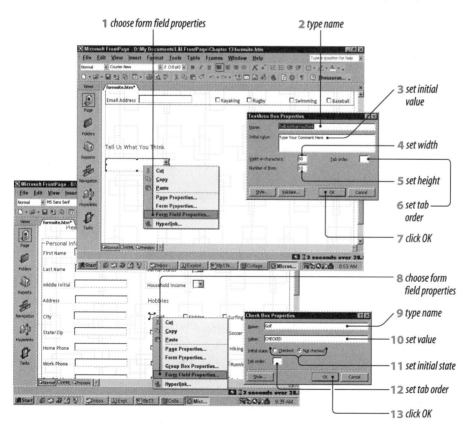

1 *choose form field properties*

2 *type name*

3 *set initial value*

4 *set width*

5 *set height*

6 *set tab order*

7 *click OK*

8 *choose form field properties*

9 *type name*

10 *set value*

11 *set initial state*

12 *set tab order*

13 *click OK*

9 type name

Type a name in the **Name** box; this name appears in the form results.

10 set value

Type a value, such as **CHECKED**, to associate with the checkbox. If the visitor selects the checkbox, this value appears in the form results file.

11 set initial state

Specify whether the checkbox should be checked or unchecked by default when the form opens in the visitor's browser.

12 set tab order (optional)

If establishing a custom tab order, specify the checkbox's position in that order.

13 click OK

Click **OK** to apply your settings.

14 choose form field properties

Right-click the drop-down list whose properties you want to set and choose **Form Field Properties.** The **Drop Down Box Properties** dialog box opens.

15 type name

Type a name in the **Name** box, this name helps you locate the data from this list in the form results.

16 click add

Click **Add** to add an option to the drop-down list that site visitors can then select.

tip You can make your first option in the list a command, such as **Select an Option.** This option appears in the visitor's browser by default.

17 type choice

In the **Choice** field of the **Add Choice** dialog box, type an option to appear in the drop-down menu.

tip What you type in the **Choice** field is, by default, what appears in the form results if the site visitor selects that option. To specify a different value for the form results, select the **Specify Value** checkbox and type the value you prefer in the accompanying textbox.

18 set initial state

Choose **Selected** if you want this option selected in the list by default or **Not Selected** if you don't.

tip Unless you specify otherwise, the first item in your list of options appears in the drop-down list by default.

19 click OK

Click **OK** to add the choice to your list. Repeat steps 16–19 until you've added all the options you want to your drop-down list.

tip Change the order of the options in your drop-down list by selecting an option you want to move and clicking **Move Up** or **Move Down**.

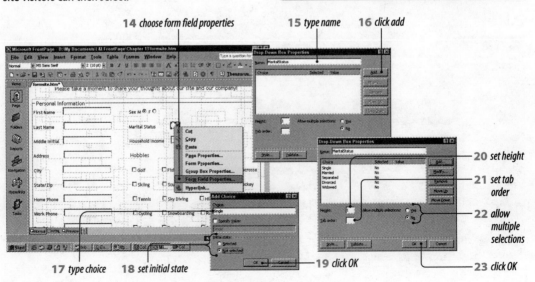

14 *choose form field properties*　　**15** *type name*　**16** *click add*

20 *set height*
21 *set tab order*
22 *allow multiple selections*
23 *click OK*

17 *type choice*　**18** *set initial state*　**19** *click OK*

20 set height

Usually, drop-down boxes require site visitors to click the down-arrow button next to the box to view its options. You can, however, make it so that the contents of the drop-down box are completely visible on the form by default. Type the number of choices in the list in the **Height** field to display the list in full.

21 set tab order (optional)

If establishing a custom tab order, specify the drop-down box's position in that order.

22 allow multiple selections

Click **Yes** or **No** in the **Allow multiple selections** area to allow multiple menu choices.

23 click OK

Click **OK** to apply your settings.

24 choose advanced button properties

Right-click the advanced button whose properties you want to set and choose **Advanced Button Properties.**

25 type name

This name appears in the form results.

26 set value

Type the text that you want to appear on the button in the **Value** field.

27 specify button type

Choose **Normal, Submit,** or **Reset** from the **Button type** drop-down list.

> *tip* If you select the **Normal** option, you probably need to write a *script* to be associated with the button in order for the button to function correctly.

28 set tab order (optional)

If establishing a custom tab order, specify the advanced button's position in that order.

29 set button size

Set the width and height of the button, in pixels.

> *tip* The size of the button adjusts automatically to fit the text you type in the **Value** field (step 26); for this reason, it may be counterproductive to adjust the button size unless you have a good reason to do so.

30 click OK

Click **OK** to apply your settings.

> *tip* If you need to delete a form field, click the field to select it, and then press the **Delete** key on your keyboard.

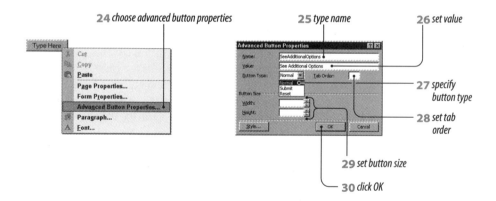

24 *choose advanced button properties* **25** *type name* **26** *set value*

27 *specify button type*

28 *set tab order*

29 *set button size*

30 *click OK*

Selection Options

Normally, visitors must click a checkbox to select or deselect it. If you also want visitors to be able to select or deselect a checkbox by clicking its label, select the label text and the checkbox and choose

Insert➡Form➡Label. (This also applies to option buttons.)

To designate one letter in the label as a *keyboard shortcut*, allowing the viewer to press **alt+the letter you**

specify to select or deselect the field, select the letter and then click the **Underline** toolbar button. (You must have taken the steps outlined in the preceding paragraph before you can assign a keyboard shortcut.)

The Form Field Validation Dialog Boxes

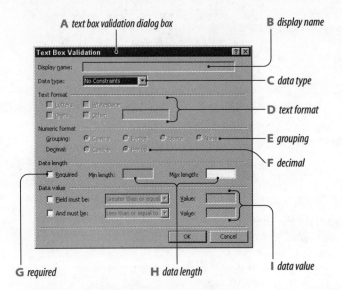

A *text box validation dialog box*

B *display name*

C *data type*

D *text format*

E *grouping*

F *decimal*

G *required*

H *data length*

I *data value*

The textbox, text area, option button, and drop-down box fields let you set rules for *data entry*. These rules, which vary from form element to form element, include the ability to specify what types of characters a visitor may enter in the field, the length of the character string, parameters for any values entered, and whether visitors are required to fill in the field.

A text box validation dialog box

Set the data-entry rules for textboxes and text areas.

B display name

If a visitor tries to submit a form without filling in a certain field, he or she may, depending on the rules you set, receive a warning message. That message instructs the visitor to fill in the field; the name you enter in the **Display name** box is the name the warning message uses to identify the field.

> *tip* This field is grayed out unless you choose a data type from the **Data type** drop-down list (C). If you choose the **Text** data type, you must also check one of the **Text format** checkboxes to activate the **Display name** field.

C data type

Specify the type of data you want the text field to contain. Your options are **No Constraints, Text, Integer,** and **Number.**

D text format

Specify whether you want the text field to allow letters, digits, whitespace (such as tabs, spaces, and carriage returns), or other characters (such as commas or hyphens) by checking the checkboxes in the **Text format** area. (The **Text format** area is grayed out unless you choose the **Text** option in the **Data type** drop-down list.)

E grouping

Specify whether numbers or integers are grouped using a comma (123,456,789), a period (123.456.789), a space (123 456 789) or nothing at all (123456789). (The **Grouping** option buttons are grayed out unless you choose the **Integer** or **Number** option in the **Data type** drop-down list.)

F decimal

Specify whether to represent a number's decimal point by a comma or a period. (The **Decimal** option buttons are grayed unless you choose the **Number** option in the **Data type** drop-down list.)

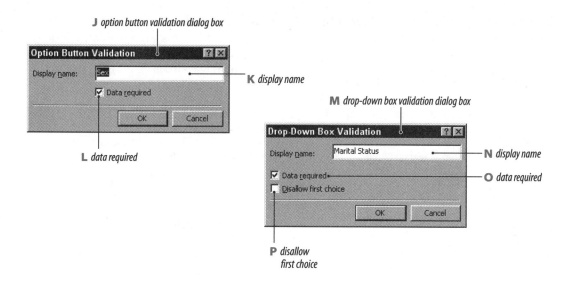

J *option button validation dialog box*

K *display name*

L *data required*

M *drop-down box validation dialog box*

N *display name*

O *data required*

P *disallow first choice*

G required

To require visitors to fill in the text field, check the **Required** checkbox.

H data length

Set a minimum and maximum length for the character string in the text field.

I data value

Specify a *value constraint* in the **Data value** area. When you set up a value constraint, your form performs numerical or alphabetical comparisons using the conditions you specify.

> *tip* A value constraint limits the available acceptable input for a field. For example, to specify that visitors may not enter a number less than 1865, you select **Greater than or equal to** in the drop-down box and type **1865** in the **Value** box.

J option button validation dialog box

Set the data-entry rules for option buttons.

K display name

The name you enter in the **Display name** box refers to the group of option buttons; the name also appears in

warning messages instructing visitors that they must make a selection from the group. Visitors only get such a message if the **Data required** checkbox (L) is checked.

L data required

Specify that users must select one of the option buttons in the group before submitting the form.

M drop-down box validation dialog box

Set the data-entry rules for drop-down boxes.

N display name

The **Display name** box works like the same-named box in the **Text Box Validation** dialog box (A).

O data required

Specify that users must select one of the options in the drop-down list before submitting the form.

P disallow first choice

Select this option if the first entry in your drop-down list, which appears by default, offers an instruction to site visitors, such as **Choose an item.** That way, users must select an option other than the instruction to submit the form.

Set Rules For Data Entry

You use a **Validation** dialog box to set data-entry rules for textboxes, text areas, option buttons, and drop-down lists.

1 choose form field properties
Right-click the textbox or text area for which you want to establish rules and choose **Form Field Properties**.

2 click validate
The **Text Box Validation** dialog box opens.

3 select data type
Open the **Data type** drop-down list and choose **No Constraints, Text, Integer,** or **Number.** (If you choose **No Constraints,** skip to step 8.)

4 set text format
If you chose **Text** in step 3, specify whether the field allows letters, digits, whitespace, or other characters.

5 set grouping
If you chose **Integer** or **Number** in step 3, specify whether numbers or integers should be grouped by commas, periods, spaces, or nothing.

6 set decimal
If you chose **Number** in step 3, specify whether to represent decimal places with commas or periods. (If you chose **Comma** or **Period** in the Grouping area, you can't select **Comma** here.)

7 type display name
If you chose **Text, Integer,** or **Number** in step 3, type a name for the field for warning messages sent to visitors if they neglect to fill in the field.

8 check required (optional)
Check to require visitors to fill in this field.

9 set data length
Specify the minimum and maximum lengths of the text string entered by the visitor. (You can set a maximum length for the visitor's text string even if the field isn't required.)

10 set data constraints (optional)
Check the **Field must be** checkbox and choose an option in the drop-down box. Then type the value constraint in the **Value** field. To set a second value

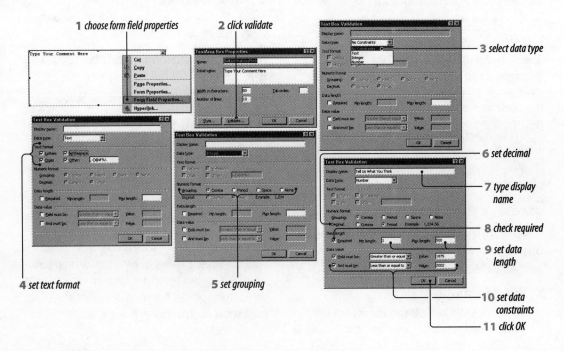

1 *choose form field properties*   2 *click validate*   3 *select data type*

4 *set text format*   5 *set grouping*

6 *set decimal*

7 *type display name*

8 *check required*

9 *set data length*

10 *set data constraints*

11 *click OK*

constraint, check the **And must be** checkbox and set the drop-down list box and **Value** field as needed.

11 click OK
Click **OK** to apply your settings.

12 choose form field properties
Right-click the option button for which you want to establish rules and choose **Form Field Properties.**

13 click validate
In the **Option Button Properties** dialog box, click the **Validate** button.

14 check data required (optional)
Require users to select an option from the group before submitting the form by checking the **Data required** checkbox.

15 type name
If you check the **Data required** checkbox, type a name in the **Display name** field for warning messages instructing visitors to make a selection from the group of option buttons, and then click OK.

16 choose form field properties
Right-click the drop-down list for which you want to establish rules and choose **Form Field Properties.**

17 click validate
In the **Drop-Down Box Properties** dialog box, click the **Validate** button.

18 check data required (optional)
To require users to select an option from the list, check the **Data required** checkbox.

19 type name
If you check the **Data required** checkbox, type a name in the **Display name** field to appear in warning messages instructing visitors that they must make a selection from the drop-down list.

20 disallow first choice (optional)
If the first option in your drop-down list contains instructions, such as **Choose an item,** check the **Disallow first choice** checkbox to require users to select a different option to submit the form.

21 click OK
Click **OK** to apply your settings.

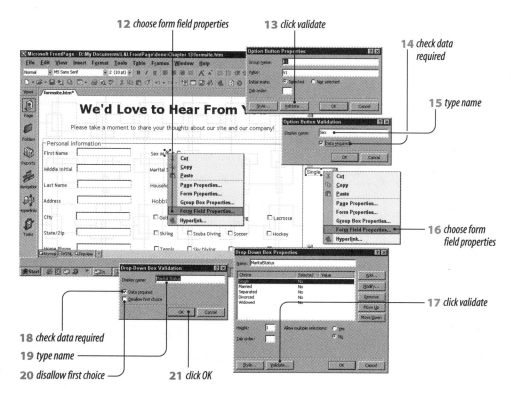

12 choose form field properties
13 click validate
14 check data required
15 type name
16 choose form field properties
17 click validate
18 check data required
19 type name
20 disallow first choice
21 click OK

Title ☐ ▼ ● Region

(13) **Build Forms:** Set Rules For Data Entry

Build Forms: Set Rules For Data Entry   **249**

Form Properties & Saving Results Dialog Boxes

After you establish rules for data entry, you must tell FrontPage how to collect and display data in your forms. FrontPage lets you save form data in text files, e-mail messages, and databases, or you can use custom scripts to handle the data.

A form properties dialog box
Specify how your form should handle input data and other properties here.

B send to
Store your form results in a file or have them sent to you by e-mail.

C file name
Specify the text or HTML file in which data should be saved. A form results file, **form_results.csv**, is automatically saved in your Web's **_private** folder when you create a form page; click Browse and locate it.

D e-mail address
If you want form results sent to you via e-mail, type the e-mail address here.

E send to database
Store form results in the Microsoft Access database of your choosing (click the Options button to locate the database file).

> *tip* When you save results to a database, file, or e-mail message, FrontPage uses *form handlers* to handle form input. To use these form handlers, the Web server hosting your site must have **FrontPage Server Extensions** or **SharePoint Team Services** installed.

F send to other
Use your own custom scripts to handle form results. Alternatively, you can choose to handle data using either the Registration or Discussion form handler, which are helpful for pages that allow visitors to register with your site or conduct discussion groups.

G form name
Type the name of the form.

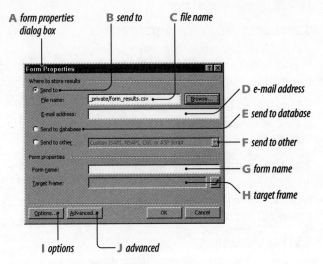

A *form properties dialog box* B *send to* C *file name*

D *e-mail address*

E *send to database*

F *send to other*

G *form name*

H *target frame*

I *options*   J *advanced*

H target frame
Specify the frame in which form results appear, such as in a confirmation page.

I options
Configure the selected form handler.

J advanced
Create or modify hidden fields.

> *tip* Consider adding a *hidden field* to a form if you have multiple forms whose results are saved to the same file. Then, you can assign each form a unique number, and place that number in a hidden field in each form. When you receive results from the form, they contain the information from the hidden field so that you can determine which form was used to gather the information.

K saving results dialog box
Specify settings for results saved to a file or an e-mail message, and for confirmation pages.

L file results tab
Set preferences for results sent to a file.

M file name
Specify the file in which results should be saved.

N file format
Set the results file's format.

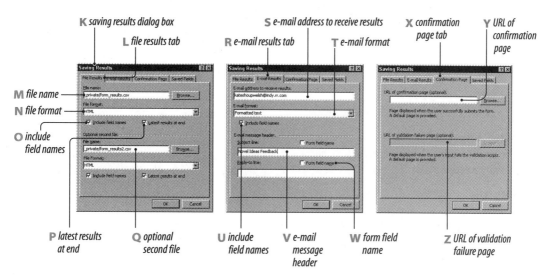

K *saving results dialog box*

L *file results tab*

M *file name*

N *file format*

O *include field names*

P *latest results at end*

Q *optional second file*

R *e-mail results tab*

S *e-mail address to receive results*

T *e-mail format*

U *include field names*

V *e-mail message header*

W *form field name*

X *confirmation page tab*

Y *URL of confirmation page*

Z *URL of validation failure page*

O include field names
Specify whether the results file includes field names *and* input provided by the site visitor.

P latest results at end
Place newest results at the bottom of the file.

Q optional second file
Enter a file name, format, and other options to send results to a second file.

R e-mail results tab
Set preferences for results being sent via e-mail.

S e-mail address to receive results
Enter the address to which results are sent.

T e-mail format
Specify the e-mail message's file format.

U include field names
Specify whether the results e-mail includes field names *and* input provided by the site visitor.

V e-mail message header
Type the text you want to appear in the results message's subject and reply-to (sender) lines.

W form field name
Display the results from a particular field in the e-mail message's **Subject** or **Reply to** line (type the field's name in the textbox).

X confirmation page tab
Set preferences for a *confirmation page*.

Y url of confirmation page
Enter the path of the confirmation page you want to display to visitors after they submit a form; click **Browse** to locate the page on your Web.

Z url of validation failure page
Display a *validation failure page* if any field in your form isn't filled in correctly; type the address or click **Browse** to locate the page.

The Saved Fields Tab

The Saving Results box's **Saved Fields** tab lets you select the form fields whose results you want displayed in your file or e-mail, the order in which you want them to appear, and more.

⟨steps⟩ **Port Form Data To A File**

If your Web is a simple one, transferring, or *porting*, data that users enter in a form to a file in your Web (the default method for storing such data) is probably adequate for your needs.

1 choose form properties
Right-click the form, and choose **Form Properties**.

2 select send to
Click the **Send to** option button at the top of the **Form Properties** dialog box.

3 type file name
FrontPage automatically saves a form results file, **form_results.csv**, in your Web's **_private** folder when you create a form page; this name appears in the **File name** box by default (simply add it if it doesn't).

4 click options button
Click the **Options** button to open the **Saving Results** dialog box. (The file name you entered in step 3 appears in the **File Results** tab of the **Saving Results** dialog box by default.)

5 choose file format
In the **File Results** tab, choose a file format from the **File format** drop-down list.

6 include field names
Check **Include field names** so the results file shows field names alongside input provided by site visitors.

7 place latest results at end
Check **Latest results at end** to place the newest results at the bottom of the file.

> *tip* You can't uncheck this option if you opted to port form results to a text file.

8 set up second file (optional)
You can port form data to two separate files; set the second file's name, format, and other options just as you did for the first file.

> *tip* If you type a name for a file that doesn't exist, FrontPage creates the file the first time the form is submitted.

9 click OK
Click **OK** once to close the **Saving Results** dialog box, and again to close the **Form Properties** dialog box.

1 *choose form properties*

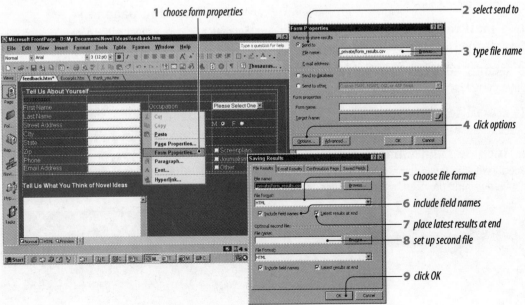

2 *select send to*

3 *type file name*

4 *click options*

5 *choose file format*

6 *include field names*

7 *place latest results at end*

8 *set up second file*

9 *click OK*

You don't have to set up a file for storing form data; instead, you can have form results e-mailed directly to you each time a visitor submits a form. This method of retrieving form data is especially useful for feedback forms because you can quickly and easily respond to visitor feedback via e-mail.

> 📌 You must publish your Web to a Web server with **FrontPage Server Extensions** or **SharePoint Team Services** installed before setting up your Web to port form data to you via e-mail. Chapter 14, Publish A Web, tells you how to get your Web to a server.

1 choose form properties
Right-click the form and choose **Form Properties**.

2 select send to
Click the **Send to** option button at the top of the **Form Properties** dialog box.

3 clear file name field
Unless you want form data ported to a file as well as sent to you via e-mail, delete the contents of the **File name** box.

4 type e-mail address
Type the address you want form data sent to.

5 click options button
Click the **Options** button to open the **Saving Results** dialog box.

6 click e-mail results tab
Click the **E-mail Results** tab in the **Saving Results** dialog box.

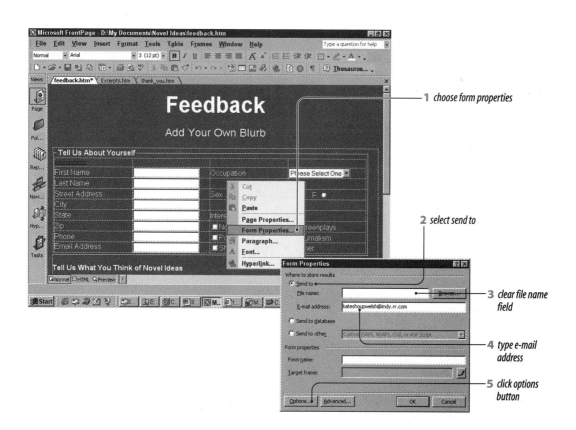

1 choose form properties

2 select send to

3 clear file name field

4 type e-mail address

5 click options button

7 **choose e-mail format**

Choose an e-mail format from the **E-mail format** drop-down list.

8 **include field names** (optional)

Check **Include field names** if you want the results file to include field names in addition to input provided by site visitors.

9 **set subject**

The subject of e-mail messages containing form data is "Form Results" by default. To change the subject, type the text that you want to appear.

10 **set reply-to line** (optional)

If you want a specific e-mail address to appear in the Reply-to line, type it here.

6 click e-mail results tab

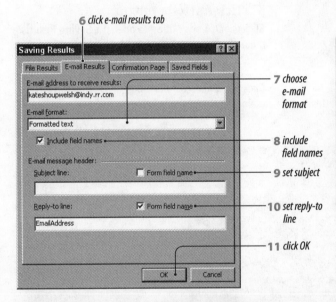

7 choose e-mail format

8 include field names

9 set subject

10 set reply-to line

11 click OK

11 **click OK**

Click **OK** once to close the **Saving Results** dialog box, and again to close the **Form Properties** dialog box.

Send Form Data To A Database

You may decide that you want to store the information you collect from site visitors in a database. If so, you have a few options. If you've already created the database you want to use to store form information, use the Database Interface wizard to create a form using the fields in the database. (Start this wizard from the **Web Page Template** dialog box.)

Alternatively, if the database you created is *ODBC compliant*, you can create your form page as outlined in this chapter, but configure it to port data directly to the database when a visitor submits a form. For information on doing so, consult Microsoft FrontPage Help.

Finally, if you haven't yet created the database, you can use FrontPage to create one to store form results. To do so, select the **Send to database** option in the form's **Form Properties** dialog box, and then click **Options**.

In the Database Results tab of the **Options for Saving Results to Database** dialog box, click the **Create Database** button. FrontPage creates an Access database, then displays a confirmation message listing the database's name and location. Click **OK** to close the confirmation message, **OK** to close the **Options for Saving Results to Database** dialog box, and **OK** to close the **Form Properties** dialog box.

Create A Confirmation Page

Many Web sites display a *confirmation page* to visitors after they submit a form to confirm the selections made in the form. Although FrontPage displays a default confirmation page automatically, you can create your own. Before you start, write down the display names of all the fields in your form whose input you want the visitor to confirm. This section outlines creating a confirmation page for a Web whose form results are stored in a file or sent via e-mail.

1 create page

On a new page in your Web, add content, such as a page header and a brief message thanking visitors for submitting their input. Format the page as desired.

2 choose web component

Click in the spot on your page where you want the confirmation information to appear and choose **Insert➥Web Component** to open the **Insert Web Component** dialog box.

3 choose advanced controls

In the left-hand pane of the **Insert Web Component** dialog box, choose **Advanced Controls**.

4 choose confirmation field

In the right-hand pane of the **Insert Web Component** dialog box, choose **Confirmation Field**.

5 click finish

Click **Finish** to close the **Insert Web Component** dialog box and open the **Confirmation Field Properties** dialog box.

6 type name

Type the name of the first form field whose input you want to confirm. This name must match the name you typed in the **Name** box in the form field's **Properties** dialog box.

7 click OK

Click **OK** to add the confirmation field to your page.

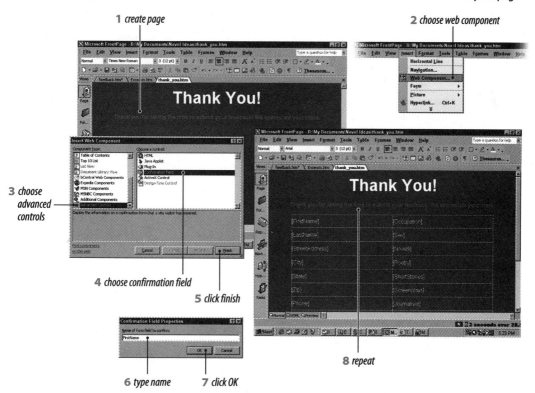

1 *create page*

2 *choose web component*

3 *choose advanced controls*

4 *choose confirmation field*

5 *click finish*

6 *type name*

7 *click OK*

8 *repeat*

> **tip** Format the confirmation field just as you would any other text.

8 repeat
Repeat steps 2–7 for each confirmation field you want to add.

9 save page
Choose **File→Save As.** In the **Save As** dialog box, type a name for the confirmation-page file and place it in the folder for your Web; then click the **Save** button.

10 choose form properties
Open the page containing the form whose results appear in the confirmation page you just created; right-click the form and choose **Form Properties.**

11 choose send to
Make sure the **Send to** option in the **Form Properties** dialog box is selected.

12 click options
Click the **Options** button to open the **Saving Results** dialog box.

13 click confirmation page tab
Click the **Confirmation** tab in the **Saving Results** dialog box.

14 enter page address
Enter the name and location of the confirmation page you just created. If you're not sure of its address, click the **Browse** button to locate it.

15 click OK
Click **OK** to close the **Saving Results** dialog box, and again to close the **Form Properties** dialog box.

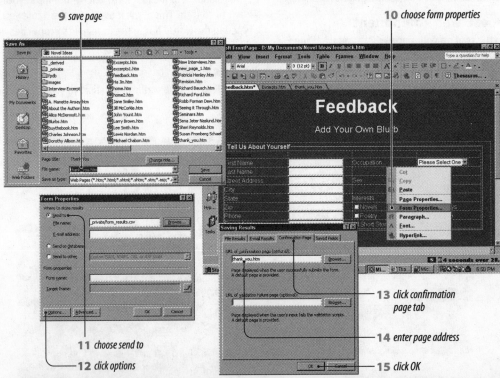

9 *save page*

10 *choose form properties*

13 *click confirmation page tab*

14 *enter page address*

11 *choose send to*

12 *click options*

15 *click OK*

Confirm Database Input

If you plan to save your form results in a database, select the **Send to database** option button in the **Form** Properties dialog box before clicking the **Options** button. The **Options for Saving Results to Database** dialog box opens; in the **Database Results** tab, type the location of the confirmation page.

chapter 14

Publish A Web

When you finish building your Web, and you're ready for people on the Internet to visit it, you must copy the files that comprise the Web to a Web server, or *publish* it.

Before you publish your Web, check your site for broken hyperlinks or other problems, and make sure the pages look the way you want them to. (See The Site Summary Report on page 258 to find out how to check your links and preview your site.) Then, locate an Internet service provider—preferably one whose Web servers have **Microsoft FrontPage Server Extensions 2002** installed—to "host" your site. (Make sure you get the server's Internet address, plus your username and password, if necessary.) FrontPage Server Extensions 2002 are an absolute must if your site includes any dynamic elements, such as forms, Web components, and the like.

Depending on whether the server you publish to has the server extensions installed, you can use either FTP or HTTP to get your site on the Internet. After you publish your Web, FrontPage maintains all its links, theme information, shared borders, and so on.

The Site Summary Report

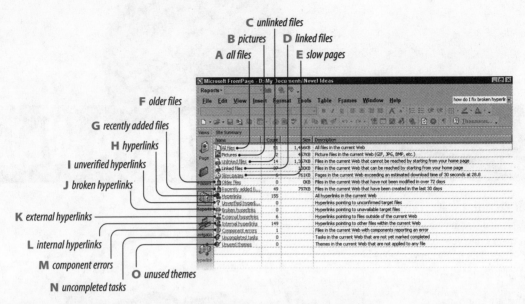

C unlinked files
B pictures
A all files
D linked files
E slow pages

F older files
G recently added files
H hyperlinks
I unverified hyperlinks
J broken hyperlinks
K external hyperlinks
L internal hyperlinks
M component errors
N uncompleted tasks
O unused themes

The **Site Summary report** lets you see the status of the components of your Web, and link to more details about them. To view the report, choose **View➥Reports➥Site Summary.**

A all files

View a summary of all the files in your Web, including name, size, type, date last modified, and more.

B pictures

Tells the number of picture files in your Web.

C unlinked files

Tracks the number of files that can't be reached by users starting at your Web's home page.

D linked files

Tracks files that can be reached via the home page.

E slow pages

Lists pages that exceed an estimated download time of 30 seconds over a 28.8Kbps modem.

F older files

Lists files that haven't been altered in more than 72 days.

G recently added files

Lists files that have been added within the past 30 days.

H hyperlinks

Lists the total number of hyperlinks in your Web.

I unverified hyperlinks

Lists links that point to unconfirmed files.

J broken hyperlinks

Lists links to unavailable or non-existent files.

K external hyperlinks

Lists links that point to files outside your Web.

L internal hyperlinks

Lists links that point to files within your Web.

M component errors

Lists files on your Web that have at least one component reporting an error.

N uncompleted tasks

Lists tasks in your Web that aren't yet marked completed. (You create *tasks* to keep track of what needs to be done on your site; see Chapter 15, Manage A Web.)

O unused themes

Lists any themes you apply to your Web that haven't been used in any files in the Web.

The Publish Web Dialog Box

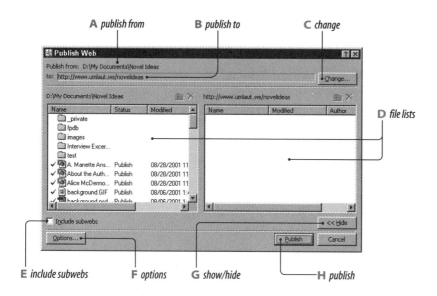

A *publish from*   **B** *publish to*   **C** *change*

D *file lists*

E *include subwebs*   **F** *options*   **G** *show/hide*   **H** *publish*

Using the **Publish Web** dialog box, you specify the Web source, destination, and more.

A publish from
Indicates the directory on your computer that contains the Web you want to publish.

B publish to
Points to the server and folder in which you plan to publish your Web.

C change
Click the **Change** button to enter a different publishing destination.

D file lists
View the files you're about to copy to the server in the left-hand file list. After you copy the files, they appear in the pane on the right.

E include subwebs
Check this checkbox to include subwebs when you publish your Web. (A *subweb* is a complete FrontPage Web that exists within another Web.)

F options
Click this button to open a dialog box (I though N) that lets you specify which pages in your Web you want to publish.

G show/hide
This button toggles between **Show** and **Hide;** click it to display or hide a pane containing a list of files and folders on the server you are publishing to.

H publish
Click this button to publish your Web to the server you specify.

I changed pages only
Publish only the pages that have changed since the last time your Web was published.

J all pages
The **All pages, overwriting pages already on destination** option button lets you publish all the files on your Web.

> *tip* When publishing your Web, you can specify that certain pages not be published; if you do, those pages aren't published when you select **Changed pages only** or **All pages, overwriting pages already on destination**, even if the pages have been changed since the last time the Web was published.

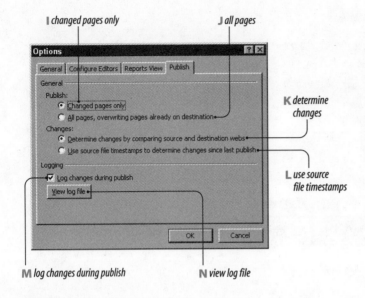

I *changed pages only*

J *all pages*

K *determine changes*

L *use source file timestamps*

M *log changes during publish*

N *view log file*

determine which pages were changed by comparing the files on the server with the files on your computer.

L use source file timestamps

With the **Use source file timestamps to determine changes since last publish** option button, FrontPage determines which pages were changed by using *source file timestamps*.

M log changes during publish

FrontPage creates a *log file* to log changes made during the publishing process.

K determine changes

The **Determine changes by comparing source and destination webs** option button lets FrontPage

N view log file

View the log file generated by FrontPage (M).

Web Hosting Services & Domain Names

Before you can publish your Web, you must locate a Web-hosting service, also called a *Web provider*. If you don't require much in the way of support or add-ons, such as video-streaming capabilities, you find companies to host your site free of charge or for a nominal monthly fee. If, however, you want to reach tech support 24/7, and you require substantial add-ons, you need to spend some money to have your site hosted. In any case, make sure the hosting company you select supports all the features of FrontPage 2002. Microsoft makes it easy to find such Web hosting services; simply visit http://www.microsoftwpp.com/ to locate one. Another good source for locating hosting services is CNET (visit www.cnet.com, and, under **Internet Services** in the list of CNET services, click **Web Hosting**).

After you find a Web provider, it's time to register a domain name for your site. A *domain name* is the part of your URL that identifies your site—for example, in the URL www.yoursite.com, *yoursite.com* is the domain

name. Several companies, called *registrars,* help you register domain names, the most popular and venerable of which is Network Solutions (www.networksolutions.com). Before you can register a domain name, however, you must make sure that someone else hasn't already registered it. Most registrars contain a search feature to help you find out if a name is available. Be flexible; many domain names have already been taken, so you may need to think up some alternatives.

After you find an available domain name, register it. Depending on which registrar you choose, it can cost anywhere from $30 to $60 per year to register your domain name (note that for some of the cheaper services, you must agree to display ads on your Web pages). When you register your domain name, you supply the registrar with your Web provider's domain name servers and their IP addresses. That way, when people type your Web address in their browser, they are directed to the server hosting your site.

Publish To A Server

If the server that you have selected to host your site has **Microsoft FrontPage Server Extensions 2002** or **SharePoint Team Services** installed, you can use FrontPage to publish your Web via *Hypertext Transfer Protocol* (HTTP), the underlying protocol of the World Wide Web. Otherwise, you can use FrontPage to publish your Web via *File Transfer Protocol* (FTP).

In either case, you should obtain the server name, your username, and your password from the Web hosting company before you begin the process of publishing your site. You must be connected to the Internet in order to complete this task.

1 choose publish web
Open the Web you want to publish and choose **File➡ Publish Web.** The **Publish Destination** dialog box opens.

> *tip* If the **Publish Destination** dialog box doesn't open, the Web has been published already; instead, you see a Web server's location in the top-left corner of the **Publish Web** dialog box. To specify a different server, click the **Change** button in the **Publish Web** dialog box to open the **Publish Destination** box. Then type the new server's location.

2 enter publish destination
Type the path to your host server. (You get this path from the service provider.)

3 click OK
Click **OK** to close the **Publish Destination** dialog box.

4 enter username & password
Type your username and password, and, if necessary, the network domain name assigned to your account (check with your Web-hosting service for more information).

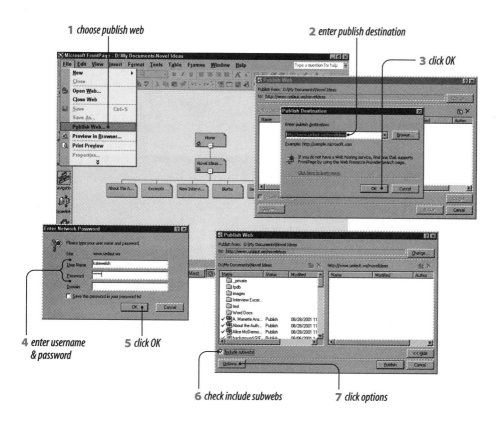

1 *choose publish web*　　**2** *enter publish destination*　　**3** *click OK*

4 *enter username & password*　　**5** *click OK*

6 *check include subwebs*　　**7** *click options*

5 click OK

Click **OK** to close the **Enter Network Password** dialog box. The **Publish Web** dialog box opens.

6 check include subwebs (optional)

Check the **Include subwebs** checkbox if you want to include *subwebs* (any complete FrontPage Webs that exist within your primary Web) when you publish your Web.

7 click options

Click this button to open the **Options** dialog box, where you can specify which pages in your Web you want to publish.

8 click publish tab

If it isn't already displayed, click the **Publish** tab.

9 select pages

Choose **Changed pages only** to publish only pages that have changed since the last time your Web was

published; choose **All pages, overwriting pages already on destination** to publish all files on the Web.

10 detect changes (optional)

If you chose **Changed pages only** in step 9, specify how FrontPage should determine which pages have been changed since you last published your Web— by comparing files on the server with files on your computer or by using file timestamps—by choosing the appropriate radio button under **Changes.**

11 click OK

Click **OK** to close the **Options** dialog box. The **Publish Web** dialog box reappears.

12 click publish

Click **Publish** to publish your Web to the server.

13 view file transfer

A file-transfer dialog box keeps you apprised of the progress of the file transfer. (Depending on the size of your Web, the file transfer could take some time.)

14 click done

Click **Done** to complete the publishing process.

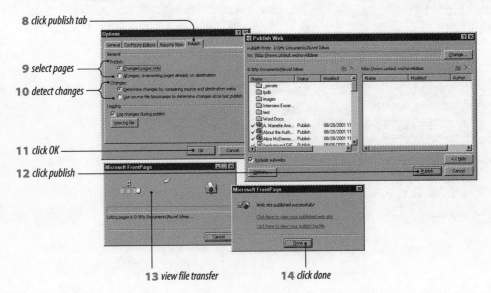

8 *click publish tab*

9 *select pages*

10 *detect changes*

11 *click OK*

12 *click publish*

13 *view file transfer*

14 *click done*

Publish A Backup Web

A *backup* of your Web comes in handy when disasters occur; if something happens to the files on your computer or the Web server, you can easily get your site up and running again. To create a backup of your Web, you can publish the pages to your computer or network, a process that resembles publishing a Web to a Web server. By publishing, rather than simply copying, your Web, you ensure that your Web's structure is maintained.

> **tip** For all the FrontPage components in your Web site to work properly on your computer, you have to set up your computer as a server with **FrontPage Server Extensions 2002** or **SharePoint Team Services** installed.

1 choose publish web

With the Web open that you want to publish, choose **File→Publish Web.** The **Publish Destination** dialog box opens.

> **tip** If the **Publish Destination** dialog box doesn't open, it's because the Web has been published already; you see a Web server's location in the top-left corner of the **Publish Web** dialog box. To specify a different location, click the **Change** button in the **Publish Web** dialog box to open the **Publish Destination** dialog box, and then type the new location.

2 enter publish destination

Type the path to the folder on your computer or network where you want to store the backup of your site.

> **tip** If you're not sure of the exact path of the folder where you want to create a backup of your Web, click the **Browse** button to locate it.

3 click OK

Click **OK** to close the **Publish Destination** dialog box.

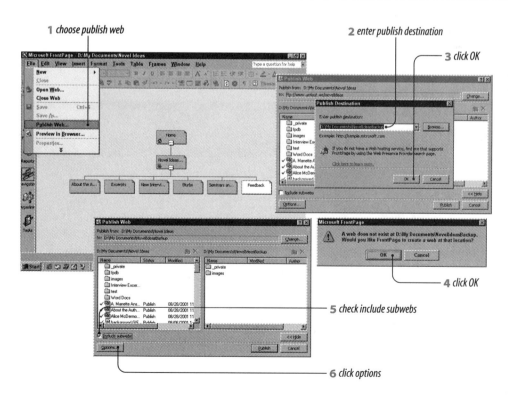

1 *choose publish web*

2 *enter publish destination*

3 *click OK*

4 *click OK*

5 *check include subwebs*

6 *click options*

4 click OK

If a Web doesn't currently exist at the location you've specified, click **OK** in the alert window that appears to create one.

5 check include subwebs (optional)

The Publish Web dialog box opens. (Click the **Show** button to view it in its entirety; this button toggles between Show and Hide.) Check the **Include subwebs** checkbox if you want to include *subwebs* (any complete FrontPage Webs that exist within your primary Web) when you publish your Web.

6 click options

Click **Options** to open the **Options** dialog box, where you can specify which pages in your Web you want to publish.

7 click publish tab

Click the **Publish** tab to specify what pages you want to publish.

8 select pages

Choose **Changed pages only** to publish only the pages that have changed since the last time your Web was published; alternatively, choose **All pages,**

overwriting pages already on destination to publish all files on your Web.

9 detect changes (optional)

If you chose **Changed pages only** in step 8, you must specify how FrontPage should determine which pages have been changed since you last published your Web by choosing the appropriate radio button under **Changes.**

10 click OK

Click **OK** to close the **Options** dialog box.

11 click publish

Click **Publish** to publish your Web to the specified server.

12 view file transfer

A file-transfer dialog box keeps you apprised of the progress of the file transfer. (Depending on the size of your Web, this could take some time.)

13 click done

Click the **Done** button to complete the publishing process.

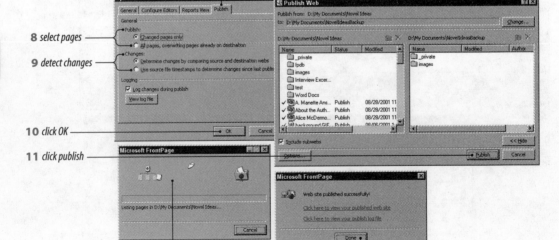

7 *click publish tab*

8 *select pages*

9 *detect changes*

10 *click OK*

11 *click publish*

12 *view file transfer*

13 *click done*

Manage A Web

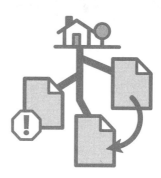

You've built your Web site and published it to the Internet; you may think your work is done at this point.

Alas, depending on what type of Web site you've created, there's a good chance that you need to perform some *Web site maintenance* from time to time—for example, you may need to update your site's content, monitor the site's usage, and more.

Fortunately, FrontPage 2002 provides several tools to aid you in managing your site. For example, FrontPage's extensive *reporting* features help you track site usage, view broken hyperlinks, and more. And using FrontPage's Task view, you can assign Web-management tasks to various people, and quickly determine what work remains to be done.

Finally, using FrontPage, you can embed keywords into your Web pages and register your site with search engines on the Internet, thus allowing people surfing the Web to locate your site.

Reports View

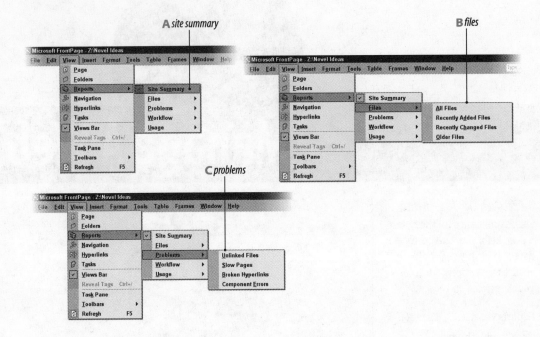

A *site summary*

B *files*

C *problems*

Using FrontPage reports, you can quickly and easily assess the state of your Web site. For example, you can monitor site usage, view a Web site summary, detect maintenance problems, and manage workflow. FrontPage gives you many report options; you access all the reports by choosing submenu entries from the **View→Reports** command.

A **site summary**

The **Site Summary report** lets you see, at a glance, the status of the components of your Web, such as the number of files, hyperlinks, and so on, and allows you to quickly link to more details about those site components.

The Site Summary report is covered in more detail on page 258 in The Site Summary Report.

B **files**

The **Files** submenu displays reports regarding the status of files in your Web—how old the files are, when they were modified, and the like. Options in the submenu include **All Files, Recently Added**

Files, Recently Changed Files, and **Older Files;** all of these options, with the exception of the Recently Changed Files report, are accessible via the Site Summary report (A).

C **problems**

The **Problems** submenu displays reports regarding problems in your Web, including slow-loading pages, component errors, and broken links. Options in the submenu include **Unlinked Files, Slow Pages, Broken Hyperlinks,** and **Component Errors.**

Learn more about using the reports in the **Problems** submenu to troubleshoot your Web in Troubleshoot Your Web on page 268. You can also turn to page 144, Fix Broken Links, for help on fixing any broken links you may find.

D **workflow**

The **Workflow** submenu displays reports regarding workflow status in your Web. If you have assigned files to certain individuals, you can

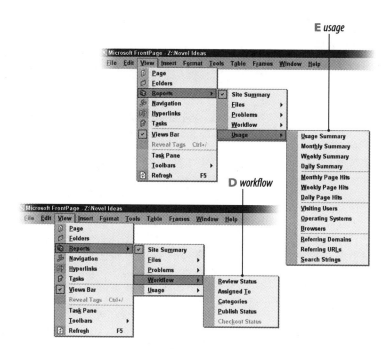

E *usage*

D *workflow*

determine who is assigned to the file, as well as whether files are checked out for use by those individuals, their review status, their publishing status, and their checkout status. Additionally, workflow reports reflect whether categories have been assigned to files. Options in the submenu include **Review Status, Assigned To, Categories, Publish Status,** and **Checkout Status.**

Learn more about workflow reports and file categories later in this chapter, in Manage Workflow on page 271.

E usage

The **Usage** submenu displays reports regarding site usage, such as page hits, the browsers used by visitors, the operating systems used by visitors, and more. Options in the submenu include **Usage Summary, Monthly Summary, Weekly Summary, Daily Summary, Monthly Page Hits, Weekly Page Hits, Daily Page Hits, Visiting Users, Operating Systems, Browsers, Referring Domains, Referring URLs,** and **Search Strings.**

Learn more about usage reports later in this chapter, in Analyze Web Usage on page 273.

The Reporting Toolbar

The Reporting toolbar helps you perform certain reports-related tasks with the click of a button. For example, click the **Reports** button to choose any report you want to generate and read. Alternatively, use the buttons on the toolbar to view a usage chart, edit a hyperlink, or verify the hyperlinks in your Web.

Troubleshoot Your Web

Using FrontPage's various **Problems reports,** you can determine whether your Web contains unlinked files, and which pages in your Web are slow to load. You can also use Problems reports to detect broken hyperlinks or component errors.

1 choose unlinked files
After you've opened the Web you want to trouble-shoot, choose **View➡Reports➡Problems➡Unlinked Files.**

2 view unlinked files report
FrontPage shows you a list of unlinked files, including information about each file such as its name, type, the date it was last modified, and more. In a perfect world, your site won't contain unlinked pages (that is, pages that aren't accessible from links elsewhere in the site) unless they are old or decommissioned. If it does, you might need to re-think your site's navigation structure and add links from other pages to the unlinked pages. (Refer to Chapter 12, Add Navigation Elements, starting on page 216, for more information.)

tip The Unlinked Files report can also be useful for identifying rogue files that hackers or otherwise bad people have put on your system.

3 choose slow pages
Choose **View➡Reports➡Problems➡Slow Pages** to open a Slow Pages report for your site.

4 view slow pages report
FrontPage shows you a list of pages it deems "slow," and includes information about each file such as its file name, file type, the date it was last modified, and more.

tip You can make slow pages faster. Open a page listed in the Slow Pages report by double-clicking it; edit it as needed to remove components, such as pictures, Web components, or other items, that slow down its loading speed.

5 choose options (optional)
If you find that FrontPage's idea of a slow page is too slow or too fast for you (FrontPage defines "slow" as

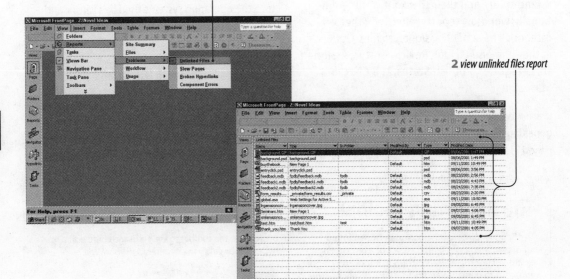

1 *choose unlinked files*

2 *view unlinked files report*

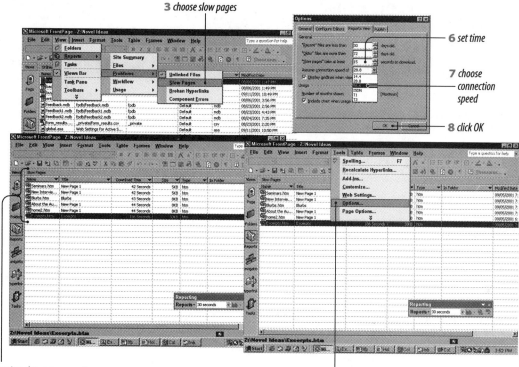

3 choose slow pages

6 set time

7 choose connection speed

8 click OK

4 view slow pages report

5 choose options

taking 30 seconds or longer to load over a 28.8Kbps modem), you can change the amount of time it takes for a page to be considered slow or change the modem speed used to calculate how long the page will take to load. To do so, choose **Tools➞Options** to open the **Options** dialog box.

6 set time (optional)
In the **Reports View** tab of the **Options** dialog box, enter the amount of time you want to use to define a slow page in the **"Slow pages" take at least** spin box.

7 choose connection speed (optional)
From the **Assume connection speed of** drop-down box, select the speed of connection you believe

most people who visit your site will use (56.6 is a safe bet).

8 click OK (optional)
Click **OK** to apply your changes.

9 choose broken hyperlinks
Choose **View➞Reports➞Problems➞Broken Hyperlinks** to view a Broken Hyperlinks report.

10 view broken hyperlinks report
This report helps you zero in on all the errant links in your Web so that you can swoop in and fix them in a flash; the list also includes information about each file, such as its file name, file type, the date it was last modified, and more.

Test Your Network Connection

Another important step in trouble-shooting your Web is making sure that your network connection is functioning properly. To do so, choose **Help➞About Microsoft**

FrontPage. Then, in the **About Microsoft FrontPage** dialog box, click the **Network Test** button. **The FrontPage TCP/IP Test** dialog box opens; click the **Start Test** button. If your

network connection is functioning properly, a box with the word "Yes" in it appears with all the entries in the dialog box. Click **Exit** and then click **OK.**

11 choose component errors

Choose **View➡Reports➡Problems➡Component Errors** to open a Component Errors report.

12 view component errors report

View the list of pages with component errors.

tip The **Errors** column contains information about the component error and how to fix it. If necessary, adjust the sizes of the other columns in the report to view the **Errors** column in full.

tip To fix a broken link, right-click it in the list of links found in the Broken Hyperlinks report and choose **Edit Hyperlink**. Enter the correct hyperlink path in the **Replace hyperlink with** field of the **Edit Hyperlink** dialog box. To replace the incorrect link in all pages, choose **Change in all pages**; to change the link only in the page or pages you've selected, select **Change in selected pages.** Finally, click the **Replace** button to apply the correct hyperlink.

9 *choose broken hyperlinks* **10** *view broken hyperlinks report*

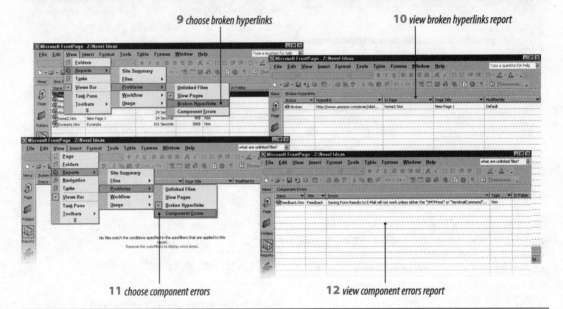

11 *choose component errors* **12** *view component errors report*

Filter Report Data

FrontPage's AutoFilter feature lets you filter reports to display only the data you wish to see. To filter report data, open the report you want to run. Then, click the down-arrow button at the top of the column that contains the item you want to filter by and choose the item from the list that appears. You can even apply multiple filters—simply select values in different columns.

To filter for rows in the report that contain specific text, for items greater than or less than another item, for items containing or not containing specific data, or the beginning or end of a text string, click the down-arrow button at the top of the column containing the text and choose (Custom). In the **Custom AutoFilter** dialog box, select the filter criterion from the drop-down box on the left; type the text you want to filter by in the box on the right. If you wish, choose And or Or and specify a second filter criterion.

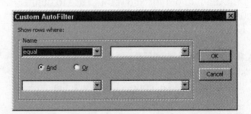

Filter settings are saved when you close the Web or FrontPage; if you want to remove them, you must do so by hand. To remove a filter from a single column (but not from the rest of the report), click the down-arrow button at the top of the column, and choose (All) from the list of options that appears. To remove all filters from a report, right-click anywhere in the report and choose Remove Filters.

 **Manage Workflow**

Using FrontPage's **Workflow reports,** you can determine which files have been reviewed by whom, how files in your site are categorized, who is responsible for each file on your site, and the site's publish status. Also, you can determine which files have been checked out by other Web authors to be edited.

1 choose review status

Open the Web whose workflow you want to manage and choose **View→Reports→Workflow→Review Status.**

2 view review status report

FrontPage shows you a list of files on your site, indicates who (if anyone) reviewed the files, and if so, whether they have been approved or denied.

> *tip* To set a file's review status, right-click it and choose **Properties.** In the **Workgroup** tab of the **Properties** dialog box, select an option from the **Review status** drop-down box and click **OK.**

3 choose assigned to

Choose **View→Reports→Workflow→Assigned To** to open an Assigned To report.

4 view assigned to report

Determine who, if anyone, is assigned to each file in your Web, when each file was assigned, and by whom.

> *tip* To assign a file, click the cell in the file's **Assigned To** column, click it a second time, and then type a name or select one from the drop-down list.

5 choose categories

Choose **View→Reports→Workflow→Categories** to open a Categories report.

6 view categories report

View the categories of the files in your Web. To set a file's category, right-click it and choose **Properties.** In the **Workgroup** tab of the **Properties** window, select a category in the **Available categories** list, and click **OK.** To add options to the **Available categories** list, click the **Categories** button, type the new option in the **New category** field, click **Add,** and click **OK.**

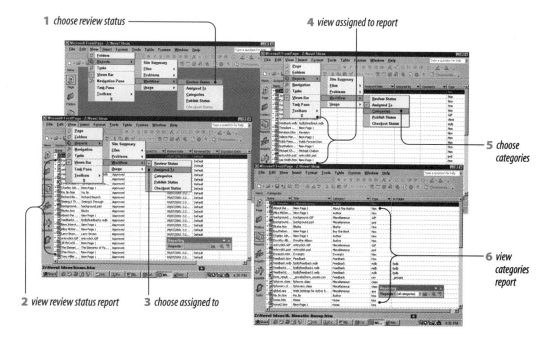

1 *choose review status*

4 *view assigned to report*

5 *choose categories*

6 *view categories report*

2 *view review status report*

3 *choose assigned to*

7 choose publish status

Choose **View**→**Reports**→**Workflow**→**Publish Status** to open a Publish Status report.

8 view publish status report

Determine which files on your Web should be published the next time you publish your Web. If there are any pages in your Web that you don't want published, click the page's entry in the **Publish** column once, and a second time; then, choose **Don't Publish** from the drop-down box that appears.) Refer to Chapter 14,

Publish A Web, for more information on getting your Web onto the Internet.)

9 choose checkout status

Choose **View**→**Reports**→**Workflow**→**Checkout Status** to open a Checkout Status report.

10 view checkout status report

Determine which files on your Web have been checked out (checked-out files are indicated by a red checkmark if they are checked out by you, or by a padlock icon if they are checked out by someone else).

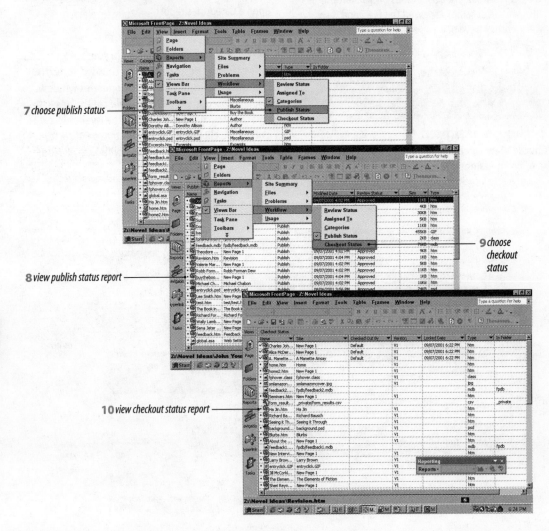

7 *choose publish status*

8 *view publish status report*

9 *choose checkout status*

10 *view checkout status report*

Analyze Web Usage

The FrontPage 2002 **Usage reports** help you quickly and easily determine how many hits your site has received, glean information about site visitors, and more. Before you can use these reports, however, you must first tell FrontPage to collect the information, how often to collect it, and how long to keep it. You must be connected to the Internet to complete this task.

1 choose administration home

After you open the Web for which you want to collect usage information, choose **Tools➡Server➡Administration Home** to open the Site Administration page in your Web browser.

2 click change usage analysis settings

In the Site Administration page, scroll to the **Configure Usage Analysis Settings** section and click the **Change usage analysis settings** link.

3 enable usage analysis

Select the **On** radio button in the **Usage Analysis** area to enable usage analysis.

4 specify recurrence settings

Specify whether usage analysis should occur on a daily, weekly, or monthly basis, and at what time. If you choose Weekly or Monthly, you must also specify the day the usage analysis should take place.

1 *choose administration home*

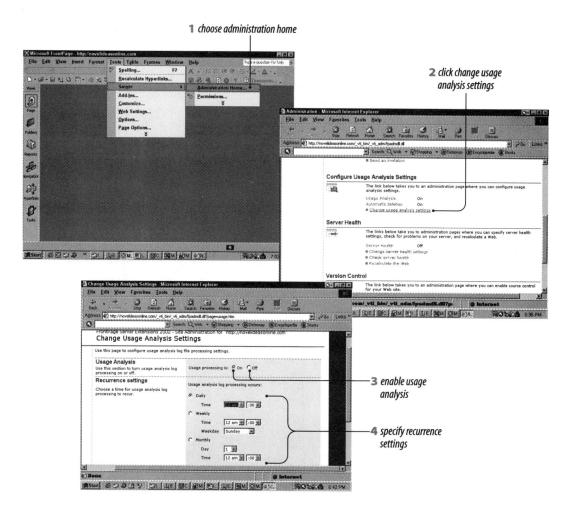

2 *click change usage analysis settings*

3 *enable usage analysis*

4 *specify recurrence settings*

5 apply additional settings

In the **Additional Usage Analysis Settings** area, specify how long usage data should be retained, and whether log file data should be processed in 24-hour increments. If you wish to receive e-mail notifications to confirm that usage analysis has occurred, type your e-mail address.

6 click submit

Click the **Submit** button to apply your settings.

7 choose usage summary

Back in FrontPage, choose **View➡Reports➡Usage➡Usage Summary** to open a Usage Summary report.

8 view usage summary report

The usage summary report contains scads of useful information, such as the total number of visitors your Web has received. For more detailed reports, experiment with the various options in the **View➡Reports➡Usage** submenu.

> *tip* The Web server hosting your site must have Microsoft FrontPage Server Extensions 2002 or SharePoint Team Services installed in order for you to collect usage data. Additionally, usage analysis must also be enabled on the Web server that hosts your site.

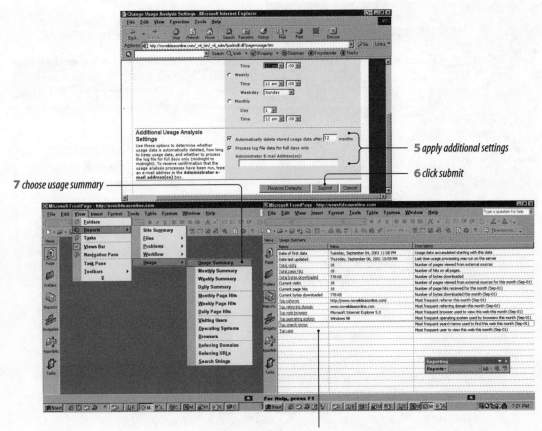

5 *apply additional settings*

6 *click submit*

7 *choose usage summary*

8 *view usage summary report*

Tasks View

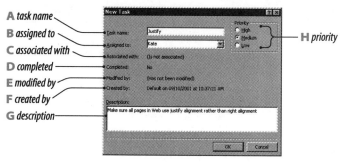

A *task name*
B *assigned to*
C *associated with*
D *completed*
E *modified by*
F *created by*
G *description*

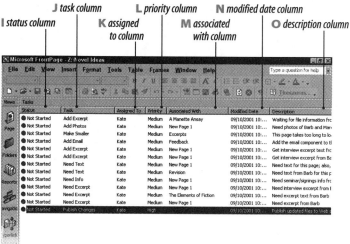

I *status column*
J *task column*
K *assigned to column*
L *priority column*
M *associated with column*
N *modified date column*
O *description column*

D completed
Find out if the task is done.

E modified by
See if the task has been modified and by whom.

F created by
View the name of the person who created the task, and when the task was created.

G description
Type a description of the task here.

H priority
High, Medium, or **Low** indicate the task's priority.

I status column
View the status of each task; options are **Not Started, In Progress,** and **Completed.**

J task column
See the name of each task you've created.

You can create and assign tasks, describing work to be completed on your Web or a specific file, to a person or group. You can then keep track of the tasks you create using **Tasks view,** which you access by choosing **File➞New➞Task.**

A task name
Type the name of the task you want to create.

B assigned to
Type or select from the drop-down list the name of the person or workgroup assigned to the task.

C associated with
The name of the file associated with this task.

K assigned to column
Determine the person or group to whom each task is assigned.

L priority column
Determine the priority of each task.

M associated with column
Determine with which file, if any, each task you've created is associated.

N modified date column
Determine when each task was last modified.

O description column
View text to describe each task you've created.

steps Create & Manage Tasks

Using tasks can really help you keep organized when it comes to completing work on your Web.

1 open file (optional)

To create a task that is associated with a particular file, open the file. If the task isn't associated with a particular file, skip to step 2.

2 choose task

Choose File➡New➡Task to open the New Task dialog box. Alternatively, choose Edit➡Tasks➡Add Task.

3 name task

Type a descriptive name for the task in the Task name textbox.

4 assign task (optional)

If desired, type or select from the drop-down list the name of the person or workgroup you want assigned to the task.

> *tip* If you're not yet certain to whom you want to assign the task, don't worry; you can assign a task after it's been created. To do so, open Tasks view. Click the cell in the **Assigned to** column of the task you want to assign, and then click it a second time. Then, type or select a name to assign the task.

5 type description

Type a description of the task. Make your description and instructions as informative as possible so that when you (or another Web author) are ready to tackle the task, you'll know what needs to be done.

> *tip* The description text may be too long to fit in the Description column. You can view a description in full by right-clicking it, choosing **Edit Task**, and reading the contents of the **Description** field of the **Task Details** dialog box.

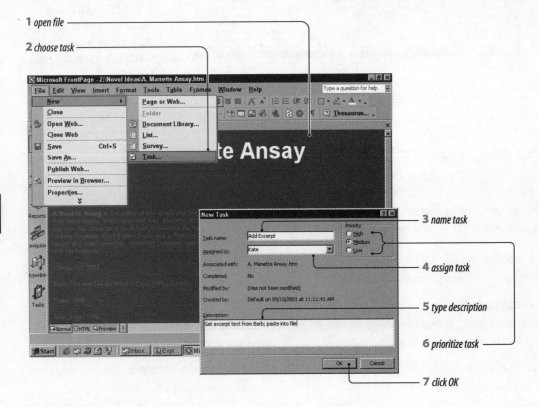

1 *open file*

2 *choose task*

3 *name task*

4 *assign task*

5 *type description*

6 *prioritize task*

7 *click OK*

6 prioritize task

Your choices are **High, Medium,** or **Low.** If you don't prioritize the task, it's set to **Medium** by default.

> 💡 To change the priority, open Tasks view. Click the cell in the **Priority** column of the task you want to change two times, and select **High, Medium,** or **Low.**

7 click OK

Click the **OK** button to create the task.

8 click tasks

Click the **Tasks** button in the **View** bar to open the Tasks pane and view any tasks you've created. If

desired, click a column heading to sort the task list by the values in that column.

9 get task details

Double-click a task in the **Tasks** list to open the **Task Details** dialog box and start working on the task.

10 start task

For tasks not associated with a file, the **Task Details** dialog box simply provides info about the task. After you find out what you need to know, click **OK** to close the dialog box.

For tasks that *are* associated with a file, the Task Details dialog box contains a **Start Task** button. Click it to open the file associated with the task, and complete the task.

11 mark task as completed

Mark a task that isn't associated with a file as completed by right-clicking it in Tasks view and selecting **Mark as Completed.** For tasks that are associated with a file, simply save your changes to the file. FrontPage asks if you want to mark the task as completed; if so, click **Yes.**

If you're not done with a task, but you want to save the changes you've made so far, click **No** when asked if you want to mark the task as completed. FrontPage marks the task as in progress.

8 *click tasks*   9 *get task details*   10 *start task*

11 *mark task as completed*

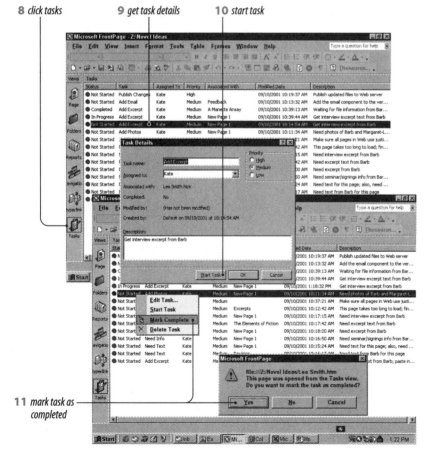

The Server Health Check

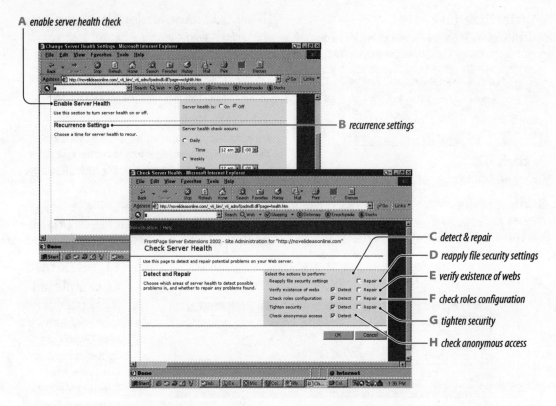

A enable server health check

B recurrence settings

C detect & repair

D reapply file security settings

E verify existence of webs

F check roles configuration

G tighten security

H check anonymous access

The **FrontPage 2002 Server Health Check** feature lets you determine whether the server hosting your Web is experiencing any problems, and whether your site is secure from hackers, viruses, and other Web villains. You must be connected to the Internet to use the FrontPage 2002 Server Health Check feature. Also, the server hosting your site must have **Microsoft FrontPage 2002 Server Extensions** or **SharePoint Team Services** installed.

A enable server health check

Turn the Server Health Check feature on and off.

B recurrence settings

Specify whether the Server Health Check should occur daily, weekly, or monthly.

C detect & repair

Use the **Detect** and **Repair** checkboxes to specify the areas of server health you want the Server Health

Check to scan for problems, and whether those problems should be repaired.

D reapply file security settings

Reapply file security settings to your Web.

E verify existence of webs

Verify that all subwebs in your site are accessible via the Internet.

F check roles configuration

Ensure that user role settings can be enforced.

G tighten security

Ensure that required Web files and directories exist, and that only users with the appropriate permissions can access them.

H check anonymous access

Make sure that anonymous users can't modify content on your Web.

Run A Server Health Check

The first time you run a Server Health Check, you must first specify Server Health Check settings for your site. You must be connected to the Internet to complete this task; also, note that the Web you open in this task is the one that resides on the Web server hosting your site, not the one you likely have saved on your computer's hard drive.

1 choose administration home

After opening the Web on which you want to run a Server Health Check, choose **Tools➥Server➥ Administration Home** to open the Site Administration page in your Web browser.

2 click change server health settings

In the Site Administration page, scroll to the **Server Health** section. If this is the first time you've run a Server Health Check on your Web, click the **Change server health settings** link (if not, skip to step 7).

3 click on

In the **Enable Server Health** area, click the **On** radio button.

4 apply recurrence settings

In the **Recurrence Settings** area, specify whether the Server Health Check should occur daily, weekly, or monthly. If you select **Weekly,** specify the time and

1 choose administration home

2 click change server health settings

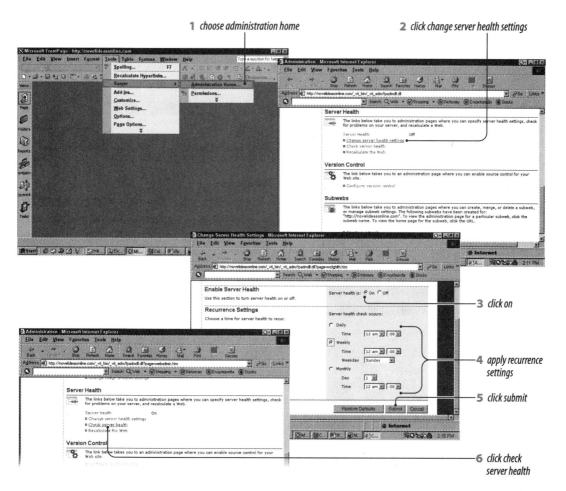

3 click on

4 apply recurrence settings

5 click submit

6 click check server health

weekday the check should occur; if you choose **Monthly,** specify the day of the month and the time to run the check.

5 click submit
Click the **Submit** button to apply your Server Health Check settings.

6 click check server health
In the Site Administration page, scroll to the **Server Health** section and click the **Check server health** link.

7 check detect & repair boxes
Use the **Detect** and **Repair** checkboxes in the **Check Server Health** window to specify the areas of server

health you want the Server Health Check to scan for problems, and whether those problems should be repaired.

8 click OK
Click **OK** to run the Server Health Check. An animation of two gears working indicate that the check is in progress; it may take a few moments to complete.

9 view server health report
When the Server Health Check is complete, a server health report appears, detailing what problems were detected and if they were fixed.

7 click detect & repair boxes

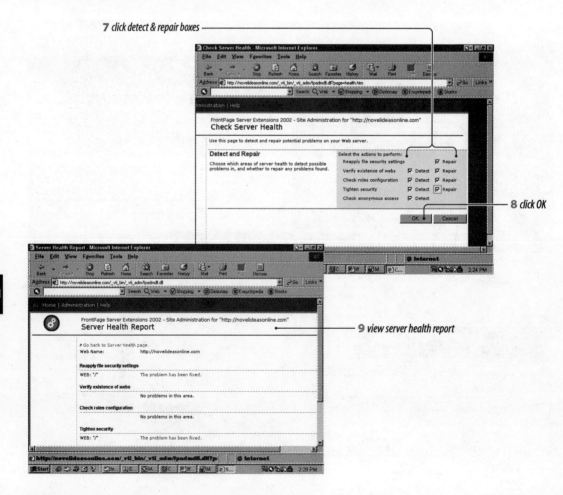

8 click OK

9 view server health report

Update & Edit A Web

Unless your site is completely static, you'll need to make changes to it at some point. To edit or update your Web, you simply use FrontPage to add or change pages in your Web (the one stored on your local computer) and republish your new-and-improved site to your Web server.

1 open web

Choose **File➡Open Web** and, in the **Open Web** dialog box, locate and select the Web on your local machine that you want to edit or update, and click **Open**.

2 make changes

Make changes to your site as needed.

3 republish site

Republish the site on your local computer to your Web server. When you republish your Web, click the **Options** button in the Publish Web dialog box and select the **Changed pages only** radio button in the **Publish** tab of the **Options** dialog box. That way, you save time by only republishing pages that have changed. Refer to Chapter 14, Publish A Web, for more information about publishing your site.

1 *open web*

2 *make changes*

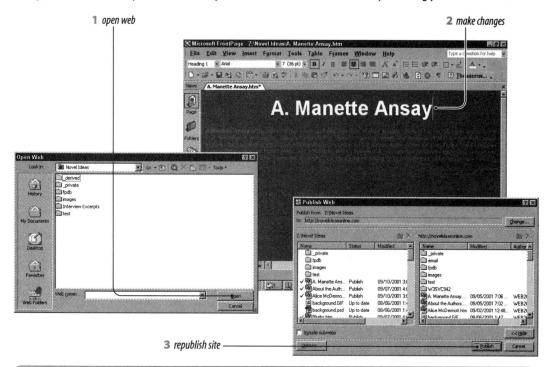

3 *republish site*

Delete A File Or Folder

You should delete any files or folders you don't need any more to conserve space on your Web server. To delete a file or folder from your Web server, even if it's already been published, click the file or folder you want to delete in the right-hand pane of the **Publish Web** dialog box and then click the pane's **Delete** button (the one with an "X" on it). Doing so deletes the file or folder from the Web on your server, but the file or folder still exists on your computer. If you also want to delete the file or folder on your computer, click in the left-hand pane and click the pane's **Delete** button.

Registering your site with a *search engine* helps people locate your site. Before you approach a search engine site to register, however, you should embed keywords into your site's home page. That way, when Internet users type those keywords into the search box at a search engine that recognizes them, your site appears in their list of search results.

Many search sites require you to undergo their own registration processes in addition to embedding keywords in your home page; review a site's documentation to find out what's required.

1 choose properties

Open your site's home page and choose **File➞ Properties** to open the **Page Properties** dialog box.

2 click add

In the **Custom** tab of the **Page Properties** dialog box, click the **Add** button in the **User Variables** area.

3 type keywords

The **User Meta Variable** dialog box opens. In the **Name** box, type **keywords.**

> **tip** If you don't want to go to the trouble of registering your site with the gazillion search engines that exist on the Web, try using a service such as the one provided by HyperSubmit (www.hypersubmit.com), which registers your site with more than 400 search engines for a yearly fee.

4 add keywords

In the **Value** box of the **User Meta Variable** dialog box, type the actual keywords for your site (use commas without spaces to separate the words and phrases). Think hard about what keywords are appropriate for your site; you can use both generic and specific words. For example, if your site is about novel writing, you might include keywords such as "books" and "writing," in addition to "novel writing."

5 click OK

Click **OK** once to close the **User Meta Variable** dialog box, and a second time to close the **Page Properties** dialog box.

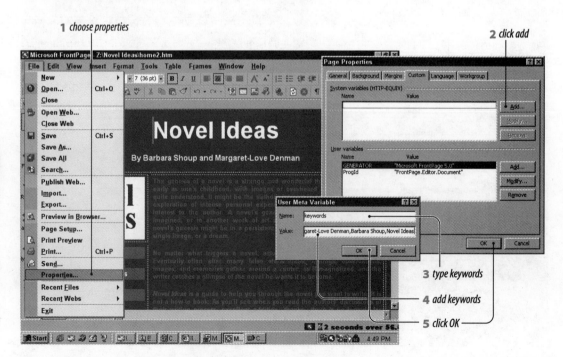

1 *choose properties*

2 *click add*

3 *type keywords*

4 *add keywords*

5 *click OK*

Customize Your Workspace

You can tweak the FrontPage workspace to better fit the way you like to work. For example, if you prefer to use toolbar buttons instead of menus to perform certain actions, you can add buttons that represent menu commands to your toolbars, or display additional toolbars on your desktop. If, on the other hand, you rarely use toolbars, you can elect to hide them, freeing up space on your desktop.

You can also specify your preferences when it comes to how items are displayed on menus. For example, you can instruct FrontPage to display font names in their fonts—that is, the Helvetica menu entry is formatted with the Helvetica font, the Arial menu entry is formatted with the Arial font, and so on. Additionally, you can set other general preferences within FrontPage, such as the default font, color-coding preferences, and more.

The Customize Dialog Box

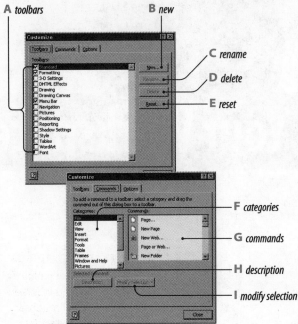

A *toolbars*
B *new*
C *rename*
D *delete*
E *reset*
F *categories*
G *commands*
H *description*
I *modify selection*

The **Customize** dialog box contains three tabs: Toolbars, Commands, and Options. The Toolbars tab lets you specify what toolbars you want visible on your FrontPage workspace. The Commands tab aids you in adding commands to toolbars. The Options tab helps you specify how you want your toolbars and menus to appear.

A toolbars

In the Toolbars tab, you find a list of the available FrontPage toolbars. Check the checkbox next to a toolbar to select or deselect it; when you close the **Customize** dialog box, FrontPage displays all the checked toolbars on your workspace.

B new

Click the **New** button to create a new, custom toolbar.

C rename

Click the **Rename** button to rename any custom toolbars you've created. The **Rename** button is grayed out unless you've selected a custom toolbar in the toolbars list (A). That's because you can change the names of

custom toolbars only. You can't change the names of those toolbars that are built in to FrontPage.

D delete

You click the **Delete** button to delete the toolbar selected in the toolbars list. Like the **Rename** button, the **Delete** button is grayed out unless you've selected a custom toolbar in the toolbars list. Again, you can't delete toolbars that are built in to FrontPage. Only custom toolbars can be deleted.

E reset

Click **Reset** to return the Toolbars list to its default configuration. That is, by clicking Reset, you undo any changes you make to the Toolbars list, and only those toolbars that are visible by default are checked.

F categories

In the Categories list, you find a list of command categories, organized by menu name or by type. Click an entry in this list to display commands in the **Commands** list (G).

G commands

The Commands list contains commands in the category you selected in the Categories list (F).

H description

View help information about the selected command.

I modify selection

Click **Modify Selection** to modify a menu, menu command, or toolbar button. You can change the menu, command, or button's name, image, and more. The **Modify Selection** button is grayed out unless you've selected a toolbar button, menu, or command from the FrontPage workspace, not from the **Customize** dialog box.

J show standard and formatting toolbars on two rows

Check this checkbox to position the Standard toolbar and Formatting toolbar on separate rows.

K always show full menus

Check this checkbox to instruct FrontPage to always show full menus. If you leave this option unchecked, FrontPage's menus display only basic and frequently used commands; you must click the down arrow at the bottom of the menu to view the remaining commands in that menu.

> 💡 If you select or clear the **Always show full menus** checkbox, the setting is applied automatically to all other Microsoft Office programs installed on your computer.

L show full menus after a short delay

Check this checkbox, which is available only if the **Always show full menus** checkbox is cleared, if you want the full menu to appear after a few moments.

M reset my usage data

Click the **Reset my usage data** button to return the items in the **Personalized Menus and Toolbars** area to their default settings.

N large icons

Check this checkbox to increase the size of toolbar buttons, making them easier to see.

O list font names in their font

Clear this checkbox to display the names of fonts using a standard font, thus speeding the display of the list. If you prefer, however, to automatically view samples of each font in the font list, leave this checkbox checked.

> 💡 If you select or clear the **List font names in their font** checkbox, the setting is applied automatically to all other Microsoft Office programs installed on your computer.

P show screentips on toolbars

Check this checkbox to turn on *ScreenTips*. That way, when you hover your mouse pointer over a toolbar button, a description of that button appears.

Q show shortcut keys in screentips

If you like to use your keyboard to navigate programs, you want to check the **Show shortcut keys in Screen-Tips** checkbox. That way, the ScreenTips that appear when you hover your mouse pointer over a toolbar button provide keyboard shortcut information.

R menu animations

Gimmick lovers everywhere will enjoy customizing how their menus appear onscreen. Options include **Random, Unfold, Slide,** and **None.**

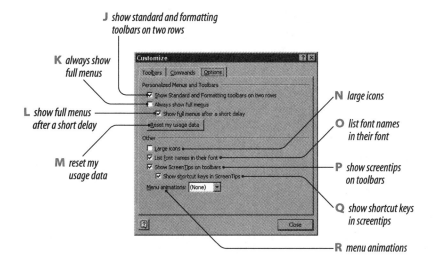

J *show standard and formatting toolbars on two rows*

K *always show full menus*

L *show full menus after a short delay*

M *reset my usage data*

N *large icons*

O *list font names in their font*

P *show screentips on toolbars*

Q *show shortcut keys in screentips*

R *menu animations*

steps Customize Menus

You can change a menu command's name and accompanying image, specify whether the entire menu be shown by default, and even decide whether the menu is animated.

1 choose customize
Choose **Tools→Customize** to open the **Customize** dialog box.

2 click commands tab
Click the **Commands** tab in the **Customize** dialog box.

3 open menu
Open the menu you want to modify. To modify a menu command, select the command after opening its menu.

4 click modify selection
Click **Modify Selection** to view your options.

5 select option
Select the option you want.

6 click options tab
Click the **Options** tab in the **Customize** dialog box.

7 click always show full menus (optional)
Clear this option to view only basic and frequently used menu commands.

> **tip** Clearing the **Always show full menus** checkbox enables the **Show full menus after a short delay** checkbox. Check that box if you want the full menu to appear after the shortened menu has been open for a few moments.

8 choose menu animation (optional)
If you want your menu to slide open or unfold (rather than simply opening), choose **Random, Unfold,** or **Slide** from the **Menu animations** drop-down list.

9 click close
The **Customize** dialog box closes.

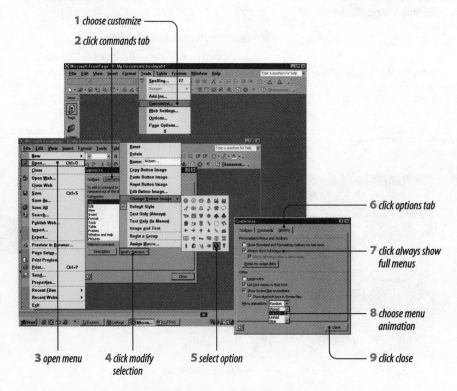

1 *choose customize*
2 *click commands tab*
3 *open menu*
4 *click modify selection*
5 *select option*
6 *click options tab*
7 *click always show full menus*
8 *choose menu animation*
9 *click close*

steps Customize Toolbars

Using the **Customize** dialog box, you can specify which toolbars appear on your workspace, where they are placed, how large toolbar buttons are, and whether they feature ScreenTips.

1 choose customize

Choose **Tools➡Customize** to open the **Customize** dialog box.

2 choose toolbars

The **Toolbars** tab of the **Customize** window lists the FrontPage toolbars. Check the checkbox next to a toolbar to select or deselect it; repeat for all the toolbars you want to add or remove.

> *tip* You have only a limited amount of workspace when you use FrontPage. If you display a gazillion toolbars, you won't have any room to actually work. If you discover that you don't have enough room to work, deselect a few toolbars in the **Toolbars** list.

3 click commands tab

To add buttons to toolbars on your workspace, click the **Commands** tab in the **Customize** dialog box.

4 choose category

The **Categories** list features categories of commands, organized by menu name or by type. Click an entry in this list to display commands in the **Commands** list.

5 choose command

The **Commands** list contains commands in the category you selected. Click the command you want to add to a toolbar on your workspace.

> *tip* If you're not sure what a particular command does, select it and then click the **Description** button to view information about the command.

6 drag command

Drag the command to a toolbar on your workspace; a button representing that command is added.

> *tip* If you find you never use a particular button on a toolbar, you can easily remove it. With the **Customize** dialog box open, drag the toolbar button you want to remove from the toolbar.

1 *choose customize* —

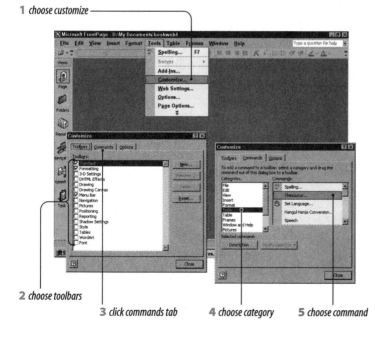

2 *choose toolbars*

3 *click commands tab*   4 *choose category*   5 *choose command*

7 click options tab

To specify how toolbars are displayed on your workspace, begin by clicking the **Options** tab.

8 check show standard and formatting toolbars on two rows

To position the Standard and Formatting toolbars on two separate rows, click the **Show standard and formatting toolbars on two rows** checkbox.

9 check large icons

If toolbar buttons seem a little small to you, check the **Large icons** checkbox to increase the size of toolbar buttons, making them easier to see. Be warned, though: Enlarging the toolbar buttons can greatly diminish the amount of space you have to work with.

10 check show screentips on toolbars

Select this checkbox to enable ScreenTips.

11 check show shortcut keys in screentips

If you check the **Show ScreenTips on toolbars** checkbox, you have the option of checking the **Show shortcut keys in ScreenTips** checkbox. Check this box if you like to use your keyboard to navigate programs. That way, the ScreenTips that appear when your mouse pointer hovers over a toolbar button provide keyboard shortcut information.

12 click close

Close the **Customize** dialog box and you're done.

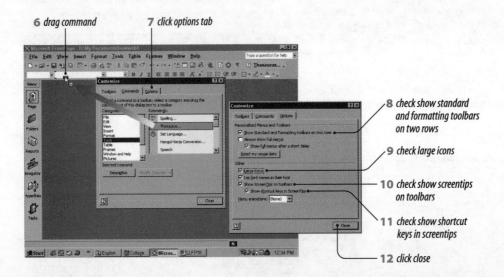

6 *drag command*   7 *click options tab*

8 *check show standard and formatting toolbars on two rows*

9 *check large icons*

10 *check show screentips on toolbars*

11 *check show shortcut keys in screentips*

12 *click close*

Create Toolbars

If you use the same toolbar buttons over and over, consider creating a custom toolbar containing all those buttons. To do so, click the **New** button in the **Toolbars** tab of the **Customize** dialog box. The **New Toolbar** dialog box opens; type a descriptive name for your new toolbar. Then click the **Commands** tab in the **Customize** dialog box, and add buttons to the toolbar using the method described in steps 4, 5, and 6. (Continue dragging commands until the toolbar contains all the buttons you need.)

Custom toolbars are automatically displayed on your desktop. If you don't want a custom toolbar to be displayed at all times, deselect it in the **Toolbars** list in the **Customize** dialog box.

Look It Up & Learn

3-D effects, 125

About Microsoft FrontPage
    dialog box, 269
Access and Web publishing, 31
actions, undoing and redoing, 8, 48
active graphics, 172
ActiveX controls, 196

Add Browser dialog box, 72
Add or Remove Buttons➥Customize
    command, 9
Add to Dictionary command, 61

Advanced Button Properties dialog
    box, 242, 245
Align Left button, 83
Align Right button, 83

> ▦ **left aligned**
> ▦   **right aligned**
> ▦   **centered**
> ▦ **justified text is where
>   margins are even on
>   both the left and right**

aligning
    graphics, 121
    horizontal lines, 52
    objects, 125
    paragraphs, 83
    pictures, 120
    tables, 146, 148, 154, 156
    text, 75, 83
    WordArt, 129
All caps special effect, 81

289

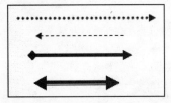
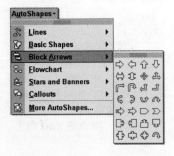

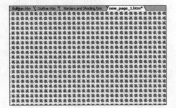
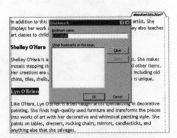

Index

C ***continued***
(begins on page 291)

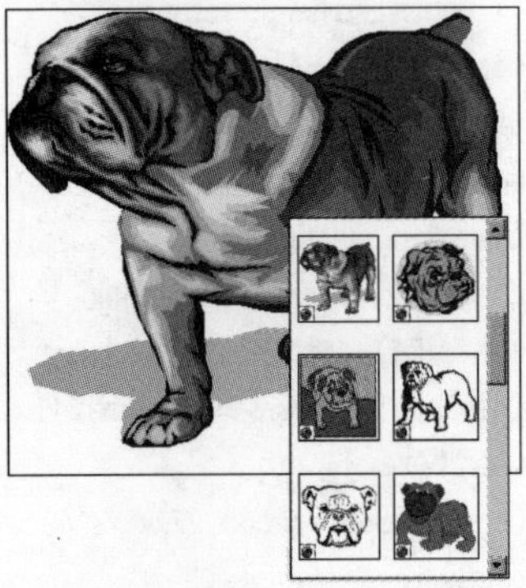

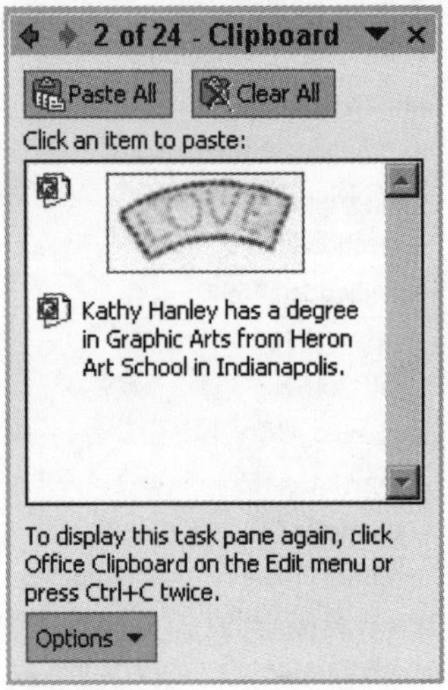

2 of 24 - Clipboard
Paste All
Clear All
Click an item to paste:
LOVE
Kathy Hanley has a degree in Graphic Arts from Heron Art School in Indianapolis.
To display this task pane again, click Office Clipboard on the Edit menu or press Ctrl+C twice.
Options

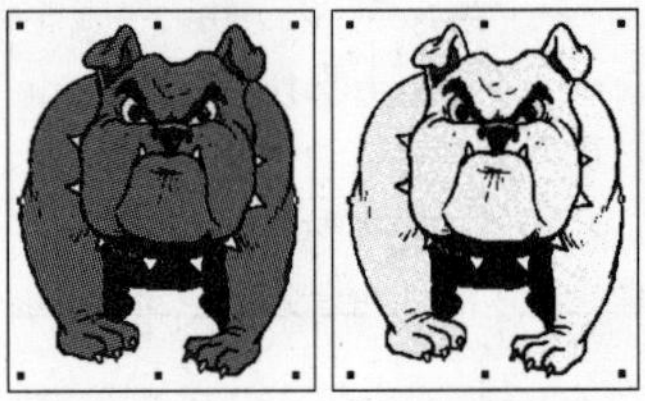

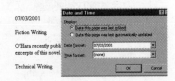

continued
(begins on page 294)

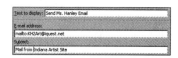

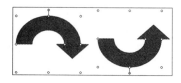

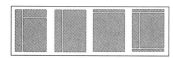

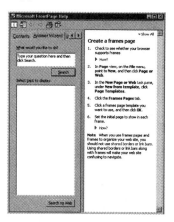

help window, 16–17

continued
(begins on page 299)

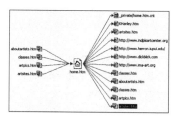

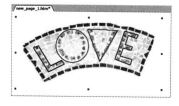

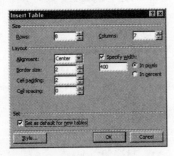
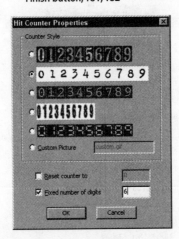

```
Copy  = ctrl + c
Paste = ctrl + v
Undo  = ctrl + z
Save  = ctrl + s
```

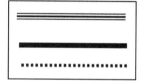

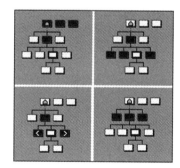

M *continued*
(begins on page 303)

N

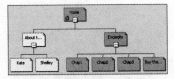

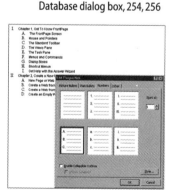

Index

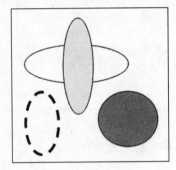

O *continued*
(begins on page 305)

ovals, 123
Overline special effect, 81

 P

padding, 92
Page Enter transition effect, 199
Page Exit transition effect, 199
page icon, 141
Page Options dialog box
    Check spelling as you type
      option, 61
    Compatibility tab, 180, 206
    Default Font tab, 78
    Frames checkbox, 206
    General tab, 61
Page Properties command, 58, 98
Page Properties dialog box
    Add button, 282
    Background Sound area, 201
    Background tab, 98, 100
    Custom tab, 282
    Forever checkbox, 201

Page Properties dialog box, *continued*
    Frames section, 212
    Frames tab, 214
    General tab, 201
    Loop spin box, 201
    Margins tab, 58
    Open button, 201
    Show Borders checkbox, 214
    Specify left margin checkbox, 58
    Specify top margin checkbox, 58
    User Variables area, 282
page scroll buttons, 4
page size tables, 157

page tabs, 4
Page Templates dialog box, 45, 170
    Form Page Wizard option, 234
    Frames Pages tab, 41, 206
    General tab, 40
    Just add Web task option, 41
    Style Sheets tab, 169
page title, 31, 42

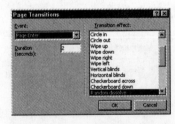

page transitions, 199, 202
Page Transitions dialog box, 199, 202
Page view, 4, 10, 32, 33
page-element styles, 164
page's Properties dialog box, 229

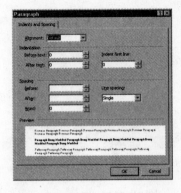

Paragraph dialog box, 166
    1.5 option, 85
    After spin box, 82, 85
    After text indent boxes, 82
    After text spin box, 84
    Alignment drop-down list, 83
    Double option, 85
    Line Spacing drop-down list,
      82, 85
    Preview area, 82
    Single option, 85
    Before spin box, 82, 85
    Before text spin box, 84
    Before text spin box, 82
    Word spin box, 82
paragraph-level styles, 164, 165
paragraphs
    aligning, 83
    background color, 93
    borders, 75, 92
    ending, 46
    foreground color, 93
    formatting, 82
    indenting, 82, 84

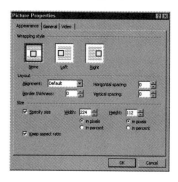

continued
(begins on page 306)

previewing
  borders, 92
  bullets, 88
  clipart, 105
  fonts, 77
  frames pages, 207
  paragraphs, 82
  styles, 165
  table formats, 152
  themes, 173
  video, 201
  Web pages, 33, 41, 72
  Web pages before printing, 59
  Web pages in browsers, 8
Preview/Properties command, 105
Print dialog box, 58, 60

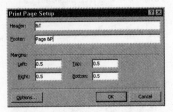

Print Page Setup dialog box, 58
Print Preview command, 59
printers, selecting, 60
printing
  headers and footers, 58
  help information, 16
  number of copies, 60

printing, *continued*
  page ranges, 60
  previewing Web pages before, 59
  Web pages, 8, 60
_private folder, 237, 252
program windows, 3–4
programs
  buttons for, 4–5
  listing name of, 2
  switching between, 5
  text from other programs, 49
  Web page creation in different,
    30–31
Project Web template, 27
Properties command, 5, 70, 229
Properties view, 110–111
Publish Destination dialog box, 263
Publish Status report, 272
Publish Web Destination dialog
    box, 261
Publish Web dialog box, 259–260,
    262, 264, 281
publishing
  backup Web, 263–264
  to servers, 261–262
  Webs, 8, 257
Push Button Properties dialog box, 242
push buttons, 237

Recalculate Hyperlinks dialog box, 143
recalculating hyperlinks, 143
Rectangle tool, 123

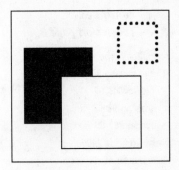

rectangles, 123
redoing actions, 8
refreshing Web pages, 9
registering with search engines, 282
regrouping objects, 125
Remove Formatting (ctrl+shift+Z)
    keyboard shortcut, 71
Rename command, 70
renaming Web pages, 70
replacing text, 67
Reporting toolbar, 267
reports, 10, 32, 265
  filtering, 270
  listing, 142
  sorting, 142
  viewing, 142
Reports view, 10, 32, 266–267
resizing
  columns, 161
  fonts, 74, 75, 76, 78
  frames, 213
  graphics, 120, 130
  images to thumbnail, 116
  objects, 6
  rows, 161
  task panes, 11
  windows, 3

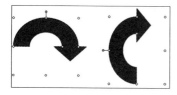

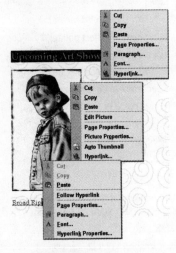
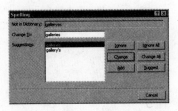

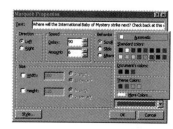

Index

continued
(begins on page 311)

Text Box Validation dialog box, 246–247, 248–249

text files, inserting, 50

text shortcut menu, 15

Textarea Box Properties dialog box, 241

TextArea Properties dialog box, 243

Textbox tool, 123

textboxes, 14, 46, 123, 236, 239

themes, 25, 163, 172

   active graphics, 172

   applying, 172, 173

   background pictures, 172

   built-in, 172

   color schemes, 176

   colors, 172

   CSSs (Cascading Style Sheets), 172

   default, 173

   deleting, 172, 178

   elements, 177

   fonts, 177–178

   graphics, 172, 177

   modifying, 172, 174–178

   naming, 178

   pre-defined, 172

   previewing, 173

   removing, 173

themes, *continued*

   saving, 178

   styles, 178

   templates, 27

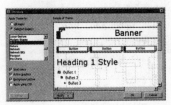

Themes dialog box, 172

   Active Graphics checkbox, 173

   Background picture checkbox, 173

   Modify button, 174, 176

   Sample of Theme area, 173

   Vivid colors checkbox, 173

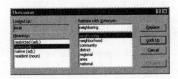

Thesaurus, 68

Thesaurus dialog box, 68

Thumbnail view, 106

thumbnails, 116

Thumbnails view, 110–111

title bar, 2

toolbar buttons, 2

toolbars

   button equivalent of command, 12

   combining, 3

   creation of, 288

   custom, 5

   customizing, 287–288

   customizing display, 8

   navigating combined, 9

Tools menu, 13

Tools on the Web command, 105

Tools➡Customize command, 3, 8, 286, 287

Tools➡Page Options command, 61, 78, 206

Tools➡Recalculate Hyperlinks command, 143

Tools➡Server➡Administration Home command, 273, 279

Tools➡Spelling command, 62, 63

Top-Down Hierarchy template, 205

transition effect, 188

transparent colors, 117

trigger effects, 197

troubleshooting Webs, 268–270

.txt files, 195

U

unavailable pointer, 7

Underline button, 51

Underline (ctrl+U) keyboard shortcut, 51, 76

Underline special effect, 80

Undo button, 48

Undo (ctrl+Z) keyboard shortcut, 211

undoing

   actions, 8, 48

   changes to images, 117

ungrouping objects, 125

Unindent (ctrl+shift+M) keyboard shortcut, 84

Unlinked Files report, 268

Update (F9) keyboard shortcut, 54

updating

   links, 70

   Webs, 281

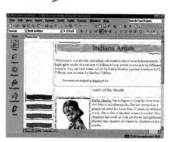

Index

continued
(begins on page 315)

Web pages, *continued*

editing, 57
elements, 13
empty or blank, 21
from existing Web pages, 45
formatting text, 39
headers and footers, 58
hyperlinks, 39, 134–135, 141
inserting text files, 50
list form, 236
location for, 42
managing, 13
margins, 58
moving among, 13
naming, 4, 39, 42, 43
new, 8
no-frames, 207, 209
opening, 8, 26, 56, 57
opening options, 38
page tabs, 4
pictures, 39
previewing, 33, 41, 72
previewing before printing, 59
previous or next, 11
printing, 8, 60
recently used, 21
refreshing, 9
renaming, 70
replacing filler text, 41
retitling, 70
saving, 8, 36, 42, 43
saving as template, 44
spell checking, 63
stopping display of, 9
tables, 39

Web pages, *continued*

templates, 40–41
text, 39
views, 4, 32–33
Web providers, 260
Web publishing, 31
Web site maintenance, 265
Web Site Templates dialog box, 28

Web sites

frames, 205
hyperlinks to, 136–137
table of contents, 227–228
URL, 133
viewing hyperlinks, 141
Web Task task pane, 11

Webdings font, 53
Webs, 19

adding content, 25, 27
adding pages, 29
analyzing usage, 273–274
appearance, 29
assigning tasks, 29
audience, 29

Webs, *continued*

backup, 263–264
clear-cut purpose, 29
closing, 36
collecting pictures for, 29
collecting text for, 29
combining, 27
as containing folder, 42
copying or cutting text
between, 48
creation of, 20–21
default name for, 28
default pages, 26
default view, 25
empty or blank, 21, 28–29
feedback, 29
filler text, 24
listing contents, 29
location for storing, 22, 29
location of links, 24
managing, 13
mapping pages, 29
naming, 28, 31
opening, 26, 35
overview of structure of, 26
page listings, 29
page structure, 29
path for storing, 26
planning, 29
publishing, 8, 257
recently opened, 35
relationship of pages within, 10
shared borders, 224–226
status of components, 258
storing, 22–23, 29
structure of, 32
switching between, 35

Index

 continued
(begins on page 315)

template creation of, 26–27
templates, 21
themes, 25
title, 31
troubleshooting, 268–270
updating, 281
wizard creation of, 22–25

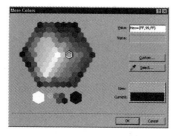

Web-safe color, 99
What's This?, 80
window menu, 13
windows, 3–4
Wingdings font, 53
wipes, 199

wizards, 19, 21, 23–25
Word, 30–31

WordArt, 46, 123, 128–129
WordArt Gallery dialog box, 128
workflow, 271–272

Zoom In button, 59
Zoom Out button, 59